STATE OF
WAR

STATE
OF
WAR

MICHIGAN IN WORLD WAR II

Alan Clive

The University of Michigan Press
Ann Arbor

Published in the United States of America by
The University of Michigan Press and simultaneously
in Rexdale, Canada, by John Wiley & Sons Canada, Limited
Manufactured in the United States of America

1983   1982   1981   1980   5   4   3   2

Library of Congress Cataloging in Publication Data

Clive, Alan, 1944—
   State of war.

   Bibliography: p.
   Includes index.
   1. World War, 1939-1945—Economic aspects —Michigan.
2. Michigan—Social conditions.
   I. Title.
   ISBN 0-472-10001-7

*Grateful acknowledgment is made to the following publishers and insti-
tutions:*

The National Geographic Society for copyrighted photographs. Reprinted
by permission of the National Geographic Society.

People's Song Library Collection, Archives of Labor and Urban Affairs,
Wayne State University, for "UAW-CIO," by Baldwin Hawes. Copyright ©
by Baldwin Hawes.

The publishers of the *Detroit News*, for photographs from the files of the
Detroit News. Reprinted by permission.

Wayne State University, for photographs from the Wayne State University
Archives of Labor and Urban Affairs. Reprinted by permission.

To the people of Michigan

Acknowledgments

A number of individuals, libraries, and historical depositories were of assistance during the research for this work and it is my pleasure to acknowledge their aid. I wish to thank the staffs of the following: the various branches of the University of Michigan Library, especially the late Ann Gale; the Michigan Historical Collections, especially Mary Jo Pugh; the G. Flint Purdy Library, Wayne State University, Detroit; the Archives of Labor History and Urban Affairs, Wayne State University; the National Archives and Records Service, Washington, D.C.; the Washington National Records Center, Suitland, Maryland; the Michigan State Archives, Lansing, Michigan, especially Geneva Wiskemann; the Harry S. Truman Library, Independence, Missouri; and the State Historical Society of Wisconsin, Madison. A grant from the American Council of Learned Societies aided in the completion of the manuscript.

Many persons have inspired or encouraged me during the research and writing of this study. My wife Mary has made all of the plowing through statistics and obscure reports worthwhile. Professor Sidney Fine has made many significant contributions through careful reading at various stages of progress, and has provided a model of scholarly integrity. Gerald Linderman's friendship has been a constant support and his suggestions on style and content have been unfailingly sound. Others who have made contributions through their readings include Shaw Livermore, Alexander Saxton, Albert Hermalin, and Richard Dalfiume. A complete list of others who have helped me would tax the reader's patience, but the following

must be mentioned with special thanks: Dorothy Arvidson,
Ann Bobroff, Julia First, Beatrice Freedberg, John Gilbreath,
Louise Gilbreath, Peter Holtje, Randy Jacob, Robin Jacoby,
Dorothy Keilt, Sophie Levin, Eleanore Soja Miller, Elizabeth
Pitman, John Shy, Alice Smuts, Judith Zendell Souede, and
Jane Wheeler. Joan Thorne's excellent typing considerably
eased the burden of proofreading.

Contents

Abbreviations x

Introduction: Michigan in World War II 1

Chapter

1 "Victory Is Our Business" 18

2 The Worker's War 55

3 Communities: Breathing under Water 90

4 Race: Change and Resistance 130

5 "Tennessee and Kentucky Are Now in Michigan" 170

6 Women, Youth, and the Limits of Wartime Change 185

7 End and Beginning: Victory and Reconversion 214

Conclusion: War, Change, and Continuity 234

Notes 245

Bibliography 273

Index 291

Photographs *following page* 178

Abbreviations

AFC	America First Committee
AFL	American Federation of Labor
BAE	Bureau of Agricultural Economics
BLS	Bureau of Labor Statistics
CCPA	President's Committee for Congested Production Areas
CHPC	Detroit Citizens' Housing and Planning Council
CIO	Congress of Industrial Organizations (formerly Committee for Industrial Organization)
CMP	Controlled Materials Plan
CPA	Congested Production Area
CRC	Civil Rights Congress of Michigan
DHC	Detroit Housing Commission
DSR	Detroit Street Railway Company
DSW	Michigan Department of Social Welfare
DUL	Detroit Urban League
DVC	Detroit Victory Council
EMIC	Emergency Maternal and Infant Care Program
FEPC	President's Committee on Fair Employment Practice
FES	Federal Extension Service
FHA	Federal Housing Administration
FPHA	Federal Public Housing Authority
FWA	Federal Works Agency
GM	General Motors
MCD	Michigan Council of Defense
MCF	Michigan Commonwealth Federation
MESA	Mechanics Educational Society of America

MGS	Minority Group Service
MOWC	March on Washington Committee
MUCC	Michigan Unemployment Compensation Commission
MYGC	Michigan Youth Guidance Committee (later Commission)
NAACP	National Association for the Advancement of Colored People
NDAC	National Defense Advisory Commission
NDMB	National Defense Mediation Board
NHA	National Housing Agency
NIRA	National Industrial Recovery Act
NLRB	National Labor Relations Board
OCD	Office of Civilian Defense
OCWS	Office of Community War Services
ODT	Office of Defense Transportation
OPA	Office of Price Administration
OPACS	Office of Price Administration and Civilian Supply
OPM	Office of Production Management
OVA	Michigan Office of Veterans' Affairs
OWI	Office of War Information
PAC	CIO Political Action Committee
PW	Prisoner of War
PWA	Public Works Administration
REA	Railway Express Agency
RWLB	Regional War Labor Board
SDCC	State Day Care Committee
SLMB	State Labor Mediation Board
UAW	United Automobile Workers
UCWOC	United Construction Workers Organizing Committee
UE	United Electrical Workers
UMW	United Mine Workers
URW	United Rubber Workers
USCB	United States Children's Bureau
USDA	United States Department of Agriculture
USES	United States Employment Service
USHA	United States Housing Authority

USO   United Service Organization
USPHS United States Public Health Service
VFV   Victory Farm Volunteers
WLB   War Labor Board
WMC   War Manpower Commission
WPA   Work Projects Administration (formerly Works
       Progress Administration)
WPB   War Production Board

Introduction

Michigan in World War II

★ 1 ★

The Second World War was a total war. The principal belligerents raised armies numbering in the millions and mobilized every sector of their societies, by voluntary action or coercion, into one great effort in support of their combat troops. Although the United States created a military force that eventually swelled to sixteen million men and women, the overriding objective of the American mobilization was maximum production of the weapons of war. The nation's industrial output was its signal contribution to the European phase of the conflict and enormous productive capacity enabled the U.S. to carry on the simultaneous struggle in the Pacific. A year before Pearl Harbor, President Franklin Roosevelt set forth America's wartime role in a single phrase: "We must be the great arsenal of democracy."[1]

No geographic, social, or economic element of American society escaped the impact of total war, but the production mobilization affected certain areas more than others. A handful of states bore the brunt of the national war effort. California, its relatively small prewar aviation industry expanded almost beyond recognition, became a manufacturing giant. Industrial plants in New York, Illinois, and Indiana were enlarged and converted to war production. As the capital of the automobile industry, the nation's mightiest prewar manufacturing endeavor, Michigan played a central role in the war of machines.

Watching Detroit scrap its passenger car assembly lines in early 1942, a reporter wrote: "Just as Detroit was the symbol of America in peace, so it is the symbol of America at war. Other towns make arms, as other towns made automobiles, but whether we win this war depends in great measure on Detroit."[2]

What follows is a narrative and analysis of how the society and economy of Michigan met this production challenge. It is a story of people and institutions confronting a supreme crisis. It would be an incomplete story, however, without some reference to and analysis of the meaning of that wartime experience. By 1945 Americans understood that events of profound significance had transpired at home as well as abroad during the six years of world war. Students of the period begin with the assumption that an understanding of the contemporary United States depends upon a comprehension of that wartime interval. Unfortunately, the first synthetic accounts of home-front America did not appear until the early 1970s. Large areas of wartime social and economic history remain unexamined or uninterpreted even at the level of dissertation literature. Over the past thirty years, however, a debate about the domestic consequences of the world conflict has sputtered on. The argument, when reduced to its essentials, is about the degree of change that took place in the United States during the war years and, to a lesser extent, about the character of that change, whether benevolent or malign in nature.[3]

In 1951, Eliot Janeway voiced the then prevailing academic and popular belief that the war had created "a many-sided social revolution," restoring national prosperity and confidence and giving people a sense of security about their future. Women, blacks, and farmers made remarkable economic and social strides. Meanwhile President Roosevelt deliberately chose to ignore many home-front problems, trusting—correctly, in Janeway's view—that they would resolve themselves. The nation, Janeway wrote, "had regained all its historic dynamism and more: it was on the march." Geoffrey Perrett emphatically reaffirmed this view of the war in 1973. The 1939–45 period, he asserts, brought "the closest thing to a real social revolution the United States has known in this century. . . . No other six years in this century have brought so much real change in the lives of Americans." Wartime prosperity erased social injustice where New Deal reforms had failed, and the war effort molded the people into a happy, confident, social collective, reassured of the worth of their institutions. The war, Perrett concludes, "was a boon to people's hearts and ideals. It was also good to their pocketbooks."[4]

Other scholars have suggested that, far from having undergone radical change during the war, the United States missed an opportunity to join the world movement toward greater social and economic freedom in the postwar era. In 1948 Bruce Catton scourged the business-oriented "war lords of Washington"—including President Roosevelt—for defeating or undermining such progressive concepts as labor-management committees and the Reuther Plan for automotive conversion. "We retreated from democracy," Catton asserted, "because democracy means Change—if it means anything worth the life of one drafted sharecropper. . . ." Two decades later, Barton J. Bernstein rejected an affirmative view of wartime events. Conceding that the war had ended the depression, he nonetheless contended that the conflict created only a limited prosperity. Labor and agriculture became "effective partners in the political economy of large-scale corporate capitalism," but big business tightened its grip over American life. Social welfare legislation languished, and blacks received only a few benefits, while racism endured.[5]

Continuity figures more significantly than does change in John Morton Blum's 1976 reassessment of the war era. "The American way of living returned, during the new prosperity of the war years," Blum writes, "to patterns that Americans liked to believe had marked national life before the depression, patterns they wanted to preserve and to project into the postwar period." The return of the old ways of thought was hastened by the adoption of what Blum describes as "necessitarian" values by almost all Americans, from President Roosevelt to the men and women in the war plants. The need to produce vast quantities of war goods seemed to necessitate

complete reliance on giant industries as well as the relinquish-
ment of control over the domestic economy to the representatives of those industries. The need to preserve domestic
tranquility dictated that the black call for equality be ignored.
Necessitarian values and the popular desire to preserve wartime economic gains created a society dedicated by 1945 to the
maintenance of abundance for the middle class through consumer spending, a society selfishly willing to shrug off the
claims of deprived or outsider groups.[6]

Several historians have offered modifications or alternatives
to the polar perspectives represented by Janeway and Perrett
on the one hand or Bernstein and Blum on the other. James
MacGregor Burns declares that "World War II cut deep into
the bone marrow of American life." A powerful Presidency
emerged, to which client groups would be forced to turn for
aid in the future. A permanent defense industry arose, linked
to the great universities. Burns places the emphasis of his account on change rather than continuity. He taxes Roosevelt
and the federal government, however, for blunting the thrust
of the social revolution unleashed by the war. Like Blum, Burns
takes disapproving note of the reliance on expedient measures
in the formation of domestic wartime policy.[7]

To David Brody, "World War II . . . finished old business so
that the country could turn unencumbered to the postwar
world." That business was the final acceptance by corporate
America of a significant role for the federal government in the
promotion of prosperity and the recognition that industrial
unionism had come to stay. President Roosevelt, eager for business cooperation, downplayed liberal social measures save in
the waning months of the war. Broad national support for the
war obviated the need to hold lofty visions before the people as
an incentive to unity. Brody stresses the continuity of the "essentially reactive" New Deal which lacked a coherent vision of
the society it was intended to promote, and the expedient policies of the war period. The consolidation of the New Deal,
however, facilitated by the very expediency others criticize,
constituted a positive achievement.[8]

Richard S. Kirkendall observes that "many old parts of

American life, including the basic political and economic institutions, remained in place [during the war]. American leaders had ... deliberately preserved those institutions, protecting them against serious challenges at home and abroad, and the American people had resisted as well as demanded change." The rise of a huge military establishment, however, marked a radical departure from previous American history. Following Janeway and Perrett, Kirkendall assesses the war's domestic impact as a positive one. Finding wartime phenomena to be essentially continuous with those of the prewar past, he ends his account on a note of uncertainty, writing: "It appeared that the nation now knew how to avoid a depression, but it was not certain that the United States would do so. Pressure for change in race relations seemed likely to persist, but the success that it would enjoy could not be predicted."[9]

"World War II radically altered the character of American society and challenged its most durable values," Richard Polenberg asserts. The federal government assumed a central role as the arbitrator between and dispenser of favors to competing interest groups and a military-industrial complex emerged, but the wartime economy "preserved important features of capitalism," and the crisis-born system of controls simply codified many extant informal rules and regulations. "Only the first cracks in the armor of segregation had appeared by 1945." The wartime production boomtowns experienced many of the same problems of family dislocation suffered by communities in depression days. Internal hostility was replaced by a spirit of national unity, and the war had a generally therapeutic effect on the American psyche. Polenberg stresses the war's importance in creating "a more urban, technological, and industrialized society" than that of 1941. Setting out to demonstrate that America was transformed during World War II, Polenberg instead describes an experience in which change and continuity intermix in ambiguous fashion.[10]

There are wide areas of agreement among the historians of the home front. Most, for instance, maintain that the war restored prosperity and national confidence. The conflict stimulated the growth of the federal bureaucracy and the powers of the presidency and heightened the influence of labor and business. Industrial and military representatives established close ties. A hopeful beginning was made in the struggle for black equality. Some argument can be generated even on these points, however, and there is considerable disagreement as to whether these and other developments add up to a radical alteration of American life, reflect the acceleration of trends and forces already present, or constitute some combination of both. Debate has centered on the impact on the nation—whether for good or ill—of the government's admittedly expedient wartime policies. In addition, some scholars are at odds with others about the nature of the long-run consequences of the war.

The interpreters of the period base their conclusions largely on national developments, especially those arising in Washington. They refer occasionally to significant events in particular states or cities, but never dwell long on a single geographic area. The present study, besides being an account of Michigan at war, is an effort to chart the interplay of continuity and change in the social and economic community of this single and most important state. It can be said of Michigan—as it can be said of few other states—that events that transpired within its borders during the war affected the entire nation. The Michigan of 1939 contained within its fifty-eight thousand square miles all the elements that characterized mid-twentieth century America: giant industry, an ambitious labor movement, large-scale agriculture, great cities, diverse and often antagonistic ethnic and racial groups, and thousands of people in want. In undertaking its vital military production task, Michigan had become by 1945 the focus of every force and motivation that shaped the years of total war. Michigan's homefront experience reveals much about the impact of the Second World War on American life then and now.

★ 2 ★

The automobile created modern Michigan. The production of motorcars transformed the state into an industrial colossus and gave world renown to the name of Detroit. Michigan's leadership of the industry derived in part from the fact that

Detroit and Flint long had been centers of carriage and wheel construction. Ransome E. Olds began large-scale production of motorcars in 1901, and Henry Ford, the enigmatic genius who personified the automotive revolution, introduced the Model T in 1908. Six years later Ford installed the first complete moving assembly line in his Highland Park plant, and upon the opening of his enormous River Rouge complex in 1919, the making of automobiles entered the stage of giant enterprise. Motor vehicle manufacturing grew into the nation's largest industry, and the automobile rolled across the United States, leaving in its trail profound social and economic change. By 1929 Detroit had become the most potent symbol of modern American life—to one commentator, the harbinger of a "utopia on wheels." It was the capital—and Michigan, the richest province—of a dominion ruled by a force mightier than kings, "the new Messiah," in Henry Ford's phrase: production.[11]

Between 1900 and 1930 the industry enormously influenced the demographic map of Michigan. Manufacturing replaced mining, lumbering, and farming as the state's chief source of employment. Migration flowed from the northern half of the state and from the eastern, north central, and southern regions of the United States into twenty-six lower peninsula industrial counties. Dearborn, site of the Rouge, grew from a village of less than a thousand to a community of fifty thousand. Detroit's rise from 285,704 inhabitants at the turn of the century to 1,568,662 in 1930 was not the largest in the state in percentage terms, but was the most spectacular in absolute numbers.

In the 1890s, Detroit was "a quiet, tree-shaded city, unobtrusively going about its business of brewing beer and making carriages and stoves." Two decades later many a Georgian mansion either had been converted into a boardinghouse or demolished for road-widening. The city abandoned the slogan "Detroit the Beautiful" for "Detroit the Dynamic." It sprawled quickly and haphazardly, east and west for ten crowded miles along the river, north and south up Woodward Avenue until nearby suburban communities were surrounded by new subdivisions and a network of concrete. A visitor to Detroit in

1920 described "a cluster of new sky-scrapers thrusting gawk-
ily up out of a welter of nondescript old buildings. . . . Automobiles are everywhere."[12]

The automobile industry, voracious for manpower, drew
new elements into the population of Michigan. A tide of immigrants from southeastern and southcentral Europe, including many Catholics and Jews, swept into the expanding
industrial centers, peasantry and urban poor alike seeking opportunity in the assembly plants. Detroit's foreign-born population tripled between 1900 and 1920 to some 290,000 persons
in a city of nearly a million, a proportion far in excess of the
national average. The passage of restrictive legislation effectively halted European immigration after 1925, but as late as
1940, the foreign born comprised 10 percent or more of the
inhabitants of several Michigan cities. These immigrants settled into tightly packed urban enclaves, establishing institutions to preserve a vigorous ethnic consciousness. Many old-
stock Americans despised the religion, language, and customs
of the newcomers and their seeming unwillingness to forsake
Old World ties. The longtime residents found the newcomers
inferior to earlier Anglo-Saxon immigrants; a Detroit executive expressed the common opinion that "one German is worth
half a dozen Polacks or Dagoes."[13]

Few blacks had settled in Michigan before 1914. When the
First World War temporarily halted immigration, however, recruiters for the auto companies scoured the South, urging
black laborers and field hands northward with the lure of high
wages and better living conditions. By train, car, and on foot,
the migrants arrived in the state's industrial centers. Between
1910 and 1920 the black population of Michigan increased
more than 300 percent, and tripled again by 1930 to 169,452
persons, most living in the Detroit area. Before the migration,
a rigidly enforced color line had barred blacks from practically
all employment save the most menial. Thanks to the wartime
manpower shortage, black industrial employment increased
sharply. But employers wanted black workers for the most arduous, dirty, and low-paying jobs. Only the individualistic Ford

broke the unwritten sanction against the use of blacks on the assembly line, and then solely at the River Rouge plant.

Blacks were compelled to live in the city's most deplorable housing as well as to hold its worst jobs. Confined before 1914 within a narrow zone on the near east side of Detroit, they had nonetheless lived in close proximity to white immigrants. During the wartime migration and into the 1920s, the black population filled and overflowed vacant homes as whites moved north and west into the periphery of the city. A wholly black district emerged, known ironically to its inhabitants as "Paradise Valley." Rents were exorbitant for the crowded, run-down dwellings available to blacks. The white community meanwhile built a paper wall around its neighborhoods by the use of restrictive covenants against occupancy by blacks and other "undesirable" tenants. Black rates of disease, death, and crime far exceeded those of whites, while black school attendance, proprietorship, and proportion of doctors and lawyers all fell below city-wide averages.

Southern whites also travelled the roads to Michigan. So great was the influx of both races after 1910 that the historic pattern of movement into the state shifted from an east-west to a north-south axis. By 1930, 165,926 southern whites lived in Michigan, three-fifths of them in Detroit and Flint. Small towns in Missouri, Arkansas, Tennessee, and Kentucky served as the major focal points for the migration. Although many southerners left their native region for good, most kept in close touch with their birthplace, and many returned during seasonal layoffs. The white migrants, like the blacks and the immigrants, sought enlarged economic opportunities. The southerners, too, established homogeneous residential areas, such as Flint's "Little Missouri." They assimilated more easily than the Europeans did and moved more freely than blacks, but a number of southerners resisted quick adaptation to big-city, northern ways. Many Michigan natives regarded them with no more sympathy than the other recent arrivals, contemptuously referring to southern whites as "hillbillies" or worse.

Michigan was no Eden of toleration before the automotive age; in 1863, whites had rampaged through Detroit's black district and the presence of federal troops had been required to restore order. The anti-Catholic American Protective Association found eager sympathizers throughout the state. The forces of enmity and discord intensified in the early twentieth century, however, because of the economic competition of culturally hostile groups and because of the anonymity of urban life. Throughout the 1920s, Henry Ford fanned sparks of anti-Semitism with articles in the *Dearborn Independent.* Michigan became a stronghold of the refurbished Ku Klux Klan. In Detroit's increasingly charged atmosphere an outbreak of violence seemed inevitable. It flared during the spring and summer of 1925 as white mobs frightened away blacks seeking homes distant from Paradise Valley, and one black family defended its new home with gunfire, killing a white bystander. Racial tension ebbed in the late 1920s, but the potential for renewed conflict remained.

The catastrophe of the Great Depression now fell upon a state that already had endured three decades of wrenching social and economic change. Motor vehicle production fell from more than 5,000,000 units in 1929 to a low of 1,300,000 units in 1932. Only the Big Three (Ford, General Motors, and Chrysler) and four smaller firms survived the decade. Urban growth and in-migration came to a virtual standstill. Thousands abandoned the fruitless quest for employment, leaving the cities for a more self-sufficient and less expensive life in the countryside. "The employment agencies and soup kitchens are crowded," Edmund Wilson reported from Detroit in 1931, "and people without jobs gloomily make their way from one factory gate to another in the hope that somebody may be hiring again. . . ." In the last quarter of 1934, nearly one in every six citizens of the state depended upon relief. Farmers suffered severe losses and the Upper Peninsula's mining industry all but collapsed.[14]

It became evident as the depression wore on that the state's black population, increased by 1940 to 208,000, had suffered more than the whites. Black unemployment statewide stood at a demoralizing 16.7 percent on April 1, 1940, in contrast to a white jobless rate of 9 percent. The bars against expanded black employment and housing opportunity remained as high as ever. Blacks, moreover, continued to suffer harrassment and persecution. Although the Ku Klux Klan virtually disappeared from the state by 1934, it was succeeded by an even more sinister organization, the Black Legion. Founded in 1932 or 1933 and dominated by in-migrant southern factory workers, the group espoused a vicious brand of white supremacy, anti-Catholicism, and anti-communism. The reign of the Legion, punctuated by murder and torture, ended in 1936 with the group's exposure and collapse, but pockets of organized prejudice persisted. Detroit's frustrated blacks often answered violence in kind: "On the night when Joe Louis would win a fight," an observer remarked, "a white man was not safe in Paradise Valley." Louis, who had grown up and perfected his boxing skills in Detroit, provided the black community rare moments of exultation in the cheerless depression years.[15]

The political impact of the depression was cataclysmic. Republicans had dominated Michigan politics since the party's founding. Disillusioned, thousands of voters chose Franklin Roosevelt by substantial margins in 1932 and 1936. Democratic success hinged on the participation of new voters, especially in the automotive centers. Although the Republicans retained a Senate seat and won the state narrowly for Wendell Willkie in 1940, the social upheaval of the 1930s forever cracked the political monolith that had been Michigan.

For some Americans, New Deal programs of relief and reconstruction were an insufficient remedy for the nation's ills. Many adhered to groups and personalities on the political extremes. The most controversial of the champions of the desperate was Father Charles E. Coughlin, pastor of the Shrine of the Little Flower in Royal Oak, a Detroit suburb. Allying himself with Roosevelt at first, the "radio priest" moved steadily rightward throughout the decade, backing an unsuccessful third-party venture in 1936. Millions of the faithful, however, continued to tune in weekly to his broadcast diatribes against Communists, Jews, and the president.

The most furious storms of Michigan's depression era broke not over Paradise Valley or Coughlin's church, but over the automobile plants. There, the struggle for unionization exploded in violence. Unionism had scarcely penetrated the industry before the 1930s. The American Federation of Labor (AFL) organized a few craftsmen, but refused to deal with the great majority of unskilled production workers, who could not be parceled out among the various craft jurisdictions. The auto manufacturers, convinced that the open shop was crucial to their success, made Detroit the "graveyard" of organizers. Lacking any protection, workers could be laid off or fired for a moment's tardiness, an angry gesture at a foreman, or for union talk. Management promoted and transferred without regard to seniority. The end of each model year brought long layoffs. The work was often monotonous and exhausting, and was made worse by the speed-up, the punishing increase in the tempo of the assembly line ordered from time to time. With the onset of the depression, hours of work grew more irregular and average weekly earnings fell steadily. The speed-up became the way of life in many plants, as owners sought to reduce costs.

Automotive workers grew increasingly restive as the depression deepened. Three thousand of the unemployed marched on the River Rouge plant in March, 1932, demanding jobs from Henry Ford, only to be met by tear gas and gunshots from the Dearborn police, which killed four and wounded two dozen. Spontaneous and generally unsuccessful strikes broke out in several Detroit auto factories in January, 1933. Workers gained new hope from the passage of Section 7(a) of the National Industrial Recovery Act (NIRA) of June, 1933, which authorized employees to organize without employer interference and to bargain collectively through self-chosen representatives. But the AFL renewed organizing efforts in the auto plants without skill or enthusiasm. The automakers fought 7(a) by establishing company unions and expanding and intensifying espionage aimed at union disruption. Section 7(a) died when the Supreme Court invalidated the NIRA in 1935. Later that year Congress replaced the defunct law's labor provisions with the Wagner Act, which explicitly recognized the principle of representation by majority rule and established the National Labor Relations Board (NLRB) to conduct representation elections and investigate unfair labor practices. The Supreme Court upheld the Wagner Act in 1937, but its constitutionality remained in doubt until then.

In this atmosphere of uncertainty the AFL called a convention in August, 1935, to weld its various automotive locals into the United Automobile Workers (UAW). Paid-up membership in the new organization amounted to a meager 22,687 workers, only 3,610 from Michigan. Within a year, the UAW threw off the AFL's chafing jurisdictional restraints, absorbed several competing unions, and affiliated with the new Committee for Industrial Organization, later the Congress of Industrial Organizations (CIO). John L. Lewis, Sidney Hillman, and others had founded the CIO to organize the mass-production industries. The AFL shortly thereafter expelled the UAW from the Federation.

With Lewis's powerful assistance and the intervention of Michigan's governor, Frank Murphy, the UAW established itself in the auto industry by winning an epic six-week strike against General Motors, which began at the end of December, 1936. Rather than picketing GM's plants from the outside, bold UAW strategists seized key installations in Flint. During the sit-down strike, UAW forces held off an attack by Flint city police, and Murphy rushed National Guard troops to Flint to preserve order. After lengthy negotiations, company and union reached agreement on February 11, 1937, GM consenting to enter into collective bargaining with the UAW. The Flint victory was an historic one for industrial unionism, and within six months UAW membership soared to 525,000.

The sit-down triumph, however, hardly removed all obstacles in the UAW's path. Although Chrysler and many parts manufacturers capitulated to the union, auto management dealt, in David Brody's words, only "grudgingly and conditionally" with organized labor. Henry Ford, moreover, stood adamantly against the UAW. His chief lieutenant, Harry Bennett, had assembled an unsavory collection of prizefighters and thugs

into the Ford Service Department, a threatening presence
within the Rouge that effectively discouraged organizers. On
May 26, 1937, a group of servicemen brutally beat a delegation
of UAW leafleteers on an overpass leading to the main gate of
the Rouge. Through his control of the compliant Dearborn
city council, Ford secured enactment of an ordinance that prevented unionists from approaching the Rouge during shift
changes, when workers might be reached with literature. To
add to the troubles from without, the UAW was continually
torn by bitter internal dissension. The disputes culminated in
early 1939 with the breakup of the union into two antagonistic
parts. President Homer Martin took a minority faction into
the AFL, while the CIO endorsed the organization of a new
UAW under R. J. Thomas. Its dues-paying membership reduced to an unpromising ninety thousand, the UAW-CIO was
forced to undertake a series of time-consuming representation battles against its AFL rival.[16]

The recession of 1937–38 bulked large among the forces
adversely affecting the UAW-CIO. The automobile industry
appeared to be leading the nation out of the depression by
1937, production totaling nearly four million units. Late in
the year, however, President Roosevelt drew back from pump-
priming federal spending and a deep and pervasive slump set
in. By January, 1938, automotive layoffs became general, and
the industry's scheduled workweek dropped to sixteen hours
for most workers. Production fell by half, and unemployment
and dejection once more spread throughout Michigan. Not
until 1939 did state and nation begin to climb out of the recession, as car output increased by nearly a million units over the
previous year.

The heralded recovery could not disguise the effect of a
decade of stagnation. Because of the powerful upturn in auto
sales in 1939, Michigan presented a somewhat brighter picture
than did the nation as a whole. The figures, however, said nothing of the psychological decline—the attitudes engendered in
manufacturers by the long, slow depression years that had
closed plants, atrophied initiative, and numbed the will. Faith
in production as the key to American social and economic op-

portunity remained strong: Detroit's mayor Edward J. Jeffries, Jr., wrote in a 1940 article on his city that it was not engaged in "the mere mechanization of America or of the American people." The automobile, he asserted, "relieves them of much of life's drudgery, and frees them for more spiritual things." The depression, however, had convinced many American businessmen that overproduction presented a danger to their economic security.[17]

The automotive transformation had exacerbated latent tensions within Michigan society, setting group against group, occasionally with violent results. The depression created conditions that perpetuated intergroup hostility and gave rise to even more violent conflict, particularly between labor and management. Although the decline of the automobile industry apparently had been arrested by 1939, confidence had not yet fully returned. The damage to the social fabric seemed even more difficult to repair. Such were the outlines of Michigan's reviving economy and fragmented society as the nations of Europe, after twenty years of uneasy peace, once more plunged into war.

The citizens of Michigan, like those of the United States, confronted the European crisis with a particular reluctance. In the twenty-seven months following the invasion of Poland, the great majority of the American people were clearly unwilling to enter the war until the decision was forced on them at Pearl Harbor. They approved of financial and material assistance to Britain and the Soviet Union and of the president's rearmament program. They distractedly prayed for an Allied victory, but were uncertain as to how far to go without entering the war themselves. By early 1940, Michigan's press, principal ethnic groups, and major labor federations had adopted a pro-Allied position, but all remained resolutely noninterventionist. Before the Japanese attack, no influential figure or group in the state actively advocated American participation in the war. Isolationism remained a potent force in Michigan. The America First Committee (AFC) sponsored rallies in Detroit attended by thousands throughout 1941.

Government policy makers and public opinion drifted during late 1941, as the naval confrontation with Germany widened and negotiations between the United States and Japan reached stalemate. Readers of the *Detroit News* Sunday edition for December 7 found the pervasive sense of uncertainty mirrored in a plaintive editorial on the deteriorating Far Eastern situation, which said in part: "The Orient is far away. Reasons for American involvement there to the verge of war are probably not so well understood as they should be by Americans. We have no doubt that if the breaking point comes, the reasons obligating the United States to the point of war will be communicated . . . by the President. That would be action required by the circumstances."[18]

Then came Pearl Harbor. Observers noted a variety of emotions expressed on the streets of Michigan that Sunday afternoon, but above all, there seemed to be an almost palpable sense of relief. At last, the uncertainty was at an end. The closing of ranks began at once. "In harmony of action and unity of spirit is our strength," proclaimed the *Detroit Free Press.* Thousands flocked to recruiting stations and civilian defense volunteer headquarters. Output jumped at several Detroit plants on the day Congress declared war. Spokesmen for both the AFL and CIO issued statements in support of the war and pledges of no strikes for the duration. The Automobile Manufacturers Association reconstituted itself as the Automotive Council for War Production, promising to provide all the material an embattled nation might require. The AFC suspended activities, and the December 15 issue of *Social Justice,* Father Coughlin's isolationist weekly, gracelessly affirmed that "we will be no obstructionists in the pursuit of this war."[19]

Government officials and the press repeatedly stressed Michigan's critical role in the war. "It is a war where continuing production is all important," Governor Murray Van Wagoner said that December. "Detroit may well be the factor that wins it." An editor in Sault Ste. Marie reflected on the central significance to the war not merely of Detroit, but of machinery itself. "There is no talk of 'technological unemployment' today. The nation wants all the technology it can get. . . . The transition from a military to a peacetime economy again may make the machine seem fearsome, but as long as the war lasts, machinery will be the hope of this nation."[20]

The events of the six war years from 1939 to 1945 in many ways paralleled those of the previous forty. As Michigan's automobile industry grew out of carriage manufacture, so a new munitions industry arose on the foundations of automotive production. Hundreds of thousands of migrants once more streamed into the state's industrial centers. Housing, transportation, and other community facilities once more became congested. Wages and the cost of living renewed their race. Native residents, old stock and ethnics, mixed uneasily with augmented numbers of southern whites and blacks, sometimes with violent results. The transformation induced by the automobile revolution, however, took place over two score years; the forces let loose by the demands of war did their work in scarcely half a decade.

Chapter 1

"Victory Is Our Business"

★ 1 ★

The story of Michigan at war begins with production. The state played a central role in the drama of national economic mobilization. Factory and farm alike joined in the enterprise. Conversion from peace to war was hampered by technological complexity and human resistance. The imperatives of war production could be—and sometimes were—challenged; but no individual, no group, no community, could avoid confrontation with those demands. Production, in turn, was the catalyst for change throughout the economy and the society. To understand the character and quality of that change, it is necessary to comprehend the nature and scope of the production effort in Michigan.

The American military had long been interested in Michigan's arms production potential and had given "educational" defense orders to such firms as General Motors and Packard before September, 1939. Between the outbreak of war and June 1, 1940, the United States government and the Allies placed some twenty million dollars in contracts with state concerns for goods that could be produced with little or no plant conversion.[1] Michigan businessmen, however, responded less than enthusiastically to the prospect of defense work. Speaking on May 17, 1940, a day after President Roosevelt had appealed for the production of fifty thousand airplanes a year, Harvey Campbell, executive vice-president of the Detroit Board of Commerce, observed: "We must remember that war orders are a boom business, and that there is a definite end to it. . . . I don't believe that manufacturers are anxious for war business. They would rather see a steady line of production and employment."[2]

The automobile industry followed a policy toward the defense program that Barton Bernstein has characterized as "profit maximization and risk minimization."[3] Throughout the defense period, the automakers, while lifting passenger car output to near record levels, claimed that their plants could not be converted to armament production without an unconscionable loss of time, money, and equipment. Facility expansion, they also contended, might leave them at the end of the crisis with costly production capacity unwarranted by consumer demand. Suspicious of the New Deal, the industry sought to protect itself from the extension of government control certain to follow a switch to military production. The manufacturers hid their reluctance to convert behind blustering attacks, sometimes justified, upon the government's bureaucratic failings and the maldistribution of contracts and scarce materials. As patriotic Americans, the leaders of the industry pledged to do whatever they could for the national defense, but they so defined their capabilities as virtually to rule out any voluntary reduction in the flow of civilian motor vehicles. During World War I the industry had adopted the same position and had fought the War Industries Board to a near standstill over the issue of conversion.

Automotive executives, like their counterparts in other businesses, rarely made their foreign policy views widely known. Henry Ford, however, shocked the nation in June, 1940, by rejecting—after previously accepting—a multi-million dollar contract for the manufacture of Rolls-Royce aircraft engines. Ford had learned that the motors would be sent directly to England; and while declaring himself ready to work for the defense of the United States, he flatly refused to build weapons for the Allies. In contrast to Ford, William S. Knudsen, a bluff, sixty-two-year-old Dane who had risen to the presidency of General Motors, had taken his stand in May by resigning his office to accept an appointment as production specialist on the National Defense Advisory Commission (NDAC). President Roosevelt later appointed Knudsen one of two Directors-

General (the other was Sidney Hillman of the CIO) of the Office
of Production Management (OPM), the agency that superseded
the NDAC in December, 1940. Knudsen's elevation indicated
both Washington's respect for automotive know-how and the
extent of the defense role the industry was expected to play. A
man of great practical experience in manufacturing, "Big Bill"
Knudsen had little grasp of broad policy questions. Like many
other Detroit industrialists, he identified the national welfare
with that of the automobile industry. As head of OPM he
worked to shield the industry from what he considered damaging government intervention.

The automakers' reluctance to convert their facilities to defense production drew scathing criticism from New Dealers
and other liberals who complained that the industrialists were
acting on the principle of "business as usual." Industry deserved much of the obloquy heaped upon it, for as Geoffrey
Perrett remarks: "American business was simply not going to
risk its fortunes on anything so transient as the defense boom.
If it had its way, it would have concentrated on satisfying the
swelling public demand for consumer goods and let the government worry about defense, at least for a while longer."[4] For
his part, President Roosevelt moved with care and caution in
dealing with the business community. Despite his insistence on
"speed and speed now," he did not call for the full conversion
of the automobile industry prior to the nation's entry into war.

Reluctant or not, Michigan industrialists accepted an increasing number of defense contracts beginning in the summer of 1940. In July Packard picked up the order for nine
thousand Rolls-Royce engines rejected by Ford; and Briggs,
Continental Motors, and Murray Corporation started work on
various aircraft subassemblies.[5] To expedite these orders, companies opened and retooled plants that had been closed during the depression. With assembly lines still engaged in
passenger car production, however, it became necessary for
the federal government to finance and build at taxpayer ex-
pense huge new factories that were then turned over to the
auto industry for the execution of specific defense contracts.
Chrysler Corporation and Army officials agreed in August on

a contract for medium tanks to be fulfilled in an enormous, forty-one-million-dollar arsenal, constructed between September, 1940, and April, 1941, in a 113-acre former wheat field in Warren Township, seventeen miles north of Detroit. New factories rose throughout the Detroit metropolitan area and in Flint, Saginaw, and Muskegon as well.

No new plant was as spectacular as the bomber factory built by Henry Ford in southeastern Michigan. In late 1940 Ford agreed to construct 1,200 B-24 medium bombers from plans to be supplied by Consolidated Aircraft of San Diego. However, when Charles Sorensen, Ford's veteran chief engineer, discovered to his dismay that Consolidated's relatively primitive construction methods appeared to preclude mass production, he drew up a sketch of a mile-long factory in which all parts of the aircraft would be manufactured, and thus the planes, many times the size of automobiles, might be assembled on a single continuous moving line. Skeptical Army officials received Sorensen's ideas coolly, agreeing in February, 1941, only to the manufacture of about two hundred bombers a month, almost half of which would be assembled elsewhere. Sorensen and Ford took this qualified approval as the go-ahead for full assembly. On March 28, 1941, workers began clearing timber from hundreds of acres of farmland four miles southwest of Ypsilanti in Washtenaw County, some thirty-five miles southwest of Detroit. Groundbreaking at the plant-site took place twenty days later. The plant, like the township in which it was situated, took its name from a small meandering stream nearby—Willow Run.

Michigan's economic condition steadily improved throughout 1940, and the year ended as the most prosperous since the onset of the depression. Recovery did not take place at a uniform rate—Grand Rapids and Kalamazoo remained relatively unaffected by the upswing, and depression persisted in the northern half of the state—but prosperity, even if only a pallid simulacrum of the boom of the 1920s, returned to the larger industrial centers.[6] The accelerating recovery, however, resulted primarily from the increase in passenger car sales that had begun in 1939 rather than from the state's involvement in the national defense program. To be sure, the state, by January 1, 1941, had received a total of nearly six hundred million dollars in prime defense contracts, as well as uncounted millions of dollars in untabulated subcontracts.[7] But most of the defense plants were still being built, and few of the armament contracts had been completed. The automakers, meanwhile, sold a total of 3,717,385 units in 1940, a rise of 28 percent over sales in the previous year.[8] Consumer demand for automobiles rose even higher in 1941 as rumors of partial automotive curtailment became a reality.

In the winter of 1940–41, Walter Reuther, the youthful head of the UAW's General Motors department, focused new attention on the issue of automotive conversion by presenting a startling proposal. Reuther premised his plan on the assumption that the automotive industry was using only half of its potential production capacity and that almost all the idle tools and space could be adapted to the construction of military aircraft. The component parts of airplanes were to be manufactured in the inactive areas of appropriate facilities— fuselages in body plants, for example—and the completed planes would then be assembled in huge hangers. Reuther proposed a presidentially appointed nine-member industrial council, representing labor, business, and government, to supervise the entire production process. Conversion could be completed within six months, Reuther declared, whereafter the automobile factories would begin turning out five hundred planes a day, or 150,000 a year.

Reuther campaigned vigorously for adoption of the scheme, but found no interest in crucial economic quarters. The aircraft industry expressed fear that approval of the plan might lead to a permanent loss of business to the auto industry. The automakers, for their part, ravaged the proposal. Labor support for the industrial council idea was spotty; most CIO and AFL unionists had no desire to assume managerial functions, and the Communists opposed the notion from the outset, although their reasons for doing so changed with each revision of the party line. Save for a flurry of interest after Pearl Harbor, nothing further was heard of the Reuther Plan. David

Brody remarks that it was a "genuine proposal for basic change, and its rejection demonstrates not only the uncertainty attending the nation's slow advance toward full mobilization, but the unwillingness of the major interest groups to embrace any scheme that threatened to alter fundamental economic relationships, even in the name of national defense."[9]

By the winter of 1941, unrestrained automotive output had begun to create grave shortages of desperately needed machine tools and of such critical materials as chrome, copper, lead, steel, and zinc. Competition between the automakers and the defense effort for these materials produced shortages for other manufacturers, especially for small businesses and plants that could not obtain munitions contracts. As affected concerns shut down for lack of supplies, their employees became victims of priorities unemployment. WPA observers in Michigan spotted examples of the process as early as February, 1941.[10] Knudsen had ruled in January that unrestricted automotive output could continue for at least six months, but as shortages and unemployment rose together, he began to retreat from that position. After consultation with the automakers, he ordered on April 17, a 20 percent cut in scheduled automobile production between August, 1941, and July 31, 1942. Actually, since Knudsen had been expected to curtail output by up to a third, the industry had received something of a reprieve. The only limit on production until August 1, 1941, was the availability of materials, and total 1941 motor vehicle production could still exceed that of the 1940–41 model year.

The industry's persisting reluctance over the spring and summer to offer its established facilities to the defense program aroused fresh criticism both of Detroit and of Knudsen's leadership of OPM. On July 20, while Knudsen was absent from Washington, Leon Henderson, director of the Office of Price Administration and Civilian Supply, unilaterally ordered a 50 percent curtailment of auto production for the 1941–42 model year. Henderson's order provoked outraged howls from Michigan. A sudden, arbitrarily imposed cut, Governor Van Wagoner declared, would leave thousands of workers jobless, increase the welfare load, and dangerously lower the state's tax revenues.[11] Knudsen protested the severity of the curtailment, and his influence together with the pleas from Michigan moved President Roosevelt to soften the blow. At a July 23 press conference he announced that the cut, to take effect November 1, would be so structured, quarter by quarter, that the steepest drop in auto output would not come until the summer of 1942. Until the Henderson cut took effect, automobile production continued under the 20 percent curtailment ordered by Knudsen. The automakers adorned the 1942 models with vitally needed chrome and steel.

The tempo of the defense program increased rapidly in Michigan during the waning months of 1941. On October 28, Undersecretary of War Robert Paterson dedicated the Hudson naval arsenal at Centerline in Macomb County, a few miles from the Chrysler tank plant. Hudson planned to manufacture the twenty millimeter Oerlikon antiaircraft gun in the 135-acre complex, which had been erected in less than eight months.[12] Willow Run, although still incomplete, began to turn out small quantities of B-24 parts in November. The construction of the bomber factory had been delayed because Henry Ford had insisted that the entire plant, which, as planned, would have been located partly in Democratically dominated Wayne County, be redesigned so that it would be safely tucked entirely inside Republican Washtenaw County. The cost of the installation, including a large airfield, increased from an estimated eleven million dollars to over forty-seven million dollars. Toward year's end, the automobile industry finally began to approach the central position in national defense production that the government had assigned to it.[13]

The prospect of mass unemployment in Michigan, rather than the problem of manpower allocation, increasingly preoccupied government, industry, and labor officials during the last half of 1941. Priorities unemployment spread across the state, devastating small businesses but leaving the automakers still relatively untouched. Looking ahead to the fall and winter, employment experts could see nothing but gloom, for the Henderson cut was to take effect just as many plants were scheduled to close for the changeover to defense work. Thousands of workers would thus be made jobless while waiting absorption into defense employment. Automobile executives expected a brief jobless period, but most other authorities agreed that a long time, perhaps as much as a year, would be required to take up the manpower slack, a time during which most workers would probably exhaust their meager state unemployment benefits.[14]

To the very eve of war, the auto industry successfully protected its cherished factories from conversion. Certainly from mid-1941 onward, if not before, thousands of tons of critical materials and countless man-hours were wasted in the production of passenger cars. The automakers allowed concern for the preservation of their industry and for profit to obscure the very vision upon which the government was depending for the creation of production "miracles." As a result of the delay the industry was only half ready in December, 1941. Government restrictions on the automakers, of course, had begun to take effective hold by the fall of 1941. By the summer of 1942, auto production would have been reduced to 38 percent of 1940–41 output, and a firm direction of priorities by Washington away from passenger cars might have reduced output still further, forcing the carmakers into the business of defense. Pearl Harbor, of course, changed all this.

Change, however, still came with difficulty. Despite twenty years of planning for economic mobilization in wartime, the military seemed to have formulated no concerted program for utilization of Detroit's resources. At a government-industry conference held in Washington on January 5, 1942, Knudsen simply read out a list of war orders and asked for volunteers to produce the items. For their part, certain auto executives, including C. E. Wilson of GM, apparently harbored the hope that motorcar production might continue in some fashion throughout the war. That hope proving unrealizable, the industry as a whole began to press the government to reinstate the January quota, which had been cut shortly after the war began, so that the thousands of units still clogging the plants could be assembled. Leon Henderson, now director of the re-

organized Office of Price Administration (OPA), accepted the
arguments of industry leaders and of key OPM officials that
the need to retain workforces intact, to preserve investments
in expensive inventories, and to provide a pool of rationed automobiles necessitated renewed production. On January 1,
Henderson, in turn, convinced the Supply Priorities and Allo-
cations Board, yet another of the agencies Roosevelt had established to coordinate the defense effort, to double the January
quota to two hundred thousand units.[15]

A national demand had arisen meanwhile for a drastic reform of the government's production bureaucracy. The divided authority of Knudsen and Hillman and the multiple
tiers of agencies too strongly symbolized the era of "business
as usual." President Roosevelt reacted to the criticism by establishing the War Production Board (WPB) on January 16, 1942,
under the chairmanship of Donald Nelson, a former Sears,
Roebuck marketing executive. The WPB inherited the organizational structure of the OPM but was endowed with vastly
greater power over the civilian economy than had been granted
to its predecessor. Nelson rightly understood that his first major task was the full conversion of the auto industry, which had
been asked to produce one-fifth of all American war material.
On January 21, therefore, he set up an office in Detroit and
delegated supervisory authority over the conversion process to
Ernest Kanzler, a forty-nine-year-old veteran of the auto industry who had been Ford's production chief and who was
then serving as head of the WPB's Automotive Division. Kanzler's rhetoric seemed to mark him as an apostle of thoroughgoing conversion, and in later years Nelson had generous praise
for the "magnificent job" done by the director of the WPB's
Detroit office. In fact, Kanzler displayed that same solicitude
for the automakers' private interests that had characterized
Knudsen's tenure at the OPM. Toward that end, he loaded his
staff with former car salesmen and sales managers, men too
much in awe of the auto magnates to make exacting demands
upon them.

Automobile output rose as the end of civilian production
neared. A WPB order of January 20 extended the January

quota deadline to February 10, and Kanzler "buried" the fact
that the automakers exceeded that quota by several thousand
units. In quiet ceremonies in Flint, Lansing, and Detroit,
workers and reporters bade farewell to the last passenger cars,
which were promptly commandeered for government use.
Certain types of nonessential parts manufacture, however,
continued long after February 10, and customary patterns of
thought persisted among the automakers. "The dread of what
a better-prepared competitor may do to them in the postwar
market dies hard in many of the boys," William Richards of
the Office of Government Reports wrote in late March.
"Chrysler Corporation disbanded only a week ago its automobile design department, after 'finishing up plans for 1943
models.' "[16]

Labor and liberal groups attacked the industry for resuming passenger car production and for its reluctance to abandon
practices that slowed conversion. As before, the United Automobile Workers stood out as a vigorous critic of the automakers. On the evening of March 24 between ten thousand and
twenty thousand persons met in Detroit's Cadillac Square to
protest delays in conversion. Bands played patriotic music, and
the audience heard speeches by national UAW and local CIO
leaders. "The workers stand ready to do everything in their
power to assure victory, but the plants are not ready," said
UAW secretary-treasurer George Addes. "The corporations
are not rushing the changeover nearly as rapidly as they did in
the peacetime days of changing from one model to another
one."[17] A government opinion survey conducted in the latter
half of March indicated that Detroit workers agreed with their
union leaders in regarding management as a major hindrance
to war production; the rank and file, however, tended to view
the government as an even greater source of production problems than the auto companies were.[18]

While automobile executives and labor leaders argued, the
conversion of Michigan's auto plants proceeded. "Where the
assembly lines used to be," A. H. Raskin of the *New York Times*
wrote after visiting a Detroit plant, "one sees swarms of construction workers ripping out overhead conveyor systems, up-

rooting old machines, rushing discarded equipment to snow-covered parking lots. . . . Great holes are chopped in concrete floors to provide anchorage for machines big enough to be used in making four-motored bombers and sixty-ton tanks. New machines start whirring even before they have been fully bolted to the floor. Old machines are hauled to repair shops and, whenever possible, adapted to war use."[19] A cautious Knudsen had estimated in February that between five and six months would be necessary for the completion of conversion. No one really knew how much time Detroit would require to become fully engaged in war production, but even the harshest critics of the automobile industry suggested only that hidebound men and ideas temporarily were slowing the fabulous machinery. In these grimmest moments of the war, darkened by the fall of one island bastion after another to the Japanese, the productive capacity of Detroit became the chief symbol of the nation's ultimate military resurgence and, therefore, of victory itself.[20]

The early stages of conversion, as expected, resulted in massive unemployment across Michigan. The December shutdown not only winnowed the ranks of the blue collar workers but also had a disastrous impact upon the retail and service firms dependent upon the automobile industry. Unemployment rose to 225,000 persons statewide in January, but the slump, although more drastic in extent than the optimists had forecast, failed to attain either the length or severity predicted by the most pessimistic observers. Joblessness receded significantly by June, thanks largely to a huge Army truck order placed in November, 1941, the sudden deluge of additional war work after Pearl Harbor, and the need to employ workers in the conversion process itself.[21]

Begun slowly and erratically, automotive conversion was substantially complete by October. The process had taken longer—by about three months—than generally had been expected. Mass production economies, however, had begun to take effect, and numerous firms announced that previously established output goals had been attained or exceeded ahead of schedule. At the end of 1942 Detroit's annual delivery rate of war goods was running in the vicinity of eight billion to ten billion dollars. The automakers had produced sufficient ord- nance, motorized vehicles, and quartermaster gear to supply the Army through 1943. In October, 1943, the industry achieved the long-predicted delivery rate of one billion dollars in armament per month.[22] American war production as a whole reached its peak at the same time.

The motor vehicle and parts manufacturers turned out a range of articles that included engines, aircraft, tanks, jeeps, armorplate, land and naval artillery, shells, bombs, machine guns, rifles, bullets, mines, helmets, gliders, pontoon bridges, cooking pots—and 749 automobiles, produced in 1943 and 1944 for government and military use. The industry vastly ex- panded its facilities in order to fulfill its wartime task. General Motors, for example, built nearly nine-hundred-million-dollars worth of new plant between 1940 and 1944, almost all of which was paid for by the government. The figure represented 116.5 percent of GM's 1939 gross capital assets, and Chrysler and Packard recorded even higher expansion-to-gross asset ratios.[23]

To each assignment the automotive engineers and tech- nicians brought their accumulated experience with mass- production methods. None of their accomplishments, substantial though they were, could fully qualify as the "production mir- acles" expected by the American people. Miracles, after all, did not require the long, patient effort needed to perfect indus- trial processes. Nor were miracles usually preceded by false starts or poorly executed conceptions. Francis Walton has de- scribed in detail the difficulties encountered by the automak- ers in adapting custom-crafted, precision-built weaponry and military power plants to mass manufacture. Mistakes in design and planning cluttered the path to full production. After working sixty- to seventy-hour weeks, the engineers at Pontiac refashioned the Swiss Oerlikon antiaircraft gun, creating vir- tually a new weapon, which they then scrapped because of de- sign flaws. Other faults did not become evident until combat use of Detroit's output. Aircraft mechanics discovered that

Ford's mass-produced cast cylinder heads for the Pratt and Whitney engine did not last as long as previous heads, which had been forged.

Much of the industry's difficulty could be attributed either to governmental maladministration or to abrupt shifts in production demanded by the armed forces. Until mid-1943, the lack of an effective mechanism for the allocation of scarce raw materials both created and augmented shortages of vital manufacturing components. The WPB's Controlled Materials Plan (CMP) thereafter limited production scheduling to existing quantities of steel, brass, aluminum, and copper. The CMP partially alleviated the allocation crisis, but largely because of military resistance, it did not work as well as expected, and supply uncertainty still plagued industry. Throughout the war, the military demanded endless modifications in equipment and abrupt switches in production from one item to another. Entire assembly lines had to be rearranged or ripped out with each change. In November and December, 1942, for example, Detroit undertook what amounted to a second conversion to meet revised production requirements.[24] Although the annual model changeover had accustomed the auto industry to frequent retooling and redesigning, the speed and extent of the wartime process were unprecedented.

Eclipsed by Chrysler's Chicago engine plant for the title of world's largest factory, Willow Run, with its low-roofed, sixty-seven-acre main building and 5,450-foot final assembly line, nonetheless remained the premier symbol of American industrial power at war.[25] To Charles Lindbergh, who became a Ford aviation consultant in 1942, the bomber plant was "a sort of Grand Canyon of the mechanized world."[26] "It is impossible in words to convey the feel and smell and tension of Willow Run under full headway," wrote James Stermer, a researcher at the University of Michigan, who worked at the factory during the spring of 1944. "The roar of the machinery, the special din of the riveting gun absolutely deafening nearby, the throbbing crash of the giant metal presses . . . the far-reaching line of half-born skyships growing wings under swarms of workers, and the restless cranes swooping overhead."[27] In Glendon

Swarthout's 1943 novel, *Willow Run,* the "immensity, insane, overpowering immensity" of the plant seemed to reduce the human actors to insignificance.[28]

But Willow Run also incorporated within itself the manifold problems, human and technological, inherent in war production. Jigs and fixtures arrived behind schedule and tooling proceeded slowly during the first year of output. Distant from housing and transportation facilities, the factory could neither attract nor retain a stable workforce. In all of 1942, Willow Run produced only fifty-six immediately flyable bombers. Employment at the plant attained a wartime peak of 42,331 in June, 1943, a figure far below the original estimates. Production increased after the company agreed to decentralize subassembly work so that more Willow Run manpower could be devoted to the primary task of final assembly, and beginning in the spring of 1943, a procession of tools and machinery moved out of the plant to other Ford facilities and subcontractors. The work force ultimately stablized and became more efficient, while it shrank to 28,411 persons in June, 1944, and to 20,200 in April, 1945. Production totals forged steadily ahead of schedule, Liberators ultimately rolling out of the plant onto the adjoining airfield at the rate of one plane every sixty-three minutes. In the spring of 1945, the Army recognized Willow Run's belated success by awarding the plant an "E" banner, the symbol of production excellence.

Although the automakers dominated the state industrial scene, their efforts were not the whole story of Michigan manufacturing at war. Hundreds of companies in dozens of communities produced every conceivable item of war. The J. W. Defoe shipyards at Bay City built subchasers and destroyer escorts. Dow Chemical processed magnesium at Ludington and Marysville and created dozens of chemically based war products at its main plant in Midland. One such product, a plastic packaging wrap called Saran, seemed to have postwar commercial possibilities. The Kellogg Company of Battle Creek produced millions of units of its wartime specialty, the K Ration. A converted factory in Petoskey transformed milkweed pods gathered by Michigan schoolchildren into a filler for life jackets, replacing the normally used kapok, cut off by the Japanese. A company in Monroe made clay pigeons for target practice; a firm in Grand Haven built soda fountain equipment for post exchanges; and the inmates of the Jackson and Ionia state penitentiaries produced cotton shirts and twine. At sixty Detroit area companies hundreds of employees, unknowingly part of a great national network, funnelled design work, tools, and gauges into the most secret of all war production efforts— the Manhattan Project.[29]

At the outset of the defense buildup, the military had entrusted the production task to the nation's industrial titans, believing that small business was unable to play an effective part in rearmament. The OPM attempted to help smaller Michigan firms obtain defense orders but, as elsewhere in the nation, to little avail.[30] Defenders of small business argued that industry's duplication of thousands of machine tools available in idle shops resulted in a waste of both materials and time. The possibility that the war might wipe out entire sectors of small business, moreover, raised the question of whether the preservation of one of America's most sacrosanct institutions might not be worth an occasional loss of the advantages of scale. Congress established the Smaller War Plants Corporation to mobilize small business in a more effective manner, but many small businesses continued to suffer a contract drought. The "little man" could not compete on even terms with the giants for manpower or for engineering expertise, and the CMP discriminated against small firms in the distribution of vital metals.

Michigan industrialists sometimes violated laws and regulations in pursuit of business since the procurement and retention of war contracts often meant the difference between survival and failure.[31] The major scandal that involved both Michigan and national business was not the occasional payment of bribes, however, but the abuse of the cost-plus contract. The impossibility of estimating labor and material costs in the production of military equipment not scheduled to be delivered for months or years forced the government to employ the cost-plus agreement, by which Washington assumed the essential expenses of production and compensated the manufac-

turer with a stated percentage of profit or a fixed fee per unit
of output. Particularly large profits could be made under the
latter agreement when technical improvements vastly increased the number of units that could be produced. Labor
repeatedly charged that the automobile industry wasted resources because cost-plus provided no incentive to limit costs.
The automakers denied these accusations, but Congressional
inquiries bore out many union claims. "It is essential that Congress take steps now to abolish [cost-plus] contracts before they
have utterly destroyed the moral fiber of the American busi-
nessman and the American worker," Michigan's Republican
Senator Homer Ferguson, no foe of free enterprise, told a
Congressional hearing in March, 1944.[32] Abandonment of cost-
plus finally became general in the spring of 1945.

The cost-plus problem was only one facet of the question of
inordinate wartime profits. The auto industry's denial of prof-
iteering was supported by an extensive OPA survey of American business, which disclosed that automakers' rate of return
on sales fell steadily throughout the war as a result of contract
renegotiations.[33] These statistics, however, did not impress auto
workers who compared their wages with the six-figure annual
salaries of the top automotive executives. Business critics,
moreover, questioned what appeared to be unusually attractive
government inducements given to industry as an incentive to
produce for war, encouragements that included generous de-
preciation allowances, relaxation of antitrust prosecutions, and
an excess-profits tax written so as to return to industry much
of the revenue collected from it during the war. The automobile industry had demanded these perquisites as the price of
its abandonment of profitable civilian production, but as Secretary of War Henry Stimson had observed in a blunt 1940
diary entry, "If you are going to try to go to war or prepare
for war in a capitalist country, you have got to let business
make money out of the process, or business won't work."[34]

"The most important things in this war are machines." So
declared Marshal Joseph Stalin in November, 1943, at the Allied conference in Teheran, in a toast to President Roosevelt
and America's productive capacity.[35] The conflict of ideologies

and economic interests had plunged the world into mortal combat, but victory or defeat depended not upon the rectitude of doctrines but primarily upon the ability of opposing nations to manufacture the machines of war. The American nation devised means by which to manufacture those machines in overwhelming numbers so that long before its enemies surrendered, the United States won the war that counted most—the war of production.

Statistics attest to Michigan's decisive role in the winning of the production war. With 4 percent of the nation's population, the state obtained better than 10 percent, or $21,754,000,000, of the nearly two hundred billion dollars in major prime war supply and facility contracts awarded by the U.S. government and foreign purchasers from June, 1940, to September, 1945. Only New York outranked Michigan in this category. Such monetary comparisons do not reveal the full extent of any state's contribution to the war effort since the figures do not include the billions of dollars in subcontracts that were left uncomputed. No American city, in any event, carried out more war work than Detroit did. The four-county Detroit metropolitan area, the center of the state's industrial activity, accounted for more than 70 percent of Michigan's production total. In addition, Genesee and Ingham Counties each received more than one billion dollars in war orders, and nine other counties secured at least one hundred million dollars in armament contracts.[36]

The enormous war production achieved by Michigan and the United States represented a victory for industry, but victory was won no more easily within the plants than on the battlefronts. "It is a harsh judgement to say that things were so bad that it is a wonder we produced enough to win the war," three former WPB staff members wrote in 1949, "but it is sound, in terms of the inadequacies of administrative methods and procedures."[37] Certainly, the performance of the Germans in maintaining production until the last months of the war or that of the Russians in moving entire factory complexes thousands of miles to safety behind the Urals are feats no less remarkable than those executed by Detroit. The war years,

moreover, witness no fundamental change in previously established industrial methods, only a number of refinements of
those methods. Behind the "miracle" lay the ability of American factories to convert rapidly to new kinds of products; the
capacity of American men and women to learn and efficiently
perform novel and often changing industrial techniques; the
development of labor-saving devices; the standardization of
parts; and the essential belief on the part of management and
workers alike that production would bring victory.[38]

The power and prestige of American business rose as each
additional gun, ship, plane, and tank rolled off the assembly
line. The trend toward concentration of production within a
few companies in each field accelerated. Even among the automakers, the most concentrated of all industrial production
groups as of 1939, a further constriction of competition took
place.[39] A formerly hostile national administration turned over
vast areas of wartime authority to leaders of industry and finance, actions that served simultaneously to vindicate and re-
habilitate business despite the criticism of cost-plus contracts
and high profits. The dollar-a-year men who flocked to Washington to staff the production bureaucracy used their influence to shape domestic economic and social policies in a
conservative fashion that alarmed the reduced and beleaguered forces of liberalism.

In the full flush of regained public respect, the depression-
era defensiveness of corporate America was transformed into
a confidence that verged at times on arrogance, a mood aptly
reflected in the following 1943 paean to Michigan industry,
published in Detroit's leading commercial journal: "To have a
guiding hand in the magic accomplishments that have been
wrought . . . must thrill the hearts of the great industrialists of
the state. Their know-how, their patriotism and lack of self-
interest, their efficiency and initiativeness [*sic*] alone accomplished the miracle of democracy."[40] The men who had been
unable to repair the mighty production machine after its
breakdown in 1929 now—with generous assistance from the
federal government—had the mechanism in full gear, most
spectacularly in the automobile industry. General Motors, to be

sure, had the right to claim, as it did in advertisement after advertisement, that "Victory Is Our Business."[41]

<h2 style="text-align:center">★ 2 ★</h2>

Industrial manpower was an essential element of the industrial triumph. The American labor force expanded between 1940 and 1945 from 56,180,000 persons to 65,290,000 persons in response to wartime production requirements. The manpower supply grew even more rapidly in Michigan than in the rest of the nation. Total employment in the Detroit labor market area attained a wartime high during November, 1943, more than doubling to 867,000 persons from the 396,000 at work three years earlier. The size of Michigan's labor force gradually declined during the last twenty months of war, but as late as December, 1944, one out of five inhabitants of the state was directly engaged in war production.[42]

To replace the hundreds of thousands of men lost to the armed services, Michigan industry obtained workers from many little-used or previously untapped sources. Among this latter group were thousands of the physically handicapped; Ford had pioneered in the hiring of deaf, blind, and amputee workers, and the United States Employment Service (USES) opened a special recruitment drive in January, 1943, to attract more of the disabled into manufacturing. Among Willow Run's claims to fame was the plant's use of midgets, who worked within confined fuselage and wing spaces. Many professional people toiled part-time at war plants, along with retirees back at work for the duration. At the cost of twelve million dollars the state school system graduated 418,315 persons from war vocational education courses between 1940 and 1945, and an additional 123,120 students completed regular vocational training programs during the same period. Until its termination on July 1, 1943, the National Youth Administration taught war jobs to large numbers of Michigan young people. Upgraders, who underwent in-plant training, also increased the available pool of skilled and semiskilled personnel.[43]

Michigan never experienced an overall labor shortage, although spot scarcities, both qualitative and quantitative, developed from time to time. The Detroit Tigers, like all major league baseball teams, lost most of their best talent to the military, mounting their wartime pennant drives with a motley collection of teenagers, has-beens, and Selective Service rejects. Tool designers and process men, craftsmen without whose talents conversion would be impossible, were in particularly short supply during 1942. By late 1943 the scarcity of common labor had begun to pose a serious problem for the forge and foundry industry of Muskegon and Detroit. The Allied invasion of Europe hung for a time on the ability of Muskegon foundries to produce engine blocks for landing craft, and delays in Detroit during the fall of 1944 slowed truck replacements for the "Red Ball Express," which carried supplies to General George Patton's Third Army.[44] Workers shunned the hard, dirty, and traditionally low-paying foundry jobs in favor of more attractive employment. The need was only for a few thousand men, but the crisis did not ease until the advent of post–V-E Day cutbacks.

Most major war plants were subject to a high degree of employee turnover; many firms had to seek several times the number of workers actually needed to maintain an adequate labor force and to replace those employees who quit for one reason or another. The draft caused the most persistent headaches for plant managers. Employers often spent days or weeks finding and training suitable substitutes for drafted skilled workers, but substitutions were sometimes impossible to make. To the annoyance of manufacturers, local draft boards doled out industrial deferments sparingly. Although the number of state men in industrial-deferred classifications rose nearly twenty-fold from January, 1942, to September, 1944, the total of industrial deferees represented less than 15 percent of the manufacturing labor force.[45] As induction neared, moreover, many men succumbed to "draftitis," staying off the job as much as two days a week, their efficiency lowered while on the job by the contemplation of an uncertain future in the military.[46]

The continued problem of pirating contributed to the difficulty of maintaining a stable workforce in Detroit. Small private shops lured away tool designers from the automakers by offering higher pay than the workers could earn under their

union contract, and then asked exorbitant fees from the previous employers for vital design work. The large concerns were
forced to employ the independents, and often found themselves rehiring their former employees at inflated wages. Labor
brokerages, sometimes set up in hole-in-the-wall offices, existed solely to hire skilled workers and to lease or rent the men
at above ceiling wages to desperate manufacturers in the Detroit area or to anyone else in the country who could afford
the price. In December, 1942, the War Labor Board (WLB)
established a special commission to police the city's troubled
market in toolmakers. This agency substantially reduced the
degree of pirating, but it proved impossible to eliminate the
brokers altogether.[47]

Labor-management conflict over seniority issues introduced
an additional element of manpower instability. During 1941,
thousands of skilled and semiskilled workers in civilian industries had refused to transfer to defense jobs for fear of losing
seniority accumulated with their existing employer. Many
skilled workers in the auto industry found themselves being
laid off because their employers were offering the new, high-
wage defense jobs not on a seniority basis but to inadequately
trained and newly hired migrant laborers. In September, 1941,
after conferences in Detroit among government, industry, and
union officials, the OPM had adopted a voluntary policy regarding transfer and seniority problems. The OPM plan allowed laid-off automotive workers to seek defense employment
with other companies without losing their seniority after their
new employment had been certified to the previous employer.
The original employer, in turn, could recall such workers for
defense jobs on a week's notice. Transfers to defense work
within firms were to be made on a seniority basis unless an
insufficient number of high seniority employees was available.
Where new employees had to be hired, preference was to be
given to workers from local industry.[48]

Throughout the war, local and national UAW leaders contended that Detroit industry generally violated both the letter
and the spirit of the OPM agreement. Some firms placed men
in lower-wage or nonwar production-related occupations after

calling employees back from their defense employment elsewhere; other companies simply refused to hire according to
seniority. Management's hoarding of labor during the conversion period also enfeebled the plan. Many firms that temporarily had no war work kept their skilled workforce intact in idle
plants lest these plants be caught short of manpower when they
did receive contracts. It was not until March, 1945, that the
automakers and the auto union arrived at a mutually acceptable arrangement that permitted employees to move into essential trades while accumulating seniority with the original
employer, instead of remaining at the seniority level attained at
the time of the transfer.[49]

Of all the problems that affected manpower stability—and
hence, production—none was more complex or intractable than
absenteeism. Critical newspapers and employers frequently
portrayed the absent worker as a slacker; Lieutenant-Colonel
Eddie Rickenbacker, returned from a three-week ordeal in the
Pacific following a plane crash, told a cheering crowd of automobile executives at a Detroit banquet in January, 1943, that
"there are no absentees in foxholes."[50] Data gathered in Detroit
war plants that May revealed an average absence rate of 5 percent, which may have been about 40 percent higher than the
peacetime rate.[51] It had been found, however, that a small percentage of chronic absentees consistently accounted for most
industrial nonattendance.

The causes of absenteeism were many. Workers frequently
became disheartened when they could not see the necessity for
their individual effort or when material shortages interrupted
production. Job shopping and work-connected illness or fatigue raised the absence rate, as did housing and transportation difficulties. Since many stores were not open at convenient
hours, some employees—especially women—had no choice
but to take time off to buy groceries or to do other shopping.
A certain proportion of the newly employed labor force adjusted poorly to industrial discipline, and numbers of men and
women lacked motivation, working irregularly because of
drinking or because they lived only for the moment. Not surprisingly, much absenteeism took place on weekends, Fri-

days, and Mondays. Despite attempted cures for the problem that ranged from coercive threats to positive incentives for good attendance, an irreducible minimum of absenteeism remained.[52]

Turnover, pirating, and absenteeism were not limited to Detroit, and their deleterious effects appeared to demand a comprehensive federal manpower policy. During the conversion period, the USES, a product of the early 1930s, stood ready as a referral bureau, but companies were under no obligation to call on it, and many employers did not. They doubted the agency's ability to meet their specific needs and desired to keep hiring entirely in their own hands.[53] In April, 1942, the USES was absorbed into the newly created War Manpower Commission (WMC) under Federal Security Administration chief and former Indiana governor Paul V. McNutt. Theoretically, the WMC assumed responsibility for the coordination of the procurement and mobilization of civilian and military manpower. The Commission, however, suffered from many administrative inadequacies that ultimately rendered it the least effective of the wartime superagencies. Its reliance on volunteerism, for example, often undercut the goals of manpower policy, since the government's purpose could be thwarted if local labor or management did not agree with a particular Washington program.

Throughout the war, government, labor, and business in Detroit and Washington tinkered with the machinery of manpower allocation in an attempt to produce an adequate supply of labor. In late 1942, representatives of the three groups drew up voluntary manpower stabilization plans for Muskegon and Detroit. Under the agreements workers in war-essential occupations could not quit to seek jobs elsewhere without receiving a clearance or certificate of availability from their previous employer.[54] The WMC imposed a mandatory forty-eight-hour week on industry in thirty-two critical war centers in February, 1943, and undertook to assess the efficiency of labor utilization by various manufacturers. Later that year, the government attempted to channel all applicants for certain essential occupations through the USES in a system of controlled referral, and in 1944 ceilings were imposed on the number of workers factories and other types of businesses could hire. Some of these initiatives were simply irrelevant to a Detroit in which many war plants already worked more than forty-eight hours weekly and where no vacancies existed in most of the occupations that controlled referral had been designed to fill. Unions and companies alike strenuously objected to and weakened the application of both utilization studies and referral hiring. Other devices did not work as well as the manpower planners had hoped; after a short period of success in limiting turnover, the Muskegon and Detroit stabilization plans lost effectiveness. By September, 1943, national manpower officials had concluded that the Detroit labor allocation setup, in the words of one news report, "had no teeth."[55]

The most serious weakness of federal manpower policy lay in military control over procurement. Washington manpower officials sought to restrict the flow of war work into Detroit and to remove some contracts already awarded because of their concern that labor supply problems might slow production. Neither the WMC nor the WPB, however, exercised final jurisdiction over the placement of production facilities or war contracts; that power rested within the procurement agencies of the armed forces. Believing that Detroit firms were best equipped to meet its needs, the military insisted that contracts be continuously directed into the city regardless of difficulties. Detroit labor and management united to oppose any curtailment of contracts, not because they feared that the city would lose a great deal of business, but because the area's designation as a center of extreme labor scarcity and instability invited unwanted federal interference with employer and employee prerogatives. Through the issuance of regulations and the establishment of special committees, the WMC attempted to rationalize contract distribution, but the agency could not withstand combined civilian and military pressures, and war work poured virtually unrestricted into Detroit's already overburdened factories until the collapse of German resistance in the spring of 1945.[56]

The nation's vast manpower resources assured that enough

people would always be found to do whatever work had to be done. This enormous labor force did not materialize in the war plants by magic, of course, and spot deficiencies in certain occupations, industries, or communities necessarily required immediate government attention. But the WMC array of ceilings, priorities, and controls lacked sufficient power to be of effective assistance to many localities. An observer's comment on Detroit's contract allocation and manpower priorities system could be applied with some force to the machinery of national labor controls: "I am convinced that, insofar as contracts and manpower are concerned in this area, the situation would be no different [if any WMC committees] had ever been set up."[57]

★ 3 ★

Dazzled by the spectacle of Detroit war production, most Americans did not realize that Michigan was also one of the great agricultural centers of the nation. Farms and cropland occupied more than half of the state's 58,216 square miles; and according to the 1940 census Michigan ranked among the ten leading states in output of dairy and livestock products, feed grains, field vegetables (such as sugar beets, asparagus, celery, and carrots), and fruits. The state's most important agricultural land lay in the southern Lower Peninsula, but every county produced some type of crop. The war thrust an expanded production task upon the farmers of Michigan. Food was a weapon, and the farmers were encouraged to produce as much of that weaponry as possible. Food, farmers across the country were told in one of the oft-repeated slogans of the day, would win the war and write the peace.[58]

The state's farmers had reacted with narrowed eyes and thinned lips to the prospect of more extensive agricultural production to assist either the United States or the Allies. Farmers painfully recalled the experience of World War I, when they had expanded acreage to meet national and world demand only to see the bottom fall out of agricultural prices in the surplus-ridden 1920s. The United States Department of Agriculture (USDA) began a campaign during the fall of 1941 to induce Michigan farmers to produce more vegetable and dairy products. In July the Department established in every farm county of the nation a Defense Board (known after Pearl Harbor as a War Board) comprised of the local heads of such federal agencies as the Agricultural Adjustment Administration and, most importantly, the county agent. These boards sought with uneven success to organize and facilitate farm production to meet annual crop quotas decided upon in Washington. After the spring of 1943 a War Food Administration within the USDA set these goals, placed limits on food distribution, and supervised a national Emergency Farm Labor Program.

Exhortations to greater effort resulted in a modest 3 percent increase in total Michigan farmland and an expansion of nearly 9 percent in acres harvested between 1939 and 1944. Retirement of elderly farmers, the draft, and land consolidation reduced the number of farms within the state from 187,589 in 1940 to 175,268 five years later.[59] The amount of land devoted to certain crops almost doubled, however, and total agricultural production in 1942 broke all previous state records. Crops in succeeding war years did not match 1942 levels, but were substantial nonetheless.

If crops did not always meet expectations, there were reasons enough. Materials shortages limited the availability of supplies and services. Rural electrification proceeded at a much slower pace than during the depression. For two years after November, 1942, the government rationed a wide range of farm implements, from combines and haybailers to milk cans. Purchasers of farm machinery had to prove need to a county rationing board, which reinforced customary farmer neighborliness on the applicant by making the sale conditional upon his promise to lend the machine to, or do custom work for, other farmers. Some farmers returned to the use of the buckrake, a wide, long-toothed harvester that had served their grandfathers seventy years before. Many a buckrake was mounted on a tractor or car, however, and despite war-imposed restrictions, the ongoing trend toward farm mechanization accelerated. But neither the buckrake nor tractor could always contend successfully with a contrary Nature. The war

years brought some of the most forbidding weather ever in-
flicted on the local countryside. Too much rain fell in 1942
and 1943, too little in 1944, and a killer frost in April, 1945,
destroyed much of the fruit and vegetable crop.[60]

Neither the absence of supplies nor the quirks of weather
created as many problems for Michigan farmers as did the
procurement of manpower. State farm groups complained of
a serious labor deficit as early as 1941, although federal reports at the time denied the seriousness of the situation. The
agricultural labor problem certainly worsened once the nation
entered the war. In their desperation, farm operators raised
the pay and improved the treatment of the long-abused hired
man. Even so, the monthly wage for a married farm employee
in 1944 averaged no better than $96.00 as compared to a De-
cember, 1944, weekly average wage of $56.57 for Michigan in-
dustrial workers, and the number of hired men declined. As
ever, farmers could not easily compete with the high wages
and glittering attractions of the city.[61]

One possible solution to the agricultural labor shortage lay
in the deferment of vitally needed farm workers. The Selective
Service Act of 1940 did not authorize group exemptions, but
the powerful farm bloc secured what amounted to partial class
deferment for agriculture when Congress passed the Tydings
Amendment in November, 1942. Local draft boards were authorized thenceforth to defer indefinitely any registrant in an
occupation deemed essential to farmwork as long as the se-
lectee remained at his job. To determine the essentiality of
each farmer and farmworker, the USDA devised the war unit
system, based on the humble cow. The care and milking of one
cow constituted one unit, and by some arcane method the Department computed the difficulty—and the unit value—of all
other farm chores in relation to that basic activity. Sixteen units
of work were generally required for deferment, although local
draft boards were allowed wide discretion, and the magic
number gyrated in response to political pressure until the entire system was abolished in 1944. Between 1,500,000 and
1,750,000 men received agricultural deferments nationwide;
the number of Michigan residents so deferred reached a peak

of 47,666 in August, 1943.[62] This deferment policy kept many youths on the farm and induced thousands of other men to abandon their draft-vulnerable factory jobs to renew their acquaintance with milk pails and manure spreaders.

Deferment not only froze manpower on the farm but sheltered thousands of boys and young men—a large proportion of an entire group—from the rigors of Army discipline and combat overseas. Throughout the war, farm representatives found themselves on the defensive in regard to the draft issue. One Michigan county agent wrote in his 1943 annual report: "It has been said agriculture has become a haven for draft dodgers. If there is anyone who wants a good argument, send them to Sanilac County. We can show them a great number of men on deferred farms who are producing plenty for the war effort."[63] The number and proportion of Michigan agricultural deferments fell both absolutely and relatively after September, 1943. Rural draft boards, however, evinced a regard for their registrants all but unknown in urban areas. Selective Service panels in farm counties cooperated amicably with local USDA War Boards and extension agents, who often personally interviewed selectees, assisted them in filling out questionnaires, and counseled them on improving their work efficiency. Men were moved from farm to farm in St. Joseph County to ensure that as many youths as possible could claim the required number of war units. All these activities helped to raise crop production but they also constituted a form of special consideration for Michigan farmers.[64]

During the prewar decade Michigan farmers and agricultural processors had become dependent for labor upon migratory workers, especially some twenty-seven thousand to thirty-seven thousand Chicanos, Mexicans, and southern whites.[65] Farmers preferred migrants to resident labor since the former could be paid less—an entire family might make no more than $150 to $640 for seven or eight months' work. Migrants, moreover, provided a usually docile and easily coerced workforce. Arkies and Chicanos departed at the end of each harvest season. Each spring the migrant from Texas to Michigan—not infrequently a "wetback," or illegal entrant into the United

States—traveled in a rickety car or truck, often journeying nonstop by night to avoid hostile state police. Once in Michigan, the migrant received from the farmer only the barest of housing—tents, cleared spaces in barns, or wretched hovels on wheels constructed especially for the transients. Decent sanitation and medical care were denied. The farmers did their best to hide the misery of migrant life from the eyes of the fastidious, for the ill-usage of the migrants constituted, in Cary McWilliam's words, "a dark and devious traffic, disgraceful in its every detail."[66]

Wartime manpower stringencies enhanced the importance of migrant labor in Michigan agriculture. It became necessary to give special gas rations to the migrants, and many who continued to work tried to take advantage of their presumably increased bargaining power. "This year, we have had more than the usual amount of trouble with our Mexican laborers," the extension agent of Oceana County noted in 1944. "From the start of the cherries, they were continually striking for higher rates and moving from one farm to another, eventually ending up either in groups on the streets or congregated in a tavern."[67] Yielding to demands by growers in the southwestern states, the federal government concluded an agreement with Mexico in 1942, whereby more than sixty thousand Mexican nationals entered the United States to work on farms and railroads. Portions of the Mexico-U.S. agreement guaranteed those braceros housing and medical care equivalent to that supplied to domestic agricultural workers. Farmers sometime ignored these clauses or carried them out half-heartedly. Some two thousand braceros provided a large proportion of the labor in the 1944 Michigan cherry and sugar beet harvests.[68] Nearly two thousand West Indian workers also came to the state under the sponsorship of various farm groups, and a few areas experimented gingerly with the use of Nisei internees from relocation camps in the western states.[69]

Farmers received a variety of assistance in bringing in their crops as a result of private initiative and government action. A group of businessmen in Fowlerville, a Livingston County farm center, helped bring in the 1942 harvest. In July, 1943,

hundreds of people responded to an offer by fruit and vegetable farmers permitting willing hands to carry away all they
could pick. The Michigan Council of Defense (MCD) organized a Women's Land Army, complete with a uniform that
could be acquired by any member who did thirty consecutive
days of farmwork. The USES allowed employees to quit war-
essential jobs in order to take up agricultural occupations and
sponsored training courses in Detroit high schools for city
youths who volunteered to spend part of the summer on the
farm. Children long had been an integral part of the rural
labor force, many youths taking time off from schools that had
revised class schedules to allow teacher and pupil alike to en-
gage in farmwork. The fifty-five thousand members of the
state 4-H organization adopted projects with war themes, and
in October, 1942, the USDA announced plans for a youth bri-
gade, later known as the Victory Farm Volunteers (VFV), to
form part of the emergency labor supply.[70]

Undoubtedly grateful for the volunteer help they received,
Michigan farmers nevertheless expressed doubts that city-soft
women, children, and businessmen possessed the necessary
stamina and experience to do field work without damaging the
crops and themselves. Lyle Tompkins observed in his 1943 extension agent's report from Oceana County that "most of the
children had never picked cherries and our efforts in super-
vising and acting as a mediator between grower and worker is
one part of the program we are trying to forget."[71] Nor could he
sustain the patriotic zeal of his VFV contingent. "Local merchants and restaurants made impressive inroads on our local
VFV group," Tompkins lamented in 1944. "Out of one squad
of ten teen-age girls, eight were employed in stores this year,
my own daughter being one of the eight, in spite of my best
efforts to keep her in the orchard."[72] Some farmers, however,
expressed pleasure at meeting city folk and working alongside
them and many an urbanite experienced a similar feeling of
accomplishment and friendship. "We had accidents, poison
ivy, and the beds were not the most comfortable I've slept in,"
wrote Nettie McCartney, a Ferndale college student, after a
summer working in the fields of lower Michigan, "but the

grand personnel and delicious food make up for the little inconveniences. It's been one of the best summers in my life."[73]

The mobilization of community manpower resources did not alleviate the farmer's concern for an adequate labor supply. A meeting of fruit growers held in May, 1943, at Traverse City endorsed the idea of using German or Italian prisoners of war (PWs) in the upcoming cherry harvest. United States forces during the war took 425,806 enemy prisoners, who, under the provisions of the 1929 Geneva Convention, could be put to work by the captor nation in safe, healthful, and nonwar-related occupations. The Army distributed 135,000 PWs in various forms of employment, mostly in agriculture. In a totally mobilized society, farming was as much a war industry as was munitions-making, but those in charge of the PW program assiduously overlooked this point. The first squad of farm-bound PWs to reach Michigan arrived by train in Benton Harbor from Camp Grant, Illinois, on October 2, 1943.[74]

Michigan farmers and processors employed between four and five thousand PWs in 1944 and 1945.[75] Sent first to a base camp at Fort Custer, the prisoners then proceeded to satellite camps, some of which operated for as few as two months or as long as two years. The camps usually consisted of groups of tents surrounded by simple wooden fences. Little more seemed necessary, for as one PW explained, "It's not the guards or snow fence that keeps us in—it's the Atlantic Ocean."[76] The farmers purchased the prisoners' services by paying the government the prevailing local wage for agricultural labor, funds which were then used to maintain the camps. The PWs, in turn, received eighty cents a day in scrip, redeemable for items at the camp commissary. Prisoners usually worked six-day, forty-eight-hour weeks in details of ten, each detail guarded by a single soldier. Even this perfunctory guard generally was discontinued after a few days. The drably clad Germans and Italians soon became an accepted part of the local landscape. All PWs in Michigan had been repatriated by the end of 1946.

Like the industrial labor force, the disparate agricultural workers of Michigan proved generally adequate to their task, if not always skilled in planting and harvesting. Michigan

farmers—and farmers elsewhere in the country—sometimes
fell short of the precise production targets set for them in
Washington, but the output of crops nationwide rose 22 percent during the war in the face of a 4 to 10 percent decline in
total agricultural manpower. Farmers discovered that their
prewar fears of expansion had been baseless, for farm prices
and profits soared. From 1939 to 1943 alone, the price of agricultural commodities rose three to four times as fast as the
cost of manufactured items; wages and salaries climbed 111
percent during the same period, but net farm income, fattened
by rich parity payments, increased 186 percent. The cash income of Michigan farmers from dairy products, livestock, and
all crops doubled between 1939 and 1945. The farmers not
only fed the American people, the armed forces, and a significant proportion of the Allied population, but, thanks largely
to government production and rationing policy, greater emphasis than ever before was placed upon the growing of nutri-
tive foods.[77]

Michigan farmers could not claim a production triumph as
smashing as that of Detroit industry, but the state's agricultur-
alists still could point to considerable achievements. Like Detroit, they accomplished their task with the aid of work-tested
methods combined with the latest refinements rather than as
the result of dramatic technological or scientific break-
throughs. (Wartime biochemical research, however, did produce revolutionary developments in insect and weed control
that greatly affected agriculture after 1945.) As the influence
of giant industry increased during the war, so did that of large
commercial agriculture and its principal spokesmen—the
American Farm Bureau Federation, the county agents, and
the land-grant colleges.

The war years may have wrought no fundamental revolution in farming technique, but they significantly changed the
circumstances in which many farm families lived. Farmers
used their increased income to pay off mortgages and other
long-term obligations; the rate of tenancy declined, and total
acreage owned by operators rose. The number of telephones
installed on Michigan farms jumped nearly 10 percent be-

tween 1939 and 1944, mitigating the isolation of rural living.[78]
Even in the record crop year of 1942, of course, farm income
averaged only $1,505, less than half the sum earned by many
war workers.[79] Still, agricultural prospects appeared encouraging. "Butter prices went up, the Guernsey herd was flourish-
ing, and perhaps we would have money at last," Curtis Stadtfeld
recalled of his wartime youth on a Mecosta County farm. "One
good crop of potatoes, one healthy harvest of wheat, and if all
should come in the same year, the mortgage would vanish forever, and the dream come true at last."[80]

★ 4 ★

That dream, the dream of prosperity, had come true not for
Michigan farmers alone but for an entire nation. "Perhaps
never before had the implications of American plenty been so
patent," John Morton Blum observed of the years between
1940 and 1945.[81] From its unequaled store of human and natural resources—so self-evidently, it seemed then, without an
end—the United States fashioned the world's mightiest war
machine and lifted 135,000,000 Americans out of a decade of
depression. In 1940 an annual average of 8,100,000 persons
in the United States and 301,000 persons in Michigan had
been without work or on WPA projects, a jobless rate for state
and nation of some 15 percent. By 1944 unemployment across
the country had decreased to an average of 700,000 (1.2 percent of the total workforce) and to a corresponding figure of
12,000 (0.6 percent) in Michigan. The federal food stamp program, inaugurated in Michigan in March, 1940, came to an
end three years later and when the Work Projects Administration, abolished by Congress in late 1942, wound up its affairs
in June, 1943, the event passed with little notice. That November, Detroit's volunteer charity societies announced the cancel-
lation of their traditional free Thanksgiving and Christmas
dinners for the needy since even many of the residents of Skid
Row were now employed.[82]

Even after the effects of a 28 percent rise in the overall consumer price index are taken into account, the wartime growth
of Michigan personal income is staggering. The state's per cap-

ita income rose from \$591 to \$1,273 between 1939 and 1945.
(United States per capita income rose in these years from \$539
to \$1,192.) Astronomical increases in federal expenditure pri-
marily accounted for this phenomenon. "Muskegon is Rolling
in Money," said the foundry town's newspaper in a 1943 head-
line that could have been reprinted almost anywhere in Michigan with a mere change of city name. More cash was in
circulation and more was being saved; bank deposits for the
average Detroit family doubled between 1937 and 1944. The
Detroit area led the United States in per capita war bond purchases. Institution of the withholding tax and various forms of
"victory" taxes swelled the total federal revenue collected in
Michigan: taxes paid by state corporations quadrupled and
those paid by individuals multiplied thirty-fold during the war.
The broadened revenue base now included hundreds of thousands of Michigan people whose incomes had not been previously taxed, as well as uncounted others who, for the first time
in their lives, were making enough money to know the privilege and pain of being a taxpayer.[83]

When they were not buying bonds or paying taxes, the people of Michigan found a variety of other outlets for their ready
cash. The press patronizingly worried about the spending habits of war workers, fearing the outbreak of the alleged self-
indulgence that had characterized the World War I era, a time
when every factory hand supposedly boasted a ten-dollar
candy-striped shirt. Luxury goods were not abundant during
World War II, but they were by no means scarce, and Detroit
department stores enlarged the thin wartime newspapers with
advertisements for furs, doeskin gloves, and seventy-five dollar
watches. Customers responded eagerly to such appeals, as the
forward bound in sales indicated. Yet the pall of the 1930s
hovered too close in the memories of too many to encourage a
careless attitude toward suddenly plentiful money. War workers not only saved but, like the farmers, put much of their
weekly wage into the retirement of mortgages and debts. Families made long-overdue visits to doctors and dentists, bought
sturdier furniture for their homes (appliances such as refrig-
erators and radios, of course, were not manufactured during

the war), and chose better food to eat on the new kitchen table. At their leisure, they jammed all sporting events—boxing, horseracing, hockey, baseball—and even a game between the Detroit Lions and Chicago Bears of the anemic National Football League drew record crowds in 1943.[84]

Even this most widespread of American prosperities had its soft spots. Thousands of employees continued to work for substandard wages and faced a constant struggle to meet the cost of living. Many small retailers were devastated: gas stations, garages, car dealerships, and other automobile-connected companies fared worst of all, but grocers voiced the loudest complaints. They charged that rising wages for inexperienced help, government paperwork, and inelastic price ceilings had made commercial life intolerable. Too often, these accusations had weight, but the OPA had no answer for the merchants save a plea to hold on. For a time, the fear of gasoline rationing threatened the stability of tourism, the second largest sector of the state's prewar economy. The number of resorts and like facilities fell nearly 40 percent between 1941 and 1943, but rationing delays and the husbanding of coupons by vacation-hungry workers sustained the greater portion of the state tourist industry.[85]

Grand Rapids, Michigan's second largest city, and long the center of the national furniture industry, had suffered severely during the depression. The community obtained few defense contracts before Pearl Harbor, and only four of the area's more than eighty factories operated full time during 1942. Civic officials and business leaders, faced with an unemployment rate in excess of 10 percent, simply could not convince the military that their ample supply of light machine tools, small plants, and skilled woodworkers could turn out the type of equipment the armed services required. Grand Rapids was not the only contract-starved community in the United States, but the cries of anguish that welled up from around the nation did not move the WPB to take action until 1943. On February 10 the Board announced that Grand Rapids would become the test site for a plan to channel between two and four billion dollars in war work into previously ignored production areas. Thanks to this

Grand Rapids Plan, by early 1945 the city's factories were producing—among other items—Diesel injectors, radio equipment, and subassemblies for the B-29 bomber.[86]

The Upper Peninsula, the wildly beautiful northernmost
third of Michigan, shared unevenly in the good times underway downstate. The Great Lakes shipping fleet, caught in economic doldrums since 1929, set new carrying records during
the war, the long, low-decked freighters racing across Lake Superior and through the lock canal at Sault Ste. Marie to deliver
vital ore cargoes before the winter freeze closed operations for
another year. But it seemed that nothing could save the Upper
Peninsula's mining district, the scene of so much community
and personal hardship during the depression. Low world prices
had induced a decline in state copper output after 1939. Peninsula mines produced a wartime high of ninety-three million
pounds in 1943, but production thereafter tailed off.[87] Most
mineowners refused to pay the increased wages ordered by the
WLB, and a manpower shortage crippled operations as workers flowed southward in search of better opportunities. Several
workings shut down permanently. A similar fate overtook the
peninsula's deep-shaft iron mines, which could not compete
with the open pits of the Mesabi Range.

None of the foregoing exceptions invalidated the overwhelming reality of revival and prosperity. The newly glowing
factory chimneys signified more than the fact that men and
women were back at work. During the 1930s not even the master politician Roosevelt had been able to lift the people out of
a sense of self-doubt and uncertainty. "The depression," Eliot
Janeway asserts, "had left a residue of feeling that America was
finished, that expansion was at an end." The war demonstrated
that the economy, at least when fueled by enormous federal
funding, had not yet lost its capacity for renewal. Production
had achieved victory abroad and prosperity at home. America's
rising confidence in businessmen was only the outward manifestation of its restored faith in the soundness of the entire
economic structure. Less than seven months after Pearl Harbor, Governor Van Wagoner had told his fellow state chief executives assembled for their annual conference: "When Hitler

sneered at democracy, and when we ourselves began to wonder if perhaps we were incapable of uniting to do the job that
had to be done, the war gave us the chance to prove to ourselves that America still has the best economic and political
system on earth . . . a system that we can all believe in and
work for, and fight and die for." The people had found a cause
to believe in and in so doing, once more had come to believe
in themselves and in the nation.[88]

Chapter 2

The Worker's War

In America at war, the workers were the "soldiers of production," second in importance to the GIs themselves. It was now patriotic, not socially demeaning, to take a factory job. In March, 1943, the *Detroit News* praised the nearly spotless absenteeism records of six workers at the GM Ternstedt Division plant whose names were Kowalski, Netkowski, Bugai, Lugari, Bauer, and Pavolik. "Look at the names . . . ," the reporter declared, "the sort of names one finds on an all-American football team . . . and at Ternstedt's, management and workers alike are hailing them as the plant's all-American production team." But many of these soldiers already had been through one war, the battle for unionization, a conflict that had its own defeats and victories. Nowhere else had the struggle reached such heights of violence and bitterness as in Michigan. Now the nation insisted that the workers of Michigan and the unions that represented them unite with the former adversary to face a greater foe. The 14,471 strikes called nationwide between Pearl Harbor and V-J Day, more than in any comparable period of American history, testified to the problems of achieving that alliance.[1]

After years of turmoil, a kind of peace descended on Michigan industry in 1940. The legislature had enacted a state labor relations law in May, 1939, defining the rights of unions and establishing a mediation board empowered to intervene in labor disputes upon request. Although sections of the act proved vague or unenforceable, the statute nonetheless contributed to a relaxation of tension on the shop floor. The CIO unions offered little opposition to management during the first year of

55

the defense period because they were busy fighting the AFL and their own national leader, John L. Lewis. The UAW-CIO assured its supremacy within automotive labor when it defeated the UAW-AFL in a series of representation elections held at GM plants that year. Lewis had announced his support for Wendell Willkie in the 1940 presidential campaign, promising to resign from office if Roosevelt won the election, a pledge he was forced to fulfill at the end of the year. (He was succeeded by Philip Murray.) The unions required time to consolidate their newly won position in industry and, insofar as the UAW-CIO was concerned, time to gather resources for the last great effort of its organizing campaign. For the cry of "Organize Ford's!" had haunted the union's leadership ever since the bloody afternoon on the Rouge overpass.

The years had at last caught up with the proudest master of mass production, the septuagenarian Henry Ford. Administrative anarchy and a public boycott of Ford products had pushed the firm into third place in motorcar sales. Although the CIO had been unable to prevent Ford from obtaining the Pratt & Whitney and B-24 contracts, union pressure had resulted in the denial to the firm of a ten-million-dollar defense award early in 1941. In February, 1941, the Supreme Court sustained the UAW's contention that Ford had flagrantly violated the Wagner Act. The union had put its internal house in order. The workers of the Rouge, restive after years of intimidation and substandard wages, had begun to turn against Ford.

The UAW's drive began on October 1, 1940, under the direction of Michael F. Widman, Jr., a Lewis subordinate. The union won an important victory when a Dearborn judge struck down the city's antihandbill ordinance as unconstitutional. Leafleteers now stationed themselves daily before the Rouge gates, finding hands eager to receive their literature. On streetcorners and in homes, bars, restaurants, and lodge halls, organizers for Ford Local 600 went about signing up members singly or by twos and threes. Following the Supreme Court ruling, Harry Bennett began to meet with worker committees to discuss individual grievances, but his position hardened at the end of March. On April 1, 1941, the eight-man grievance committee for the entire plant was dismissed, an action that provoked a spontaneous strike effectively shutting down the Rouge by day's end. The union issued a retroactive authorization shortly after midnight on April 2. Thousands of workers left the plant, their exhilaration leading one observer to remark that "it was like seeing men who had been half dead suddenly come to life."[2]

The only major violence during the strike took place on the morning of April 2 as workers still within the Rouge pelted strikers outside with nuts bolts and then twice tried unsuccessfully to break the picket lines with mass charges. These strike-breakers were young, recently hired, and, most chilling for the UAW, black. The union leaders realized that if Ford could use racism to divide the workers, the strike might be broken and the UAW irreparably damaged. By early 1941, however, thousands among Ford's black labor force had become animated by the same spirit of rebellion that moved their white coworkers. The black community of Detroit, no longer enamored of Henry Ford, lined up in a broad common front to support the UAW. Joint community and union action prevented further racial trouble.[3]

Barricading the street entrances to the Rouge, the UAW converted the plant into a beleaguered island. Governor Van Wagoner dispatched a detachment of state police to the scene empowered solely to preserve the peace. By April 3 it had become clear that Ford stood alone. Acceding to the demands of his son Edsel, the nominal head of the company, the elder Ford authorized Bennett to begin negotiations with a UAW team. Van Wagoner acted as mediator, with the assistance of an officer from the United States Conciliation Service. On April 10 the governor announced a settlement, the terms of which included a resumption of work at the Rouge without discrimination against strikers and a federally sponsored representation election to be held at Ford plants at the earliest opportunity.

The UAW-CIO overcame a weak AFL challenge in the May 21 NLRB balloting, securing almost 70 percent of the votes at the Rouge and well above that percentage at the other principal Ford plants. After preliminary doubts, Ford signed a contract with the union on June 20. The agreement guaranteed Ford workers the highest wages in the industry and established the union shop, a dues checkoff, and a host of other benefits neither GM nor Chrysler had conferred on the UAW. "Give 'em everything," Ford had said. "It won't work."[4] The union, he believed, would fall victim to its need to keep the company's goodwill in order to retain the major elements of the contract. That remained to be seen; but Ford had been organized at last.

The Ford strike symbolized the resurgence of labor conflict that punctuated 1941. All across the nation workers walked out in record numbers. Disputes often centered on the refusal of important defense contractors to obey the Wagner Act. Labor leaders learned that, although the government was unwilling to coerce these evaders into compliance, a strike usually achieved the desired result. The sudden and alarming national rise in defense-related strikes led President Roosevelt to establish the National Defense Mediation Board (NDMB) on March 19, 1941. This tripartite panel, its membership representing the public, management, and the two organized labor federations, could intervene in those disputes certified to it by the Secretary of Labor following the exhaustion of other means of conciliation. The NDMB, however, could make only non-binding recommendations.

Michigan compiled one of the most spectacular records of labor turmoil in the nation during that last peacetime year. The number of strikes more than tripled that of 1940 and the number of workers involved increased thirteen-fold. The often sizable work forces of newly opened munitions plants made inviting targets for union organizers, with a resulting rise in recognition and jurisdictional disputes. Governor Van Wagoner rushed state troopers to Saginaw in January to keep order after a fight between club-wielding UAW-CIO pickets and city police in front of the Wilcox-Rich plant of the Eaton Manufacturing Company, already under contract to the UAW-AFL. A clash at the Currier Lumber Company in Detroit on May 11 between feuding AFL teamsters and members of the CIO United Construction Workers Organizing Committee

(UCWOC) resulted in the death of a Teamster picket. The Teamsters threatened to bring all trucking in the city to a halt during their battle with the UCWOC, and later that year, they endangered the flow of defense supplies by closing the docks of the Railway Express Agency (REA) in a struggle with a rival union. The still unfamiliar processes of collective bargaining and the acrimonious atmosphere of labor relations in most plants also served to instigate numerous wildcat stoppages. During the summer and fall, for instance, Great Lakes Steel Company, a major defense producer in the Detroit suburb of Ecorse, suffered a series of illegal walkouts led by dissident members of Local 1299 of the Steel Workers Organizing Committee who were unhappy with the terms of a new contract.[5]

The strike wave angered the public and the politicians. Agitation for Congressional passage of antilabor legislation gathered force during the summer and fall of 1941. Earlier in the year the UAW had unhesitatingly supported defense-related stoppages, but over the months it had responded to government pressure and to demands of such leaders as the Reuther brothers by taking an increasingly stern line on defense strikes. In September the union suspended the charter of militant Briggs Local 212 for, among other causes, the calling by the local of four successive strikes in a month.[6] Communists within the UAW had fomented several defense strikes from mid-1940 onward, but the German attack on the Soviet Union in June, 1941, compelled a change in Party policy to all-out co-operation with the rearmament effort, thus placing a further curb on militancy. Despite the turmoil and violence of the 1941 strikes, organized labor's national and Michigan leadership lined up solidly in support of the defense program. Most CIO leaders and rank and file members believed that Hitler must be defeated and that the President had chosen the only sensible course of action in providing aid to the Allies.

Labor upheaval threatened the United States by December, however, for President Roosevelt's policy of national labor-management conciliation lay in ruins. The President already had undermined the prestige of the NDMB by naming a special panel to settle the REA strike, and the Board itself completed the job of demolition in early November by refusing to grant a union shop in the longstanding dispute between John L. Lewis's United Mine Workers (UMW) and the steel companies that owned the "captive" coal mines. The Board's CIO members resigned in anger, and Lewis called the third coal strike of the year, to begin November 17. The miners' chief called off the strike only after reluctantly acceding to Roosevelt's proposal for yet another special arbitration panel, this one so stacked as to guarantee a UMW victory. With the NDMB discredited, the nation no longer possessed an effective mechanism to achieve stability within its vital defense industry.

Pearl Harbor proved the salvation of the labor policy. Ten days after the Japanese attack a joint labor-management conference opened in Washington. The representatives quickly agreed on a policy of no strikes or lockouts during the war and on the establishment of a new War Labor Board to replace the moribund NDMB. Formally organized on January 12, 1942, the WLB retained NDMB chairman William H. Davis and the tripartite structure of its predecessor. Whereas the NDMB could hand down only weighty recommendations, the orders of the new board were binding. In Michigan, meanwhile, leaders of both labor federations voiced support for the war. The Detroit municipal employees union called off a strike that would have paralyzed city government and transportation.[7] The workers had gone to war.

Detroit workers, a federal observer noted in 1942, "are completely identified with the American army and look forward with at least as great interest to their technological triumph over the enemy as to triumphs of generalship and strategy."[8] To sustain the connection between production front and battlefront, the armed forces sent morale-boosting uniformed speakers into the factories to urge the workers to greater effort. Thousands of Detroit workers heard "UAW-CIO," a song written in 1942 by Baldwin "Butch" Hawes of the Almanac Singers. Although the lyrics celebrated past union victories over management, the main intent of the ballad was to identify the autoworkers closely with the armed forces:

I was there when the Union came to town,
I was there when old Henry Ford went down;
I was standing at Gate 4
When I heard the people roar:
'Aint nobody keeps us Autoworkers down!'

It's that U.A.W.-C.I.O.
Makes that Army roll and go-
Turning out the jeeps and tanks and airplanes every day.
It's that U.A.W.-C.I.O.
Makes that Army roll and go-
Puts wheels on the U.S.A.

I was there on that cold December day
When we heard about Pearl Harbor far away;
I was down on Cadillac Square
When the Union rallied there
To put them plans for pleasure cars away.

(Chorus)

There'll be a union-label in Berlin
When the union boys in uniform march in;
And rolling in the ranks
There'll be U.A.W. tanks—
—Roll Hitler out and roll the Union in!

(Chorus)[9]

    Although few workers understood the precise significance of their often routine and repetitive tasks, most knew they were working for some transcendent objective, however variously it might be defined. Eli Chinoy found that Lansing autoworkers compared their wartime work experience favorably to that of the early postwar years. Said one worker, "Things were different. You knew what you were working for—to bring the boys back home." Workers made their feelings known in such private ways as simply staying on the job and doing their best. In a more public fashion, UAW DeSoto Local 227 announced in September, 1943, the donation of its entire three thousand dollar strike fund for the purchase of war bonds.[10]

    War workers enjoyed heightened job security and increased wages. Prosperity provided more jobs and more highly paid

jobs. Average weekly earnings in American industry rose from
$33.40 in January, 1942, to $47.50 in January, 1945, an increase of 42 percent. As was true for all other wartime economic indicators, industrial wages in Michigan shot up to a
level higher than the national norm, from a weekly rate of
$42.11 in December, 1941, to $56.57 three years later. State
industrial wages rose only 33 percent during the period, but
started from a higher base than the national wage rate. Workers earned even more in certain occupations; in April, 1943,
for instance, employees in the Michigan machine tool industry
made $70.54 per week. A Bureau of Labor Statistics (BLS)
survey conducted in late 1944 revealed that Detroit wages led
all factory pay rates for metropolitan areas with a population
in excess of a quarter million persons. Within Michigan, Muskegon frequently surpassed Detroit as the state's high-wage
capital. Michigan's average industrial wages topped out at
nearly $57.00 per week at the end of 1943, but remained in
the $50.00 range until the mass layoffs of mid-1945, after
which pay rates began a slow decline.[11]

Large increases in hourly or weekly wage rates did not fully
explain the phenomenon of high wartime pay. Economist Seymour Harris noted in 1945 that only 36 percent of the increase
in national industrial wages between 1939 and 1944 could be
accounted for by an actual rise in pay rates; the other 64 percent of the improvement was attributable to additional overall
employment, enhanced employment in already high-paying industries, and greater resort to overtime. Between December,
1941, and July, 1943, the average workweek in Michigan industry rose some 18 percent. At the same time, hourly earnings rose only 9 percent. Frequent layoffs of varying lengths
caused by materials shortages slimmed the weekly pay enve-
lope. Many smaller factories across Michigan geared earnings
to the incentive or piecework system. The more units a worker
produced, the greater his compensation. But basic wage rates
for even skilled employees were decidedly low in comparison
to those in plants that did not employ the incentive system.
Piecework, moreover, too often put cruel pressure on those
men and women who could not keep up with the pace set by

the fastest among them. The Michigan state CIO convention's decisive endorsement of an antipiecework resolution in June, 1943, prevented large-scale implementation of the plan. Piecework plans, however, remained in force both in some firms organized by the AFL and in many nonunion plants.[12]

The Michigan wage structure was distinguished by wide regional variations and was riddled with inequities. There were differences in pay for the same job between plants and between departments in the same plant. Since Michigan had converted to war production more thoroughly than almost any other state, its industrial workers shared in high wartime wages to a greater extent than manufacturing employees in other parts of the nation. Yet thousands of Michigan workers pursuing nonwar occupations earned far less than even the average industrial wage. Thousands more, especially women, earned "substandard" wages, a rate of pay defined as fifty cents an hour or less. Before their wages were raised to the fifty cent level in mid-1943, employees of Cunningham's, a large retail drug chain, made only thirty-three cents per hour in the Detroit area, and the firm's outstate employees earned only twenty-two cents hourly. A federal official wrote from Detroit in July, 1943, that "The effect of the war has been to very greatly increase the previous differentials between industries and establishments, and even within job classifications in given establishments, all of which spells discontent."[13]

Much worker and union discontent focused on government wage policy. The first dispute about wages arose in 1942 over the question of premium pay. The CIO had won the payment of double wages for weekend and holiday work during the depression to reduce the demand for labor. Once defense production began, management demanded an end to the practice, and many companies refused to operate on weekends rather than pay the required bonuses. Resistant at first, the CIO unions ultimately gave way to mounting government pressure for the abolition of double time. In April, an emergency conference of UAW local officials hastily assembled in Detroit to approve the surrender on premium pay, which the union camouflaged as part of a program for "victory through equality of sacrifice."[14]

Workers greeted the UAW's action without enthusiasm; despite—or perhaps because of—an extensive propaganda campaign on behalf of its stand on premium pay. The auto union subsequently lost a series of representation elections to the AFL International Association of Machinists, which had refused to give up double wages. Frustration within the UAW rank and file burst forth at the union's July national convention in Chicago, where rebellious delegates forced through a resolution declaring that the premium pay concession was to be rescinded within thirty days unless the president banned all double time. Responding at last to repeated entreaties from top UAW leaders, Roosevelt on September 10 issued Executive Order 9240, which forbade the payment of premiums except for the seventh consecutive day of work. The order came in time to prevent the eruption of several strikes by restive locals. Since it rendered moot an AFL challenge on the wage issue, the directive came as a much-needed lift to the UAW-CIO. Unfortunately the order was subject to conflicting interpretations, and disputes over the application of premium pay dragged on until 1944.

The WLB set off a furor when it announced its judgment in the Little Steel case in July, 1942. Under the Little Steel formula, which was extended to cover all industries, wages would be allowed to rise no more than 15 percent in excess of their January 1, 1941 levels, the same percentage by which national living costs had risen between that date and the imposition of price control in May, 1942. The CIO made no secret of its unhappiness, but its fulminations availed nothing, and the Little Steel formula remained in force until well after V-E Day. John L. Lewis won a ceiling-busting increase from the WLB in late 1943, but only after pulling his men from the bituminous mines four times during the year and forcing the federal government to seize the coal pits.

Limitations on WLB power often proved as galling to unionists as did the agency's exercise of authority. The Board had been forbidden to raise pay above the Little Steel level unless the increase corrected a maladjustment, reduced a gross inequity, raised substandard wages, or was thought necessary "to aid the effective prosecution of the war." Since the WLB walked a narrow and conservative path in the interpretation of these guidelines, unions could be certain, in most instances, of the ultimate rejection of their wage demands. President Roosevelt placed new restrictions on the agency on April 8, 1943, in Executive Order 9328, the so-called hold-the-line order stripping the WLB of most of its power to rectify wage inequalities. The UAW took the lead in demanding a modification of the directive, which was relaxed after a month. The WLB was thereafter allowed to bring wages in discrete geographical areas up to preestablished wage brackets or "going rates." This compromise was the best labor could get, but it remained unpalatable since the WLB usually calculated wage brackets by taking the average of an area's pay rates and reducing that average by 10 percent.[15]

Labor's principal argument for wage increases was that the cost of living had outdistanced pay rates. James Wishart, director of the UAW's Research Department, declared in December, 1943, that after tax deductions and bond purchases, the average Michigan autoworker's hourly pay had increased since January, 1941, from $0.95 per hour to $1.08 per hour but that the 1943 worker needed $1.18 an hour to buy what $0.95 had comfortably purchased two years before. Between April, 1943, and April, 1945, the Detroit BLS cost of living increased only 2.2 percent, as compared to a rise in local factory wages of 5.4 percent. In the last full month of war, July, 1945, Detroit living costs attained a level of 130.8, while the national average reached 129.0 (1935–39 equals 100). The city's food costs were actually slightly lower than those of the country at large, but house furnishings, fuel, rent, and miscellaneous items all registered six-year increases above the national level. Federal statistics, however, concealed as much as they revealed about the cost of living. Cheap food was often unavailable and workers were often forced to buy expensive substitutes. A dress or suit not only cost more but was more poorly made. A subdivided apartment provided half the space but rented for the same amount as it had before remodeling.[16]

No union representative wielded substantial authority in the wartime production bureaucracy. Sidney Hillman left government service shortly after the dissolution of the OPM and no labor leader of equal stature replaced him. In most instances, labor was placed in an advisory and clearly subordinate position, having an effective voice only within the War Manpower Commission, a relatively weak agency. The most talented of labor's representatives always returned to the struggle for internal union power; Walter Reuther began the war as a government consultant but soon limited such activity in order to concentrate on union affairs. Labor could spare few men of Reuther's competence to staff the office warrens in Washington. More important, however, was the fact that even if every labor leader had been equipped with the intelligence of Reuther, the will of Lewis, and the guilelessness of Phil Murray, neither business nor the public would have accepted a major role for labor in the wartime government.

Working hours and shop floor conditions created tension and resentment in the labor force, especially among new employees. Thousands of men and women never had been inside a plant gate and were unfamiliar with tools and machines. Commenting in March, 1945, on charges of slipshod work in his plants, president George Christopher of Packard declared, "The majority of persons observed in our employment increase would have been labeled unemployable for skill or attitude in peacetime. So what can you expect?"[17] By the war peak of November, 1943, Detroit industry was operating an average of 47.5 hours per week, and many factories worked fifty-four or even seventy hours weekly. Production workers, foremen, technicians, and executives alike suffered to a greater or lesser extent from a mind- and body-numbing fatigue, a weariness intensified by the often arduous travel between home and plant. Nervous tension, increased illness, absenteeism, and accidents followed. The Michigan Council of Defense sponsored noise-abatement campaigns in major production centers to provide more restful daytime hours for night-shift workers. Workers often relieved tension with bouts of horseplay, but one such instance ended in tragedy: Louis Merino, an employee at the Kercheval Avenue plant of Continental Motors in Detroit, burned to death when a match inserted in his shoe as a practical joke ignited Merino's grease-soaked clothing.[18]

Army inspectors and procurement officials strained tempers by their heavy-handed actions against both unions and companies, although the bias was usually against labor. Just as the military ignored manpower considerations in placing war orders, so it sometimes disregarded or abrogated contract provisions that did not appear to suit its requirements. The army ended paid washup and rest periods at the Rouge because it refused to pay for time not worked, and this resulted in brief work stoppages at the end of December, 1941. In June, 1942, the Army Air Force warned Detroit's Federal Engineering Company that the military would take its business elsewhere unless the firm consented to a representation election between two competing unions. The Army used its wartime authority to order the firing of several ringleaders of a Detroit strike later that year. In addition to such publicized activities, the Army also carried on an intensive intelligence effort to keep abreast of labor developments affecting production. Officers kept detailed records on the number and geographic origin of strikes, and swapped data with the Michigan State Police, which maintained informants in many plants. Detroit armed forces labor-relations personnel won official praise for their skill and sangfroid, but the officers won few friends among the workers.[19]

Wartime pressures induced a certain relaxation of tension in some areas of labor relations. Some nonunion Michigan employers retained the allegiance of their workers by honest conduct and decent treatment. Other small plants welcomed the unions because employers needed worker cooperation to bid for war contracts and to prepare for postwar competition.[20] Workers served amicably enough with business executives on jointly sponsored tire rationing boards in the larger war plants and in such patriotic efforts as war bond drives. Workers also shared the credit with engineering experts for the automobile industry's improved production record, and that record could not have been achieved without cooperation between ordinary

unionists and factory supervisors. Detroit labor and management united to oppose federal control of local manpower
allocation.

Many plants, however, were scenes of conflict. In their study
of the Willow Run factory and community, Lowell J. Carr and
James E. Stermer found that bomber plant management regarded the employees as little more than numbers on paper, to
be manipulated with no thought of consultation or explana-
tion. Behind the precision of the assembly line, they glimpsed
a streak of irrationality in dealings between people. "I wrote a
quit slip once at the Bomber," recalled Stermer, who briefly
worked at Willow Run. "It read 'Reason for discharge: caught
sitting on toilet with his pants up.' That's it, in some twisted
kind of way, which puts into words for me the whole damned
industrial picture. Outside a factory, people try not to get
caught with their pants down. But there, it's up."[21] The war did
not create such attitudes, of course, but they were not significantly softened by the presumed need for unity. Indeed, a government survey of Detroit opinion in late 1942 revealed that
labor-management disputes supposedly damped down after
Pearl Harbor had been renewed.[22]

Management intransigence took many forms. The widespread refusal to process grievances, a tactic adopted by many
firms during the conversion period, continued to exacerbate
tensions. Disputes over line speed, wage rates, and other matters went unsettled. In one factory after another, the day-to-
day round of collective bargaining ground to a virtual halt.
Factory executives seemed especially intent on restoring their
preunion right to fire without reference to seniority. Discriminatory enforcement of safety rules also stirred worker resentment.[23] On January 2, 1943, a WPB representative in Detroit
wrote Washington: "The evidence which is piling up seems to
indicate rather clearly that a well-organized and determined
effort is being made on the part of many manufacturers and
industrialists to do everything in their power to create incidents which will 'needle' and provoke labor into unauthorized
stoppage of work."[24] Most unionists naturally concurred in such
sentiments.

Certain factory executives were particular targets of union wrath. Harry Bennett, a man totally ignorant of and uninterested in production problems, reigned as Ford's chief of labor relations. He routinely made decisions without taking into account their repercussions on the assembly line.[25] John Ringwald, Bennett's handpicked labor director at Willow Run, once had been an organizer for the UAW-CIO, but that fact won him no esteem from the leadership of Bomber Local 50. "The union is of the opinion," concluded a report by the local in February, 1943, "that Mr. Ringwald does not know where labor relations begin or end."[26] No one could belittle Fay Taylor of Briggs for a lack of interest in production or for a failure to understand procedures. "I might say that the . . . strategy of the company was being masterminded by a person who I considered to be one of the most efficient and one of the shrewdest negotiators in any plant in the United States," former Local 212 president Jess Ferrazza recalled of Taylor years later. "You never knew what time of day or night you could expect to see him in the plant. So when you talk about Local 212 . . . as being a militant local union, I can truthfully say that management helped make us this way, because we had a real adversary here."[27]

Donald Nelson advanced a possible solution to the shop floor conflict when he suggested in a March, 1942, radio address that labor-management committees be established in every war plant. The WPB chairman never indicated what the precise function and authority of such committees should be, but he seems to have had in mind consultative bodies, without real power, that would sustain fervor for increased production and assess employee suggestions designed to save time and labor. It was never Nelson's intention, whatever else he may have had in mind, to grant unions a share of managerial authority. At the peak of the war, some five thousand labor-management committees functioned in the United States, representing some seven million workers. Packard's "Work to Win" committee accepted employee ideas that saved the company $1,500,000 in labor and materials between 1942 and 1944. Officials of UAW Local 155 (Aeronautical Products, Inc.) credited their "Production for Victory" committee with lessening managerial interference in routine operations. Pins, posters, speakers, and departmental competitions were features of most committee programs. Although the UAW welcomed the Nelson scheme with some enthusiasm, Michigan factories maintaining such committees numbered only 150 by December, 1943, and labor-management consultation met a cold reception from Ford and General Motors. Management believed that the plan was only another ploy to give the unions more power, a throwback to the hated Reuther industrial council idea. GM president Charles Wilson gave his answer to the program as early as March 25, 1942: "Are you going to set policy by a voice vote? As far as this equal-voice bunk is concerned, the answer is no."[28]

The Region XI War Labor Board (RWLB) stood as a shaky barrier between labor and management. The regional boards, established throughout the nation in early 1943, were an effort to cope with mounting delays in case disposition that resulted from the WLB's centralized structure. Many managements deliberately postponed settlement of grievances by "kicking it into the Board." Beginning in December, 1942, angry Michigan rank and filers vented their fury at WLB delay by taking strike action in direct defiance of the Board's insistence that no dispute would be considered so long as a walkout remained in force.[29] The RWLB was modeled closely after the parent agency: a regional director chaired a tripartite panel of public, labor, and management members that exercised jurisdiction over dispute cases and voluntary wage agreements that were not subject to appeal. Washington could intervene if the local body overstepped the bounds of set policy. The importance of Michigan labor to war production persuaded the WLB to make the state a region unto itself, the only state to be so designated. The Region XI Board opened for business in Detroit in February, 1943, under the chairmanship of Edwin E. Witte, a professor of economics and a labor arbitrator from the University of Wisconsin who had been instrumental in drafting the Social Security Act.

"Here we have the feeling of sitting on top of a smoldering volcano, which may explode at any time," chairman Witte wrote from Detroit about labor relations in July, 1943. Although Witte supported organized labor, he generally followed an ostentatiously neutral course in his role as chairman. He was succeeded in 1944 by Louis C. Miriani, a Detroit welfare official, who held the regional chairmanship until the RWLB wound up its affairs in late 1945. Nothing Witte experienced in Detroit altered his view that government should hesitate before interfering in collective bargaining, and Miriani similarly concluded that the presence of the RWLB weakened the determination of labor and management to bargain effectively. Labor and management members of the RWLB and its subsidiary hearing panels were never impartial, the public members often lacked competence, and, although the Detroit area possessed a vast fund of expertise on the auto industry, few knowledgeable people were available to advise on the labor problems of other segments of Michigan industry. The board decentralization scheme had been designed to deal expeditiously with disputes, but plagued with such problems, delays persisted.[30]

Federal law and public opinion prevented management from making an overt attempt to destroy the unions, but nothing and no one could prevent the unions from attempting to destroy one another. The national AFL and CIO, split since 1935, had been unable to reunite. The craft-versus-industrial issue, however, no longer divided them, and both federations were now busy trying to swell their memberships by raids on vulnerable opposition affiliates. Internecine labor rivalry, an established fact in Michigan before the war, continued without pause. The UAW-AFL, no longer a serious threat to the UAW-CIO, nonetheless remained entrenched in several small and medium-sized communities in the western half of the state. To undermine the stability of Detroit CIO unions, United Mine Workers District 50, a catch-all organization, set up shop in early 1943 and began to make raids on disgruntled members of both the UAW and the United Rubber Workers (URW). The jurisdictional strike remained the weapon of choice in organizational conflict. A dispute during the summer of 1942 over control of grocery clerks in Pontiac-area stores not only closed the markets, creating a food shortage, but shut down the GM Pontiac plant for an afternoon. Rivalry between AFL and CIO maintenance men in mid-1945 idled forty-five thousand workers and slowed reconversion projects.[31]

Michigan labor boasted a local version of John L. Lewis in the person of Matthew Smith, British-born secretary of the Mechanics Educational Society of America (MESA). Smith arrived in Detroit in the late 1920s and later moved to Flint, where in 1933 he organized MESA among the tool-and-die makers of the city's auto plants. Despite defections to the UAW, MESA still claimed a membership in excess of twenty thousand. A socialist and pacifist, Smith never agreed to the no-strike policy. Speaking of AFL-CIO adherence to the pledge, he declared, "They did not sell out the workers. They gave them away."[32] Smith probably understood that the war did not provide a congenial atmosphere for a small union trying to preserve craft separation within the auto industry. MESA and other small independent unions had no representation on RWLB hearing panels. To save his union from total absorption by the UAW, Smith adopted a course of direct confrontation with both his labor rival and the federal government. From 1942 to 1944, he ordered raids on UAW locals and called a series of crippling strikes against Detroit war industry to demonstrate his militancy. He gained the recognition that he sought when the RWLB agreed in 1944 to place representatives of independent unions on appeal panels whenever appropriate.[33] Smith won his wartime battle to preserve MESA reasonably intact, although he brought the entire labor movement into disrepute by his actions.

As if interunion battles and survival struggles were not sufficient elements of instability, the Michigan labor scene was enlivened by internecine warfare within labor organizations. The state AFL was divided between the Detroit and Wayne County Federation of Labor and the more conservative outstate group that ran the state federation.[34] Factionalism within the UAW-CIO leadership, suppressed during 1942, reappeared in 1943 and after with the emergence of such issues as incentive pay and the no-strike pledge. The union was split roughly into two fluid caucuses: a group composed primarily of Communists and their sympathizers, led by secretary-treasurer George Addes and vice-president Richard Frankensteen; and a loose coalition of Socialists, Trotskyites, and members of the Association of Catholic Trade Unionists that generally followed second vice-president Walter Reuther. Union president R. J. Thomas acted as a bridge between the caucuses.

The coming of war confused UAW internal politics by scrambling traditional ideological categories. The Communists, the ultraunionists and antiwar zealots of the pre-June, 1941 period, became all-out supporters of the war effort and embraced any union-weakening proposal that might increase production, such as the adoption of incentive wage plans. The Reutherites, the "right wing" of the prewar era, also supported the war, but since they refused to subordinate trade union goals, they now became known as the "left." The small group of "radical" Trotskyites denounced the war as an imperialist venture and stood with the traditionally "conservative" Reuther forces in support of bread and butter union demands. On any issue even this fairly coherent picture was nevertheless likely to dissolve and reform kaleidoscopically. The contending groups carried on their conflict through newspapers, in union elections, and, not infrequently, by the use of fists and clubs.

Industrial relations were vitally affected by the differing attitudes of workers toward organized labor. In July, 1943, the UAW-CIO surpassed one million in dues-paying membership, becoming the largest union in the nation; thousands of the new members, however, particularly blacks, women, and southern migrants, never before had belonged to a labor organization and were apathetic if not negative about the labor movement. Far from regarding the union as their protector against management, the new workers often perceived their local as a somewhat irrelevant part of the industrial structure. Carr and Stermer found that many Willow Run workers regarded union organizers, stewards, and committeemen as little better than racketeers and the UAW itself as a kind of "industrial fifth wheel" or "gyp organization." Few workers bothered to attend Bomber Local 50 meetings or to vote in union elections. They did not understand the extent to which the union was responsible for their high pay and improved working conditions, nor did they feel it necessary to stand by the union in the face of management onslaughts.[35]

While one portion of the rank and file viewed unions with indifference or hostility, another group considered organized labor insufficiently aggressive. Months before Pearl Harbor, militant unionists within the CIO had warned that their leaders might sell out the rank and file in return for a paper show of respectability and influence in Washington. As the war progressed, the ever-increasing tangle of government wage and manpower regulations and the strict adherence of the CIO leadership to the no-strike pledge seemed to justify the worst fears of the militants. These veterans of the sit-down era, who, as likely as not, were in their early thirties, could neither understand nor readily accept the rapid change in labor tactics from the wielding of the strike weapon to the calling of tripartite conferences. Throughout the war, annual UAW local elections resulted in defeat for numerous incumbent officers found wanting in militancy by aroused and suspicious elements of the rank and file. Even the autocratic Detroit Teamsters experienced great difficulty in subduing the rising anger of their membership.[36] "It is common knowledge that enthusiasm for the [UAW] has bogged down considerably in a great many circles because we have not continued to win economic gains for our members," Victor Reuther wrote R. J. Thomas in February, 1943.[37] In one way or another, the statement was valid for a great majority of workers.

The effect of the no-strike pledge, the double time concession, and the Little Steel guidelines, had been to strip the unions, particularly the UAW, of many rights and functions, making them vulnerable to the threat of massive defections by disgruntled workers. Both labor and government, therefore, had an interest in rewarding cooperative unions and in keeping local membership rolls intact. Loathe to grant an outright union shop, the board hammered out a compromise policy in mid-1942. The standard maintenance-of-membership contract clause, used in those cases in which unions did not already have stronger security arrangements, established a fifteen-day period following the date of the contract during which workers could leave the union; thereafter, they could not resign from the union unless they quit their job or the contract expired. Largely because of the maintenance clause, national union membership rose from nine million to fourteen million persons during the war. Labor generally took the position that it was automatically entitled to the application of the clause, which it accepted as partial recompense for Little Steel. The clause could be revoked, however, for such misbehavior by a local as slowdowns or strikes, and management doggedly fought the award of maintenance except as a last resort. The issue proved a constant irritation to the Michigan RWLB, its public members swaying back and forth on the matter, depending on the merits of each case. Maintenance-of-membership played a crucial part in legitimatizing industrial unions and in tightening the control of union leadership over the rank and file. But many workers saw no direct benefits for themselves from the clause, and continued in their apathy or hostility toward organized labor.[38]

The cost of living, fatigue, intransigent management, restrictive government policies, union rivalry, and worker suspicion of labor leadership all contributed to the creation of a mounting wave of wartime strikes. The year 1944 marked both the wartime peak and the all-time national high of labor unrest, with more than 2,115,000 workers idle and about 8,721,000 man-days lost; in that year, Michigan alone accounted for more than one-tenth of all strikes, more than a quarter of the workers involved, and more than a fifth of the total time lost due to work stoppages. It is possible that as many as 65 percent of all Michigan UAW members may have walked out in 1944. But Michigan strikers had not been inactive earlier in the war; the number of state walkouts marginally increased in 1942 over 1941, while the national total of strikes declined. Uncounted thousands of workers who did not down tools participated in various forms of production slowdowns. Strikes were concentrated in the Detroit metropolitan area; by contrast, Bay City, a community with several important war plants, did not experience a major strike until June, 1945.[39]

The short walkout characterized wartime strike activity. During the entire war, strikes accounted for no more than 0.11 percent of all available working time.[40] Ed Jennings has estimated that the average auto industry wildcat involved some 350 to 400 workers for a three- to four-day period.[41] The reasons for strikes changed as the war proceeded. Wage issues, traditional fomentors of walkouts, receded in importance as the WLB tightened wage controls. Maintenance of membership obviated the need for recognition strikes. Disciplinary matters, discharges, and grievances about working conditions came increasingly to the fore. Workers were especially quick to strike over arbitrary firing of a shop steward, who collected dues and dealt with management over grievances, since they perceived his or her discharge as an attack on fundamental contract rights.

Every plant contained a hard core of union militants, often led by rebellious shop stewards, who were ready to strike over real or imagined grievances. Memories of the recent past were never far from the minds of these workers. "A lot of these companies deserve to be treated pretty miserable," said a Ford unionist in 1942. "They treated us that way during the depression. Didn't even say, 'Sorry, old man, we ain't got nothing for you today.' Just said, 'Get the hell out of here.' So now it ain't no wonder if some of the boys treat the company miserable."[42] In any department of any plant on any day, conditions might be created that could ignite the anger of all employees, resulting in a simple downing of tools or a mass walkout.

Striking workers rarely could be swayed by appeals to patriotism. To be sure, the pattern of wildcats was influenced by the most critical military events: Michigan strikes dropped sharply in the invasion month of June, 1944, and fell again at the turn of 1945 in the wake of the near-disaster at Bastogne. It was generally impossible, nevertheless, to convince the few hundred employees of a single department within a mighty war plant that their three-hour work stoppage threatened production or endangered the lives of the GIs. To the contrary, militants believed that they were fighting a war against management autocracy at home that was at least as important as the battle against fascism being waged abroad. A woman member of URW Local 101 spoke her mind on a picket line at the U.S. Rubber Company in Feburary, 1945: "My brother is in Italy. . . . He wrote me before we went on strike to fight for our rights over here. That's what we're doing. . . ." Said another striker at the same plant, "We think we have some legitimate grievances. We think the grievances should be heard and acted upon. We don't think we should get speeches about patriotism."[43]

"While we have had quite a few strikes," Witte wrote from Detroit in the midst of a strike wave during the summer of 1943, "the big explosion we have been looking for has never come." Nor was it to come during the war. Out of a mixture of motives that ranged from patriotism to personal gain, most workers never struck. Perhaps as John Anderson, a leader of the UAW's Communist faction, suggested, conscription conservatized the autoworkers' union through the drafting of many younger militant leaders. Perhaps some of the dislike felt for the boss was diffused in hatred for Hitler and Hirohito. Perhaps strikes did not become more prevalent because of the fundamental patriotism of the labor force. Whatever the reason, Joel Seidman is correct in observing that "barring drastic penalties for strikes such as a democracy would not care to impose, it is doubtful that a better record could be reasonably expected in a country of such size in the absence of invasion."[44]

Although strikes never seriously imperiled war production, they threatened the future of the labor movement itself. When workers set up picket lines, they stated an emphatic if momentary objection to the justice of the unspoken compact that bound all Americans in wartime. It was easy for those who hoarded food or purchased gasoline on the black market to justify their own minor unpatriotic infractions by pointing an accusing finger at strikers. By the same token, the workers' knowledge of the extent of the black market may have strengthened their conviction that any particular walkout was not especially harmful to the war effort. But with each new stoppage, the press, conservative politicians, and a growing majority of the general public voiced new insistence that something be done to limit or halt strikes. Many were eager to go

beyond the enactment of such measures to the wholesale re-
peal of depression-era legislative gains won by labor at such
high cost in struggle and blood. Organized labor, especially the
CIO, was not yet so secure that it could lightly contemplate
such an eventuality.

Punitive legislation to prevent strikes in defense plants had
been introduced in Congress in 1941 by Representative Howard Smith of Virginia. After John L. Lewis called his coal miners out on strike in May, 1943, Congress reacted in fury. Now
cosponsored by Senator Tom Connally, a modified version of
the Smith bill achieved speedy and overwhelming passage in
both houses in late June. The law required a union local in a
war plant to give formal notice of intent to strike, to wait
through a thirty-day cooling-off period, and then to submit
the strike question to its membership in a secret-ballot election
supervised by the NLRB. The government could seize a war
plant threatened by a strike or lockout and could impose criminal penalties for the instigation of illegal work stoppages. Roosevelt vetoed the bill, harkening to the outraged protests of
both the AFL and CIO. The demand for retaliation against
Lewis and other wartime strikers prevailing, Congress over-
rode the President on June 25.

The authors of the Smith-Connally Act thought that their
legislation would restore order to the industrial scene after a
few strike votes gave the rank and file the chance to repudiate
its strike-happy and power-hungry leadership. The precise
opposite occurred: the Smith Act introduced additional instability into labor-management relations since its provisions
placed the authority for calling now-legitimated wartime strikes
in the hands of local, often militant, leaders. The cooling-off
period may have averted some walkouts, but the election feature of the law was a complete fiasco. Workers saw nothing
unpatriotic about using the threat of a strike to pressure a
recalcitrant management. The sections of the Smith-Connally
Act that restricted union contributions to political parties also
could be evaded.

The practical failure of Smith-Connally only increased conservative demands for new measures against labor. From 1943

onward, Congress annually considered the passage of national service legislation similar to Britain's manpower draft, and such a measure cleared the House in early 1945. The press, which played up every strike in an important war plant, also clamored for action. Soldiers flooded newspapers and public officials with complaints about labor turmoil. Corporal Ernest Clark and six of his buddies wrote from the South Pacific to Detroit's Mayor Edward Jeffries in June, 1944: "The mere mention of Detroit brings nothing to mind but strikes. . . . We have only one suggestion to make, Sir—perhaps a brown uniform and $50 a month, leaving them at their present jobs, would settle any disputes the guilty persons may have."[45] Among the most serious threats to unionism was the alienation of the GIs. In the summer of 1943 the UAW had staged a highly publicized exchange of visits between Detroit workers and new inductees at Camp Atterbury, Indiana, in an effort to take labor's case directly to the troops. Women workers made a similar visit to Fort Knox, Kentucky, the following year. Many soldiers did sympathize with the aims and even with the tactics of the strikers, but their voices were not the ones being heard from the battlefront.

Because the United Automobile Workers was the largest union both in the nation and within the CIO, the policies formulated and fought for by the leadership and rank and file of the UAW were decisive for industrial labor. Since more than half of the UAW's membership resided in Michigan, the future of American labor in a very real sense was determined in the war plants of that state. The principal battle within the UAW was fought over the question of continued commitment to the no-strike pledge, to which the union had publicly subscribed at the time of its premium pay concession in April, 1942. The sixth annual meeting of the Michigan state CIO Council, held in Detroit from June 28 to July 1, 1943, formed the backdrop for the first serious test of the pledge's popularity. The delegates overwhelmingly passed resolutions against incentive pay and WLB wage policy, and approved a declaration in favor of revocation of the no-strike pledge "unless the assurances that were made to labor at the time we gave up our

right to strike are immediately and effectively put into operation. . . ."[46] Meeting in Los Angeles in February, 1944, the union's
International Executive Board agreed to a strict new strike
policy. Each stoppage would have to be reported to the Executive Board, which would supersede the local in investigating
the disturbance and, if necessary, in trying the fomentors.
Union services could be withheld from ringleaders, and if local
officers participated in the walkout, they could be removed
from office for up to sixty days and the local placed under an
administrator.

The Los Angeles policy was in force barely two weeks when
it received its first test. Union activists at the Rouge discovered
written evidence that management intended to provoke a strike
if "production is in shape to take a strike."[47] On March 7 a melee
broke out at a plant labor-relations office, hundreds of workers
taking part in its destruction. The company laid off or fired
twenty workers charged with responsibility for the incident,
and R. J. Thomas backed the decision. "The UAW-CIO today
faces one of the greatest crises in its history," Thomas asserted
in a radio address that May. "Public opinion has become in-
flamed against our union. There can be no such thing today as
a legitimate picket line. Any person who sets up picket lines is
acting like an anarchist, not like a disciplined union man."[48] Despite the efforts of the UAW leadership, the rank and file not
only continued to strike but defiantly re-elected local officials
who frequently led the wildcats.

The revolt against the no-strike pledge took organizational
form during the spring of 1944 with the formation of the
"Rank and File" caucus. Several militant leaders met in Detroit
in April to lay plans for the new grouping. Among the prominent figures in the faction were Larry Yost of Ford Local 600;
Bill Jenkins, the president of Chrysler 490; John Zupan of
Bomber Local 50; Ben Garrison of Ford 400; John McGill of
Flint Buick 599; and Robert Carter of Flint AC. The movement attracted dissidents from New York and Chicago but was
centered in Detroit and Flint. The Rank and Filers were men
who, as Nelson Lichtenstein suggests, found their position as
local leaders no longer tolerable because of the conflicting

pressures for obedience to the pledge from the UAW high command, and for defiance of the policy from the shop floor. The use of the term "Rank and File" should not be misconstrued. The new movement was not composed of ordinary workers but drew instead on members of the secondary leadership (shop stewards and local presidents), who may have represented the wishes of a majority of all workers in spirit, but who did not represent a majority of the "rank and file" in reality.

The Rank and Filers took their fight against the no-strike pledge to the UAW's 1944 convention, which opened in Grand Rapids on September 11. Fist fights between members of rival caucuses already had broken out when R. J. Thomas gaveled the twenty-five hundred delegates to a precarious order. In a written message to the meeting, Roosevelt urged retention of the no-strike pledge, and Philip Murray made a personal appearance on behalf of the same cause. "The people in the shops have lost all respect for our international officers because of their no-strike policy," rebutted Ben Garrison, one of many speakers who attacked the pledge during a turbulent debate. "Yes, my friends, I want to see the boys come home after a victorious conclusion of hostilities, but I want to make damned certain . . . that a union will be here when they do come home." Nat Ganley, the so-called whip of the Communist faction, and a supporter of the pledge, answered, "I say that the . . . rescinding of the pledge wholly or partially . . . harms the war effort, and harms our chances in the 1944 . . . election."[49] A Rank and File resolution for outright revocation of the pledge lost but received a 37 percent vote from the delegates. Propledge resolves also failed to win a majority. The leadership rushed through a resolution to reaffirm the pledge subject to a mail ballot referendum of all UAW civilian and military members, to be held within ninety days after the presidential election, and the convention dispersed on September 17.

The references during the pledge debate and the timing of the referendum in relation to the 1944 presidential election were not incidental. Wildcat strikes not only endangered labor but clouded the outlook for democratic victory that fall. However much the antilabor drift of Congress and the Roosevelt war government disturbed the CIO leaders, they still owed too much to the New Deal and could expect too little from the Republicans to abandon the president. The CIO therefore sought to aid Roosevelt by moving to avoid embarrassing him and by mounting its own election effort on his behalf. During the furor over the Smith-Connally Act in the summer of 1943, Sidney Hillman had launched a new, nationally based, pro-Roosevelt labor organization, the CIO Political Action Committee (PAC). Such UAW leaders as secretary-treasurer Addes became active in PAC affairs, and the PAC soon began an intensive drive in Michigan, where, as in California and New York, a movement toward independent political action was underway within restive union circles.

Many of the same militants who later founded the Rank and File caucus had concluded by 1943 that their hope of restoring the vitality of the labor movement and of reversing the conservative national tide lay not in continued support of Roosevelt, but in the establishment of a farmer-labor party on the model of the Canadian Commonwealth Federation. The Michigan third-party men had nothing but contempt for the Democrats of their state, a conservative clique grateful for the strength Roosevelt brought to local tickets every four years but suspicious of New Dealers and New Deal reforms.

The national UAW and Michigan CIO leaders were divided on the question of independent political action in the state, but united in their opposition to any third-party movement that appeared to threaten Roosevelt. After some 350 delegates met in Detroit in March, 1944, to organize the Michigan Commonwealth Federation (MCF) and to inveigh against the no-strike pledge and the Little Steel formula, top UAW officials attacked the new organization. By direct pressure and subtle maneuver, they forced the MCF to abandon the idea of forming a national presidential ticket and to agree not to oppose PAC-endorsed candidates for Michigan state offices.

The CIO meanwhile cast its lot with the Michigan Democratic organization. When Frankensteen keynoted the state Democratic convention in April, the Detroit press declared that the CIO had taken control of the party. The conclusion was unwarranted since the UAW was too preoccupied with intra- and interunion struggle to devote the necessary time and effort to such a coup. Those internal strains had prevented the union from taking an active part in the 1942 state and federal elections, which had brought defeat to Governor Van Wagoner and to Michigan's democratic U. S. Senator Prentiss Brown. In July, however, Thomas, Frankensteen, Addes, and Walter Reuther went to Chicago to take part in the national Democratic convention. The UAW contingent worked assiduously but unsuccessfully for the renomination of Henry Wallace as Roosevelt's running mate.[50]

The CIO staged an unprecedented effort to win Michigan for Roosevelt in the fall campaign against the Republican nominee, Governor Thomas E. Dewey of New York. Each CIO local and plant was ordered to establish a political action committee, and PAC shop chairmen were not above employing coercion to induce reluctant workers to contribute to fund drives or to register to vote. The PAC, however, generally relied upon soundcars, stickers, and tons of literature to deliver its message. Recalling the poor voter turnout that had contributed to the disaster of 1942, the Wayne County PAC compiled a master list of the 450,000 CIO members in the county. Thanks largely to PAC activity, voter registration in Detroit increased sharply. On Election Day, November 7, PAC canvassers, who had trudged patiently block after block to inquire if voters were registered, returned to the neighborhoods to remind CIO unionists and their families of their civic duty and, if necessary, to provide transportation to the polls. Massive voter turnouts in Detroit and Wayne County edged Michigan's nineteen electoral votes into Roosevelt's column by a margin of 1,106,399 to 1,084,223 for Dewey. The President carried Wayne County with some 63 percent of the vote. Roosevelt defeated Dewey nationally with somewhat more than 53 percent of the popular vote.[51]

The 1944 election outcome gave the PAC a reputation for political potency, a reputation that, as James Foster has carefully documented, is less than deserved. Roosevelt probably could not have carried Michigan without the PAC's assistance, but the labor group won the state by only some four votes per precinct against a state Republican Party that undertook no comparable organizational effort. The PAC, moreover, failed to carry such industrial states as Ohio, Indiana, and Wisconsin. Although labor areas voted more heavily for Roosevelt than did the nation as a whole, Foster observes that the Democratic increase in nonlabor districts outstripped that in areas of high PAC activity.[52] The Democrats made respectable gains in Congress, but the PAC's hope for a revived liberal majority was unfulfilled. Michigan unionists suffered complete defeat in their effort to unseat such conservative Republican Congressmen as George Dondero, Clare Hoffman, Joseph Blackney, and Jessee Wolcott. Nor did the PAC's exertions confer strength on the Michigan Democratic ticket; gubernatorial nominee Edward Fry lost by a quarter million votes to the Republican incumbent, Harry Kelly, who thus became the state's first governor to win reelection since 1928. Voters elected five CIO members to the state legislature, but that body remained under firm Republican domination. None of the MCF legislative or Congressional candidates ran strongly, and the third party soon fell into decline.

For all its rhetoric about the vital importance of political action, the Michigan CIO only partially persuaded its local officials and rank and file. Local presidents, stewards, and committeemen were too busy with day-to-day problems of labor relations to be bothered with the unrewarding work of a precinct captain. The struggle to control a dynamic UAW seemed more significant than any effort to capture a moribund state Democratic Party. Shop-level PAC personnel too often carried little weight with the membership or discharged their duties incompetently. The union rank and file resisted efforts to mold it into a bloc behind a single candidate or philosophy. Still, organized labor made a respectable showing in Michigan, and within a few years the UAW would become the most powerful political force in the state.

The no-strike debate was suspended during the fall, but with Roosevelt safely reelected, the referendum campaign be-

gan in earnest. A host of public personalities, among them the
President, urged the UAW membership to vote for retention.
Walter Reuther, a nominal foe of the pledge, spoke on its behalf, and the Communists unlimbered their heaviest rhetorical
artillery in its support. No well-known union figure stood with
the militants; the chairman of the caucus's national steering
committee, Larry Yost, was merely the head of Local 600's Aircraft Division. No prominent figure outside labor came to their
aid. Opposition to the pledge alone united them, and they advanced no other common issues around which to attract a following. But Yost, Jenkins, Jess Ferrazza, and the other Rank
and File leaders continued to hold rallies and to denounce the
pledge. They argued that industrial relations would be more
peaceful without the policy, since labor and management once
more would be on equal footing. In early January, the union
mailed out the first of more than 1,250,000 referendum ballots, including some seventy-five thousand intended for UAW
members in the armed services.

The results of the no-strike pledge referendum were announced in early March. The five UAW regions within Michigan collectively voted to retain the pledge by 81,819 to 62,783
(56.5 to 43.5 percent), representing a voter turnout of only
21.9 percent. American and Canadian union members cast a
mere 281,130 votes (11,354 from soldiers), or 22.5 percent of
the total number of ballots mailed. Retention of the pledge
carried by 64.0 percent to 34.7 percent, the remaining ballots
(1.3 percent) being declared invalid. All UAW members outside of Michigan voted by about three to one to sustain the
national leadership. The low participation rate obtained uni-
formly throughout the nation, whatever the percentage of "yes"
votes in a particular UAW region.[53] Many workers, in the expec-
tation of an early Allied victory on the European front, may
have decided that the pledge issue was no longer important.
The meager return of ballots also may have testified to a general apathy toward union affairs on the part of a great majority
of the rank and file, the clamor of the militants notwithstand-
ing. Since militants were unlikely to have passed up the chance
to show their resentment against the pledge, it can probably be

concluded that full participation of the membership would have yielded an even higher percentage of affirmative votes. Then again, the mail-ballot format of the referendum may have guaranteed a low turnout.

Michigan strikes fell off in December, 1944, and January, 1945, coincident with the siege of Bastogne and with balloting in the pledge referendum, but the number of walkouts thereafter resumed an upward climb.[54] Republican lawmakers introduced a bill in the Michigan legislature providing the death penalty for war-plant strikers.[55] The German surrender brought renewed demands from the rank and file for revocation of the no-strike pledge. Factionalism within the UAW reached new levels of intensity as Walter Reuther formally called for another referendum. Reuther argued that since government travel restrictions meant the postponement until 1946 of the next union convention, the casting of a second vote was only fair. The remainder of the UAW's national leadership coalesced against him, however, and reaffirmed the no-strike pledge at a meeting of the International Executive Board in Minneapolis on July 20.

This action did nothing to quell the mounting talk in Detroit about the inevitability of a postwar labor showdown in the auto industry, a confrontation prophesied for almost as long as America had been at war.[56] When a Senate subcommittee assembled in Detroit during the winter of 1945 to hold hearings on manpower problems, labor and management attacked each other with bared fangs. Answering industry denunciations of union irresponsibility, R. J. Thomas told the senators, "There are groups in management in this community who approve of labor unions like I approve of smallpox."[57] On April 10 Charles Wilson of GM and B. E. Hutchinson of Chrysler unveiled a postwar labor program to counter the "Industrial Charter" signed on March 28 by William Green of the AFL, Philip Murray of the CIO, and Eric Johnston, president of the United States Chamber of Commerce. The automakers' plan, although following the Charter in its concession of the union shop, called for a number of crippling restrictions on and sanctions against strikes and organizing activity.[58] A UAW emergency conference in June demanded that an immediate Smith-Connally strike vote be taken in all plants under contract with the union. "Unless there is a radical change for the better," a reporter had written in March, "Detroit and the nation may see, before the year is ended, the fiercest, wildest, and bloodiest labor struggle in all history."[59]

In reality the most violent and bloody battles of automobile labor lay in the past, not the future. During the war as David Brody notes, industrial unionism came of age. Under government guidance, labor and management, which at least shared the common objective of victory over the Axis, learned to talk, if not to relax, with one another. The WLB not only placed restraints on labor but, when necessary, forced industry to bargain in something approaching good faith. Despite the large number of wildcat strikes, the nation took a long stride toward industrial stability. Brody writes that "the industrial unions grew strong and became internally stable. . . . The subsidence of the bitter rivalry between the AFL and CIO further answered the reservations of open-shop management. By 1945, no grounds remained to sustain hopes that unionization might be reversed, nor fears that responsible relations could not be established with the industrial unions."[60]

Brody's interpretation of wartime industrial labor is substantially correct but must be qualified in light of the Michigan experience. The UAW-CIO became stronger, but the achievement of internal stability waited upon the postwar era. Factionalism and interunion rivalry throughout the state hardly seemed to slacken during the 1940–45 period. Automotive executives on all levels remained extraordinarily recalcitrant toward even government-sponsored collective bargaining. They nonetheless accepted the presence of the union within their factories, and that acceptance constituted the most significant of the unanticipated benefits conferred upon labor by the war. Never again need the UAW fear destruction at the hands of an obsessed oligarch or a faceless corporate administration.

Industrial labor matured during the war not only in terms of its status on the shop floor but also in the relationship of the unions to the larger community. The UAW-CIO's involvement in Michigan politics, although still minimal in the extent of control over Democratic Party affairs, reached new heights of organizational sophistication, if not of sustained electoral success. In metropolitan Detroit, the CIO assumed many characteristics of an agency for the coordination and advocacy of social welfare. A federal observer noted that the Wayne County CIO Council supported rent control and demanded more classrooms, housing, and other community facilities, all measures of benefit to the general population, not to labor alone. "It is as if the community at large had been waiting for some smaller and more manageable unit of local government or leadership than the city as a whole," he concluded.[61] Given the social consciousness and activist outlook of many persons within the UAW's leadership and staff, the union might have developed such a varied set of new functions naturally over the years. The war, however, forced the UAW to assume many such functions and provided it with an opportunity to take up responsibility for community leadership that had never been accepted by the masters of the auto industry.

To Nelson Lichtenstein, the UAW's growth and maturity led to a "conservative shift in labor politics and trade union policy, an attack on shop floor militancy, and weakening of internal union democracy." To be sure, the International Executive Board of the UAW-CIO extended stricter control over the locals during the war than it had attempted to enforce previously. Such an increment of authority over Michigan's unruly giant union, however, was inevitable. Even if the UAW and other CIO leaders had viewed their membership as the nucleus of what Lichtenstein calls a "radical and potentially majoritarian movement"—and they did not—more centralized command structures would have been required.[62] Within the UAW, moreover, pursuit of trade union goals did not always mean compliance with democratic procedure. The violence-prone members of Briggs 212, the archetypal militant local, did not become known as the "Dead End Kids" for nothing. Typical of the intimidating methods employed by the local was the "dues drive" of December 9, 1943, during which union militants ringed the Mack Avenue plant with picket signs, ostensibly in an effort to collect delinquent dues, but also with the intention of harrassing nonunion workers. Local president Emil Mazey was arrested for assaulting a woman after one of several melees that broke out during the incident.[63] Every jurisdictional strike, flareup of intraunion factionalism, and management or Congressional pronouncement must have reminded the UAW's leadership not only of its personal insecurity at the top of a volatile union but of what then appeared to be the uncertain future of industrial unionism itself.

Chapter 3

Communities: Breathing under Water

Mobilization for war affected every community, large and small, urban and rural. Widespread disruption of peacetime patterns of life occurred in the major production centers of the nation, and the success of the industrial war effort depended to a critical extent on the ability of those centers to cope with their vastly increased burdens. In such far-flung cities, towns, and villages as Hampton Roads, Virginia, Willow Run, Michigan, and San Diego, California, private citizens, interest groups, and public officials struggled to adjust to a reality in which crisis became the norm. They fought, too, to maintain intact as much of their old way of life as could be preserved from the explosive forces of change set loose by the war.

The nation enrolled every sector of society in the creation of the home front. The government strove to convince the people that they, too, constituted an army, one charged with the vital jobs of producing for victory and of guarding and strengthening the domestic battle lines. Propaganda urged the wearing of a uniform as the symbol of participation in one or another of the many war-related activities. A federally sponsored radio play broadcast to Detroiters in 1942 portrayed a mother's reflection on her son's departure for the military as follows: "Since Ted left for the Army, I've been thinking about uniforms. Everybody should be in uniform these days—as a soldier, a production worker, a nurse, or a first-aid worker."[1] To coordinate the myriad of citizen-participation programs,

President Roosevelt established the Office of Civilian Defense (OCD), under the leadership of the mayor of New York, Fiorello H. LaGuardia. In addition to uniforms, the OCD and cooperating institutions, such as businesses and labor unions, supplied pins, badges, posters, windshield stickers, window placards, and leaflets to popularize civilian defense, bond sales, scrap drives, and so forth. Washington inspired these projects and campaigns, of course, but responsibility for their successful execution always lay in the hands of state or community leaders.

Thousands of Michigan residents participated in civilian defense activities, serving as air raid wardens, plane spotters, fire guards, auxiliary policemen, messengers, and staffers at the several emergency disaster stations established in every production center. Still more persons became volunteer aides in day-care centers, manned information desks to answer consumer questions, or functioned as block leaders of the Neighborhood War Clubs, an organization established by the OCD in 1943 to assist air raid wardens and to disseminate information about government programs. Social differences hobbled civilian defense, many lower-class people shying away from joining the Red Cross or OCD-sponsored units, because the leadership of such groups usually was restricted to the community elite. Michigan's defense program also suffered from a power struggle during late 1941 and early 1942 between Governor Van Wagoner, nominal head of the state-initiated effort, and Mayor Jeffries of Detroit, whom LaGuardia had appointed as OCD director of the Detroit region. These problems, however, did not prevent the creation of a generally efficient statewide emergency force. Interest in civilian defense waned as the threat of enemy assault dissipated, but the Michigan OCD still counted four hundred thousand enrollees in its various programs in January, 1945.[2]

It was not necessary to spend chilly evenings scanning the skies for signs of fire or of marauding Heinkels to be a part of the civilian mobilization; one could become involved in one's own home by joining in the wartime policy of conservation. Newspapers bristled with such reminders from the government or advertisers as "You ... help ... lick the enemies of freedom when you lick the platter clean," or "Don't waste soap—use it wisely."[3] Utilities that once had urged untrammeled use of gas, electricity, or the telephone now offered advice on the moderate and efficient use of such services, or recommended that use be curtailed almost entirely. "He'll drill a Jap sniper with a long distance call you didn't make," Michigan Bell told subscribers in April, 1943, explaining further that materials used by the phone system were now devoted to a more deadly form of communication.[4] The flattened tin can and bucket of kitchen fat are now only nostalgic reminders of a past era, but they once formed the foundation of a formidable collection of salvage. To be sure, the government offered inducements of cash or extra ration points for merely handing over the family refuse; still, participation in even such humble business required a degree of active commitment. Thousands surely chose not to become involved in one campaign or another, but the constant din of propaganda, the effect of neighborhood pressure, government enforcement of stringencies, and the honest desire to cooperate undoubtedly guaranteed that most citizens refrained from waste most of the time.

No arm of the wartime government held so much power over everyday life as did the Office of Price Administration. The person who neither ate, drank, wore shoes, nor drove a car could avoid contact with the agency; the rest of the population became more or less thoroughly acquainted with its numerous programs of price control and rationing. The OPA clamped ceilings on millions of different prices and restricted the supply of a large array of commodities, some for the duration (gasoline, automobiles, tires, sugar) and some for particular periods (meat, most processed foods, shoes). Because of its omnipresence and frequent blunders, the OPA was a constant target of administration critics, and the President was forced to sacrifice its successive directors to the Congressional wolves. Like other citizen-participation programs, rationing depended upon public and official compliance and assistance, since the OPA had no large enforcement staff. Every head of household struggled to keep the family's budget of ration stamps in balance. Thousands of volunteers staffed Michigan ration boards and checked merchants for price-control violations. In 1943 Detroit made black marketeering an offense punishable in local courts.[5]

Price control and rationing generally succeeded in effecting an acceptably equitable apportionment of goods among Americans. In turn, the public, despite its grumbling, generally supported OPA. That support was not fervent, however, either among the people or among the businessmen who bore the brunt of OPA regulation and restriction. As a result, black markets flourished at one time or another during the war in such commodities as sugar, gasoline, meat, poultry, and coffee. Major black market offenses included coupon counterfeiting, fraudulent record-keeping, and selling over ceiling or by extortionate means. The gasoline black market was the special preserve of organized crime, but all other black marketeers were reputable businessmen, who excused their wrongdoing on such grounds as the unfairness of OPA profit ceilings, the customary if unethical nature of the condemned practice in prewar days, or the purely technical quality of the violation. Social status played a part in assuring that only three of 132 defendants charged with violations of OPA wholesale meat regulations in Detroit from 1942 to 1946 were sentenced to jail.[6] Legally, only merchants and businessmen were black marketeers, but thousands of Michigan citizens occasionally violated one or another OPA ruling. They hoarded food, attempted to use invalid ration stamps, or willingly paid over-ceiling prices.

Civilian defense, mass participation programs, and rationing occasionally posed major problems for state and local government. But people were at the heart of the continuing community crisis—people on the move. The draft compelled millions of men to leave their homes for journeys of hundreds or thousands of miles. Some 15,300,000 persons crossed county lines during the war, many of them workers in search of employment in the production centers. Net interstate migration from 1940 to 1945 exceeded that of the previous five years by a million persons. In two broad streams, Americans moved from south to north and from east to west. Michigan counted 286,709 net in-migrants between April 1, 1940, and November 1, 1943, a yearly average movement into the state of 80,011 persons. All estimates agree that the bulk of the migration into Michigan took place before the November, 1943, war production peak.[7]

The influx of migrants placed Michigan among the dozen states (and the District of Columbia) that gained population during the war despite the outflow of thousands of men to the armed forces. A survey of population for the period April 1, 1940, to November 1, 1943, based on applications for Ration Book No. 4, revealed that the reversal of the depression-era intrastate city-to-farm movement had accelerated. Michigan grew by a total of 126,000 inhabitants during the forty-three months covered by the census, but the entire gain took place within sixteen predominantly urban counties. The four-county Detroit area (Wayne, Oakland, Macomb, and Washtenaw) expanded from a population of 2,454,633 in 1940 to 2,709,944 in 1943, a 14.5 percent advance. Sixty-seven counties, all but one predominantly rural, lost an aggregate of 10 percent of their prewar population between 1940 and 1943.[8]

Suburban growth quickened dramatically during the war, continuing a trend long underway around Michigan's major cities. A sample census of the Detroit-Willow Run area, conducted in June, 1944, reported that the population of the city of Detroit had increased by a mere 30,454 persons in four years, or 1.9 percent, while the area outside the city grew during the same period by 19 percent. (Detroit's almost static population reflected a near-balance between the hundreds of thousands of migrants who departed and entered the city.) A survey of Muskegon County, taken at the same time, also revealed striking suburban development in contrast to slower central-city growth. Small subdivisions in war production areas displayed spectacular growth: the town of Inkster grew from 7,044 to 12,708 between 1940 and 1945 (80.4 percent), and Gratiot Township (Wayne County) nearly quintupled in the same period, from 858 persons to 5,183 (498.8 percent).[9]

Attempts to limit migration into Michigan began almost as

soon as war broke out. During the defense period, government leaders worried about the impact on welfare costs of a
mass movement of unskilled workers into the state. In 1940
and 1941, the press and public officials issued warnings to migrants to stay away, and Detroit launched a campaign to urge
industry to give priority in hiring to local residents. After Pearl
Harbor, concern focused on the effect of excess migration on
already overtaxed community facilities. The feared horde of
poverty-stricken jobseekers never descended on Michigan, but
all efforts to regulate or limit migration failed. In late 1942 the
Detroit office of the United States Employment Service forbade employers to advertise for in-migrant workers without
the agency's approval; the largest of Detroit's automotive firms
continued to recruit in violation of USES directives, however,
and the employment service itself never challenged the major
companies. Agricultural draft deferments slowed out-migration to a degree after 1943 but hardly constituted a comprehensive control. There was much talk during the war of
"closing" certain Michigan communities to workers who had
migrated from labor-short localities, but this system of inter-
area clearance foundered because of local USES maladministration and continuing employer demand for manpower.[10]

Migrants of all kinds made Detroit at war a bustling, crowded
city. Legions of newly arrived war workers rubbed shoulders
on busy streets with soldiers and sailors in the sober uniforms
of the United States or in the more colorful garb of British
Commonwealth allies. Observers saw surprisingly little change
in the outward manifestations of daytime life, but in the evening, movie theaters, bowling alleys, and clubs opened their
doors, marquees brightly lit into the early morning hours, to
cater to the needs or whims of swingshifters.[11] A reporter for
Daily Variety described Detroit, after a visit in October, 1943, as
a place "where they stand in line for a glass of beer . . . where
more dames wear slacks than in Hollywood . . . where it takes
the reserves to get a vandal out of a theater, where the sidewalk
madonnas get too much opposition from home talent . . . and
where everybody has two sawbucks to rub against each other.
Detroit, the hottest town in America."[12]

Migration created a series of interlocking and burdensome problems for the war centers. By late 1940 the increase in population due to the combined industrial and military buildup had begun to strain resources and capabilities in affected localities. The shortages and deficiences ran the spectrum of facilities and functions. Unsolved community problems threatened to become a serious hindrance to war production. The nation charged the war centers with the task of absorbing the migrant host, whether soldier or civilian, without disrupting the tempo of production. In the discharge of their responsibilities, the communities required the active involvement of citizens and of every level of government, from township boards of supervisors to Congress, from court house to the White House.

The first area in Michigan to feel the effects of the defense program, Battle Creek and surrounding Calhoun County, evidenced all the symptoms of acute community congestion by the end of 1940. The army had decided to reactivate and upgrade its World War I-era facility near the city and the new Fort Custer became for a time one of the largest military installations in the country. Trailer camps sprang up throughout the vicinity. The families of construction workers and noncommissioned Army officers crowded available housing, and their children jammed city and township school systems to capacity and beyond. The situation grew worse during 1941 as Fort Custer, largely completed by the preceding November, raised its regular complement to twenty thousand troops and processed some thirty-four thousand draftees. Street traffic increased and soldiers overflowed area taverns and social clubs. Battle Creek, solidly entrenched in the western Michigan Bible belt, offered few opportunities for sin; the troops, however, created their own opportunities with local barmaids and transient girls, as the rising incidence of venereal disease all too clearly indicated.[13]

From 1941 onward, the tiny, essentially unorganized suburban communities around Detroit were overwhelmed by the vast government program of industrial and military construction and inundated by in-migration. Macomb County, north-

east of Detroit, watched its roads deteriorate under the
pounding of tanks from the Chrysler arsenal, its schools fill to
bursting, and its health and protective services fall hopelessly
behind the demands placed upon them.[14] The localities had neither the time, the leadership, nor the financial resources to
overcome their problems. Many communities forced to confront the demands of defense and war had emerged from the
depression not only lacking needed civic improvements and
services but bereft of the fiscal resources required to meet the
new crisis. Cities had fallen into debt trying to maintain minimal functions and huge tax delinquencies had resulted in reduced revenues. The state constitution restricted the property
tax to no more than fifteen mills (1.5 percent) of total assessed
valuation unless increased by popular vote in any levying jurisdiction. The national government increased the problems of
the localities by exempting from taxation all federally or Al-
lied-owned defense facilities, such as war plants or housing
projects, and the land on which these facilities stood.

While the smaller communities sank beneath the weight of
their problems, Detroit progressed financially and organiza-
tionally. By the end of fiscal 1943, the city government had
accumulated an operating surplus and had placed finances on
a pay-as-you-go basis. Since the federal government had constructed only one major war plant within the city limits, Detroit was not as affected by the taxation issue as were the
suburban communities. In October, 1943, labor, business, and
citizens groups joined to form the Detroit Victory Council
(DVC) to concentrate on manpower and housing difficulties.
However, strengthened finances and group activity yielded little coordinated and effective action. Observers explained this
fact by pointing to the rootlessness of Detroit's population, the
lack of a large middle class, and the aloof attitude of the leading automobile executives. The automakers vetoed civic projects distasteful to them but otherwise disdained to participate
in community affairs. After a tour of the nation's war centers
in 1943, journalist Agnes Meyer wrote: "In a city like Detroit,
where the enormous industries dominate, the acute competitive psychology which characterizes management also pene-

trates the city itself, to the point where cooperation in any field of endeavor becomes difficult."[15]

During the 1930s several states, including Michigan, initiated "Little New Deals" but no state could mount a "little war effort" because none possessed the resources to do so. From July 1, 1940, to June 30, 1945, Michigan state government expenditure rose 25 percent, predominently in the areas of education and public health. Once adjusted for inflation, state spending actually fell about 2 percent in these years. In July, 1940, Michigan had become the first state in the nation to create a civilian defense organization, when Governor Luren Dickinson established the Michigan National Defense Council. As migration increased and local civilian defense responsibilities grew, the legislature created the Michigan Council of Defense in May, 1941, to cope with defense-related community problems. The lawmakers limited the MCD's mandate largely to liaison work with federal agencies, educational efforts, and the undertaking of surveys. Despite reorganization in 1943 as the Michigan War Council, the agency proved of little utility outside of its unquestionably important function as coordinator of federally sponsored civilian participation programs. "A frank look at the practicalities of the situation indicates there is disappointingly little positive action which the state government can take with benefit," concluded James Haswell, political writer for the *Detroit Free Press*, in March, 1943. "Let the state government help when asked, keep Washington informed of what it can do, and stand by for orders."[16]

State and local officials quickly turned to Washington for assistance in grappling with the social and economic consequences of industrial expansion and defense migration. The United States government, most local leaders argued, had created their problems in the first place by decreeing that a military camp be established here or that a defense plant be built or a contract awarded there. As the superintendent of Saginaw's schools told a Congressional committee in March, 1941: "We look at it this way: if the government enters into the proposition of assisting manufacturers in the construction of buildings and so on to carry out this defense work, and that brings a great many people into the communities, then certainly something should be done to help the communities as well as the manufacturers."[17] More than one locality, of course, weighed honest patriotism, the desire for prestige, and a cold-eyed calculation of the economic benefits in making efforts to obtain military installations and defense factories. Mayor Jeffries complained loudly about the unfairness of asking the industrial areas to foot the defense facilities bill, but he nonetheless tried—vainly, as it turned out—to acquire a Marine training base and a naval shipyard for Detroit.[18]

The money to finance needed community facilities had to come from a Congress ill-disposed by 1940 to generous expenditures even for defense-related civilian activities. While liberals complained that President Roosevelt seemed to be selling out the New Deal by his appointment of businessmen to top government posts, conservatives fretted that the arms program might disguise an administration plot to fasten socialism upon the land. The federal octopus must not be allowed to extend its tentacles further lest it gain control over the direction of local social and economic policy. Workers, especially those who migrated with their families, must not be pampered while the nation's soldiers were subjected to a hard regimen. Debating a defense housing appropriation in the fall of 1940, Representative Earl Michener of Michigan's Second District wondered: "Am I correct in this; that this is a national defense measure; that this is not one of those social reforms or uplift measures?"[19] Such questions and objections continually surfaced during the war, often severely limiting Washington's ability to assist impacted localities.

The provisions of the Lanham Act, the principal federal statute authorizing wartime community aid, revealed the depth of conservative fears. Passed in October, 1940, and named for its chief House sponsor, Fritz Lanham of Texas, the law had been rendered as New Deal-proof as possible. The legislators placed the administration of funds in the hands of the Federal Works Agency (FWA), identified as a no-nonsense engineering organization presumably capable of spending with greater care than the "soft-headed" professorial types in the other alphabet agencies. The law bristled with rigid inspection and evaluation procedures to prevent the dispersal of appropriations to any undeserving community. Congress added a second title to the Lanham Act in June, 1941, granting federal payments for the construction in designated areas of public improvements directly related to the defense program—sewers, school buildings, streets, and so forth. An amendment introduced by Lanham himself forbade the FWA from making any funds available for nondefense projects such as slum clearance. The total Lanham Act expenditure of nearly eight billion dollars for housing between 1940 and 1945 appears large, but shrinks beside the hundreds of billions freely appropriated by Congress without vexatious amendments for armament contracts and defense-plant construction.[20]

President Roosevelt meanwhile created a phalanx of civilian-oriented federal agencies in 1941 and 1942 under the umbrella of the Office of Emergency Management, the OCD and the OPA being only the most visible components. This bureaucracy continually swelled in size and jurisdiction, although it remained a pygmy alongside the gigantic civilian military establishment. "By the end of 1943," James M. Burns observes, "virtually a new system of presidential government had grown out of the makeshift arrangements of the old. The foundation had been laid for a powerful executive office, a huge war structure, and a vastly expanded social-welfare organization, which were to characterize the presidency for decades to come."[21] The National Housing Agency (NHA), Office of Defense Transportation (ODT), Federal Works Agency, and the Office of Community War Services (OCWS), distributed hundreds of millions of dollars for the construction and maintenance of war-necessary facilities. The federal government thus became involved as never before—and, in many ways, for the first time—in the homes, schools, bus systems, and even the brothels of America.

Given the suspicion and uncertainty surrounding the demand for large-scale federal aid to defense areas, it is not surprising that the relationship between Washington and the communities was often an uneasy one. In an era of shortages, the supply of red tape appeared unlimited—and unaffected by priorities. The flow of defense migration into Detroit's sparsely settled periphery during the fall of 1941 created an urgent need for more schools, sewers, fire equipment, and recreation buildings. In September the municipal government dispatched to Washington proposals for public works improvements to be financed in whole or part by Lanham Act funds. Detroit thereafter waited, but received no definitive response from the FWA.[22] "We have had a lot of lip service . . . but no money of any sort," wrote a distracted Mayor Jeffries in February, 1942.[23] Time and again city officials laid their case before one or another federal agency, usually to retreat in bafflement, discouragement, or anger as their pleas appeared to echo without effect in the labyrinthine corridors of the new wartime government. Approval of Detroit's requests did not come until seven to eight months had elapsed.[24] Communities across the state would suffer the same delay and frustration throughout the war.

Division within cities and towns over the location of a housing project, school, or hospital, as well as the inability of neighboring local jurisdictions to submerge longstanding disagreements, could delay federal action for months. The government chose sites in southern Macomb and northern Oakland Counties for several important defense plants, including the Chrysler and Hudson arsenals. The area's partially constructed sewer system, however, was insufficient to cope with the demands of a suddenly increased population. By February, 1941, state health officials warned that residents faced outbreaks of typhoid fever and other virulent diseases unless corrective action was taken. But the various Macomb governments could not devise a satisfactory method to raise their share of a sewer project's costs, nor could they come to an agreement with Detroit on a fee for the use of the city's sewer lines and treatment plants. Although the Public Works Administration (PWA) gave tentative approval in November to a large-scale sewer system, it was October, 1942, before all preliminary obstacles to the project were overcome and final authorization granted. The system, so urgently required months before Pearl Harbor, did not reach completion until September, 1943.[25]

Although community division sometimes frustrated the government, local conflict could strengthen Washington's hand. Unable to decide on the location of a facility or the allocation of funds for a task, city and township leaders often turned in relief to federal officials, who then made the unpalatable choices. Community politicians, of course, took advantage of this procedure to lay the blame on Washington for onerous decisions; no one could doubt, however, where the power of decision now lay. In Detroit, where cooperation was so difficult to achieve or maintain, responsibility for housing, transportation, and other important areas of civic life passed into federal care. "The competence of the government bureaucracy to handle [community] problems compatibly with the aspirations of all groups is generally questioned," an observer for the Office of War Information noted in December, 1942, "but the federal government seems to be the only institution which Detroit people regard at present as just and legitimate authority in these matters."[26]

Because they lacked hard information about the future scope of the war production program and its manpower requirements, Washington, the state, the communities, and private interests made plans without a clear notion of how much to expand vital facilities. Because the facts they needed were often difficult or impossible to determine, a certain degree of confusion became inevitable. Estimates of the labor force required for the Willow Run bomber plant fluctuated between 15,000 and 110,000 persons, a range virtually meaningless as a basis for decision making. "Your guess is as good as ours as to how many men will work there," a PWA official told a meeting of perplexed Washtenaw County planners in July, 1941.[27] The NHA formulated its plan for housing in the vicinity on the upper limit of the manpower predictions, only to receive a shock in May, 1942, when Henry Ford submitted to the War Production Board a drastically reduced maximum workforce estimate of between sixty thousand and sixty-two thousand employees.[28] As it happened, the manpower peak at the plant, reached in early 1943, was less than forty-four thousand workers and the labor force decreased precipitously thereafter. Such estimation problems dogged every aspect of the national community aid program.

Housing for the thousands of in-migrant war workers remained the preeminent community need and a vital requirement for the maintenance of a stable workforce. Yet every major Michigan production center was subject to a more or less acute housing shortage during the war. The development of housing scarcities was not surprising in light of the existing situation in many areas at the outset of the defense period. Municipal officials across the nation had become concerned by 1940 about the slowing of urban growth and the spreading of slum districts throughout city centers. A 1938 WPA survey suggested the dimensions of Detroit's problem: some 70,000 of the city's 414,000 dwelling units had been found to be substandard, the proportion of inadequate housing rising to nearly 40 percent in the central core.[29] The private construction industry had not kept pace with the need to replace deteriorating housing with decent homes. Nor had the Detroit Housing Commission (DHC) completed enough federally financed housing projects.

The gross habitable vacancy rate of Detroit's privately owned homes plunged from 7.7 percent in August, 1940, to 0.5 percent four years later, well below the 5 percent level recommended by housing professionals to ensure orderly absorption of newcomers. The statistics formed only a cold composite of thousands of individual tales of pathos. The scarcity fell with particular poignancy upon newly arrived families with children, rejected time and again by landlords. "Two children! God bless 'em, I bet you wish they'd never been born," a realtor exclaimed sadly in 1942 when a reporter expressed an interest in acquiring a home for a family. By July of that year the city welfare shelter had begun to take in employed men and their families who could find no other place to live. The total housing supply in the four-county Detroit area actually rose about 15 percent between 1940 and 1944, keeping slightly ahead of the population increase. But much of this housing was not available when it was needed. In 1944, long after large-scale war housing construction had been undertaken in Detroit, the DHC still received seven requests for every dwelling available.[30]

Detroit's city government took a number of steps to bring local energies to bear on the housing crisis. The Common Council amended the municipal zoning ordinance in 1942 to allow home owners in restricted areas to rent rooms to single persons or to childless couples. Within a month, three hundred such homes had been occupied, and a backlog of permit requests from potential landlords had accumulated. The DHC began to accept applications for the conversion of vacant stores into one- or two-family units. The agency also established a War Housing Center as a clearinghouse for occupancy requests, and in late 1943 launched a "Share Your Home" drive. This campaign brought the plight of war workers to public attention, but failed to yield the required dwellings. It was typical of all locally initiated efforts to ease the housing crunch—totally inadequate in scope and execution.[31]

Rent control was a significant element in the federal government's effort to solve the crisis. Detroit rents remained relatively stable during the first year of the defense period, but rose 1 percent per month over the last half of 1941. On March 2, 1942, the OPA ordered landlords to roll back rents within sixty days to levels prevailing on April 1, 1941; thereafter, ceilings would become mandatory, and violators could be prosecuted. The OPA program proved popular and generally effective. From an index figure of 104.6 (1935–39 equals 100) in June, 1940, the average of national rents increased a mere 3.5 percent to 108.4 by July, 1945. In that five-year interval, Detroit rents rose only 6.8 percent, almost all of the increase having taken place before the imposition of ceilings. Rent control, however, did not increase the supply of housing. Many landlords refused to place their properties on the market rather than obey the OPA or rent to those they considered undesirable. Other devious landlords circumvented OPA regulations by forcing tie-in purchases such as storm windows or empty lots as part of the price for rental. Owners who sought to sell or re-

rent at a higher rate sometimes ruthlessly evicted original tenants. During the first half of 1943 renters were being evicted
faster than new housing could be constructed.[32]

To ease the housing crisis, the federal government undertook the largest homebuilding program in American history.
From July, 1940, to September, 1945, the NHA and its predecessor agencies built or assisted in the construction of more
than two million dwelling units. By contrast, the federal public
housing program, inaugurated in 1937, had produced less
than 230,000 units by 1941. Most of the war housing was managed by the NHA's principal subsidiary, the Federal Public
Housing Authority (FPHA). The FPHA spent some eighty-
four million dollars of Lanham Act funds in Michigan to erect
more than twenty-two thousand dwelling units, composed of
trailers, dormitories, and family homes. Nearly 80 percent of
the units were located in the four-county Detroit area.[33]

The temporary project symbolized the war housing program. The shortage of critical materials dictated that war
housing be built cheaply, and a temporary home required
some 78 percent less of these materials than a permanent
house did. The "demountable" units could be disassembled,
shipped to another problem housing area, and reassembled
on the spot. The temporary homes were grouped together in
units of four, five, or six one-, two-, or three-bedroom dwellings renting for between twenty-five and thirty-five dollars a
month. Typical of the several war housing projects in Detroit
was the John R. Fisher Homes, a 536-unit development situated on a 38.9-acre tract in southwest Detroit, adjacent to River
Rouge. Opened on July 13,1943, Fisher Homes was restricted
to white in-migrant war workers and their families. Row on
row, the 171 buildings stood on a treeless, grassless mud ex-
panse. Landscaping did not begin until almost a year after
the first units were occupied. A coal-fired stove and space
heater warmed each unit. A representative two-person unit included a kitchen with an icebox, stove, and tub sink; a 4-by-6½-
foot bathroom with basin, flush toilet, and shower stall; and a
nine-foot, eight-inch-square bedroom with a single large closet.
The cream-colored walls were made of light building-board,

no barrier to the sounds or smells of the neighboring family.[34]

Visiting the project in the spring of 1944, Freda Yenney heard numerous complaints from many of the 2,100 occupants—the dirt, the heat, the lack of privacy, the dilapidated state of many of the units, and the absence of a decent environment in which to raise children. These critics would have smiled bitterly at the DHC's description of temporary housing as "adequate, comfortable, and sanitary."[35] War homes were not unduly comfortable, but neither were they hastily knocked-together shanties. The surroundings of many projects were cheerless and depressing, but the homes themselves were adequate under wartime circumstances. Yenny, moreover, found threads of praise woven into the fabric of complaint about the Fisher Homes: migrants, especially those from rural areas, appreciated continuous hot water and inside plumbing, and former apartment dwellers liked being out from under the prying eyes of a landlord. For many persons, residence in a war housing project was a step up in the world.[36]

Delay and confusion dogged each step of the war housing program. Charged with responsibility for a purely civilian problem, the NHA was at a disadvantage in the struggle for influence in war-minded Washington. Because of manpower uncertainties, the number of public units projected for the Detroit area zoomed from ten thousand to sixty thousand and back to five thousand in the year following July, 1941. By the end of 1942, only four projects containing 3,036 units had been opened, two of these scheduled for years as part of the DHC's peacetime construction. The DHC, local agent for the federal housing program, often quarrelled with the government over site selection. The conflicting statements and tangle of regulations emanating from Washington left local leaders thoroughly confused. High-level functionaries frequently visited the city to assure it of continued national concern. "You need help, and you need it on a minute-to-minute basis," the WPB's Maury Maverick wrote Mayor Jeffries in July, 1943, after a flying tour of Detroit. Help, however, continued to arrive with exasperating slowness.[37]

From the outset of the defense era, Detroit's real estate interests argued that the city's housing supply was adequate and that private enterprise could fill any forthcoming demand better than the federal government. Private contractors and real estate agents condemned the Federal Housing Administration's (FHA's) system of supply priority allocation. By mid-1942 restrictions on critical materials had brought Detroit home building to a virtual halt, and other FHA rules sharply limited the disposition of completed houses. Noting the large number of vacant lots in Detroit already served by streets and utilities, realtors asked why more war housing had not been planned for such sites rather than for distant locations, to which facilities would have to be extended. This inquiry had a certain validity since the government sometimes overlooked the availability of platted lots, but in many instances transportation difficulties rendered the utilization of these lots impossible. An outside observer suggested in June, 1942, that the city's private housing lobby might be attempting to play down the seriousness of Detroit's housing plight in order to discourage the government from making further construction plans. The private interests portrayed war housing projects as potential ghost towns and as a drug on the postwar real estate market.[38]

Realtors' opposition to war housing usually reflected the general hostility of local governments and neighborhood associations. Urban planners and citizens alike worried that conversion programs or a temporary project threatened areas of single-family residences with a decline in property values, the premonitory sign of urban blight. "By leasing the land and constructing temporary dwellings which will be removed after the termination of the national emergency," the DHC assured Detroiters in 1944, "public war housing has provided the least possible threat to the permanent value of the neighborhood in which the projects are located."[39] But so great was the hostility to temporary housing that the government was forced constantly to reaffirm its policy of postwar demolition. Although localities were justified in their insistence that the essentially shoddy war housing either be upgraded or removed after the war, the initial reaction of panic and rage in most neighborhoods, tinged with regional or racial prejudice, rarely gave way to understanding or acceptance.

The war housing program provoked few controversies more heated than that which boiled up in the vicinity of the Willow Run plant during 1942. The area most affected by the presence of the giant factory comprised a strip of townships in eastern Washtenaw and western Wayne Counties and included Ypsilanti, an industrial town of about ten thousand population, and Ann Arbor, a university community of some thirty thousand inhabitants. The Willow Run locality had developed rapidly during the 1930s without a commensurate provision of supporting facilities. This fact might not have produced a crisis had Ford been able to stick to his original plan of personnel recruitment for Willow Run. He had assumed that the plant's employees would be obtained primarily from the Rouge and from small company operations around Ypsilanti. Defense orders, however, had fully occupied the main Ford complex and a general labor shortage had developed near the bomber plant. By mid-1941, therefore, Ford turned to the recruitment of in-migrant workers. Although migration flowed into the county throughout the year, little was done to replenish the dwindling supply of housing. By early 1942 no rooms for rent could be found within a fifteen-mile radius of Ypsilanti. Workers had parked trailers or raised tents on undrained land without sanitation, and health officials spoke of the potential for typhoid and tuberculosis epidemics.[40]

Newspaper stories about the spreading chaos at Willow Run at last forced government action. After preliminary meetings among federal, state, and local officials in February, NHA administrator John Blandford, Jr., made public the government's complete housing plan for Willow Run on April 26. The FPHA, he disclosed, would begin work shortly on a huge development to be ready by June, 1943, in time to house the bomber plant's expected 110,000 workers and their families. Several thousand of the units were to be constructed in a fifteen-square-mile area of Superior Township in Washtenaw County, east of

Ann Arbor and north of Ypsilanti, to be known as Bomber
City, a development of five sections, each with its own school,
park, church, and shopping facility. The original cost estimates for the entire project ran between twenty million and
thirty-five million dollars but the contemplated expenditure
eventually rose to $108,000,000, more than twice the final cost
of the bomber plant itself.[41]

The friends of public housing, especially the UAW-CIO,
welcomed the advent of Bomber City. The union had pressed
for such a project since the fall of 1941. Within a week after
Blandford's announcement, however, a whirlwind of opposition swept Washtenaw County, growing ever larger during the
summer. Newspapers decried the project and various local
governments and chambers of commerce passed resolutions of
disapproval.[42] "Hysteria of the war crisis has been seized on to
bring an unnecessary social experiment into being," county
prosecutor George Meader told a public meeting on May 12,
following an unsuccessful trip to Washington to plead the
area's case. "A diversion of extra time and materials and effort
from production of arms ought to be condemned as unpatriotic."[43] Local residents also raised the issues of the cost of
extending services to a probable postwar ghost town, the impossibility under state law of providing any municipal government for Bomber City until at least three years had elapsed,
and the expected retrograde impact of the development upon
the area's settled way of life. Never far from the center of all
discussion lay the political implications of the potential presence of 110,000 UAW members within a Republican county
that then had a population of less than a hundred thousand.
Washtenaw politicians scoffed at denials by FPHA officials that
labor had forced the government to approve the Willow Run
project.[44]

Since local protests appeared unavailing, Bomber City
seemed on its way to a successful takeoff. Suddenly it was sent
crashing to earth by attacks from two directions. May brought
the substantial downward revision of the manpower estimate
for Willow Run. Henry Ford and Harry Bennett then came
out in total opposition to the housing project. FPHA agents

who once had found Washtenaw County farmers eager to sell land to the government abruptly became unwelcome guests. Shortly thereafter, Donald Nelson confirmed a rumor that the WPB had decided to shut off all priorities for permanent housing. On July 16 Blandford submitted a much-reduced housing plan to the special Willow Run Committee within the WPB. At a hearing before the Senate's Truman Committee six days later, the NHA administrator defended the project as vital to the war effort but replied sketchily to questions about the amount of materials and manpower to be consumed by Willow Run housing. The WPB eventually approved for construction all portions of the revised and reduced development save 4,500 public housing units, the last remnant of Bomber City. Even this small plan was held up pending further study.[45]

Bomber City was dead. The scarcity of materials soon made it impossible to build even the 2,500 permanent homes that finally had been authorized as a scaled-down project. The FPHA instead decided to erect an equal number of temporary dwellings and to begin construction during the fall of a temporary dormitory for three thousand single male workers. His interests no longer endangered by the threat of the hundred thousand presumably Democratic unionists who might have resided in a vast public housing development, Henry Ford sold the government 295 acres on which to locate the homes, schools, and shopping facilities that would be needed. The housing crisis at Willow Run meanwhile worsened. After a trip to the area in the winter of 1943, Agnes Meyer described a "nightmare of substandard living conditions." Tents and shacks dotted the roadsides and trailers squatted everywhere haphazardly. In a much-cited example of Willow Run congestion, one family of five members lived on the first floor of a home, five men slept in the basement, four more in the attic, nine persons lived in the garage, and four trailers crowded the flat, badly drained backyard.[46]

As the employment level at Willow Run climbed toward its peak, the federal government worked feverishly to complete the long-delayed housing program. On February 15, 1943, the

FPHA opened the first sections of Willow Lodge, the fifteen-building dormitory containing accommodations for more than seven thousand persons. The first temporary units of Willow Village, the substitute for Bomber City, went up in June. Five other temporary projects, two dormitory complexes, nearly a thousand federally owned trailers, and several thousand private dwellings eventually followed, the whole complex capable of sheltering some fifteen thousand people. One year after the opening of Willow Lodge, the FPHA proudly announced that the availability of housing was running ahead of demand; by that time, however, manpower needs at the plant had begun to decline. Sociologists Lowell Carr and James Stermer estimate that during the period of peak labor requirements in June, 1943, the government programs housed only 2.4 percent of those living in the vicinity of Willow Run, the figure rising to 8.8 percent in December. The NHA and FPHA can be credited with speed of execution once the decision about the type of housing at Willow Run had been made, but that decision took far too long in coming to save thousands of persons from unnecessary privation.[47]

Despite controversy and shortcomings, the war housing program was a substantial accomplishment. That success inevitably made war housing an issue in the ongoing battle over the future of the American city, a debate that had been raging since the mid-1930s. Public housing advocates, a group that included the NHA's Blandford, believed that the decaying urban core could be renewed by the provision of large-scale, low-cost homes for the people who lived in that zone of decay. The war housing program dramatically demonstrated the government's ability to undertake housing projects, even if materials shortages necessarily rendered the final product inferior. Real estate brokers and land developers also maintained that the central city could be revived through a vigorously pursued plan of redevelopment; they insisted, however, that such a plan must be implemented under private auspices. There might be room for federal subsidies to private undertakings and for whatever forms of housing private interests chose to offer, but there must be no extension of public housing and of the underlying "socialist" notion of government homes for the poor. To private groups, war housing symbolized what they dreaded most—the direct entry of the government into the mass housing market. A bill providing federal aid for private urban redevelopment in combination with public housing died in Congress in 1945, a victim of each side's ability to frustrate the desires of the other. By engendering high hopes and great fears, war housing played a role far beyond that imagined by its initiators.

Housing and transportation were so intimately interrelated that they might well have been thought of as a single problem. Unlike any other community in America save Los Angeles, metropolitan Detroit had grown up almost totally dependent on the privately owned automobile for the movement of people. The great majority of Detroit workers drove to their jobs from distant homes, shunning the buses and trolleys of the city-owned Detroit Street Railway Company (DSR). The impact of transportation on production was clearly evident at Willow Run. Most workers could reach the factory only after a long, time-consuming, and fatiguing automobile trip. Conditions grew increasingly acute after the introduction of car and tire rationing in early January, 1942, and the cessation of civilian automotive production the following month. The quit rate at the plant edged upward as workers who could find neither shelter nor a means of transportation left to find employment elsewhere. The construction of an expressway between Detroit and Willow Run in 1942 and the establishment of a second road link in February, 1943, eased but did not solve the area's transportation problems.[48]

The first efforts to solve Detroit's transportation quandary focused on a redistribution of the daily traffic flow and met with limited success. Factories, businesses, and schools in the major war centers staggered the hours of their opening and closing so as to avoid the usual morning and evening rush hour jams. The result was a relatively even traffic stream throughout these critical periods. The ODT had urged that, whenever possible, drivers form car pools of four persons per vehicle. From the spring of 1942 onward war plants established joint labor-management "share-the-ride" committees. By early 1943, the statewide passengers-per-car average increased slightly. Many workers, however, took to share-riding with a noticeable lack of enthusiasm since they mistakenly assumed that their importance to the war effort assured them a replacement set of tires. Shift changes, private plans, and the unwillingness to take responsibility for a group also hampered the share-ride campaign.[49]

Gasoline rationing offered the best method of enforcing rubber conservation, but appeared to present serious difficulties for auto-addicted Detroit. In May, 1942, the OPA instituted rationing in the Eastern states and extended the system nationwide on December 1, also mandating a thirty-five-mile-per-hour speed limit. Consternation swept the city as the deadline approached. A variety of organizations petitioned Washington either to cancel or delay gas rationing in the Detroit area. Rationing opponents argued that automotive mileage restrictions would tax the DSR beyond its limits, since the share-ride program had not fulfilled expectations. Confident that rationing would create only temporary problems for Detroit, OPA administrator Leon Henderson rejected every appeal for delay. A three-day registration period for the basic "A" allotment of four gallons per week opened on November 18. On December 1 an occasional traffic tie-up and delay in bus schedules occurred, but the vast majority of war workers got to their jobs on time and in the usual manner. People generally obeyed the thirty-five-mile limit and drove more carefully. In the two following years, Michigan automobile mileage fell nearly one-quarter; reliance on the automobile remained heavy, however, and in recognition of reality, Detroit-area ration boards were liberal in their allocation of gasoline to war workers.[50]

After the introduction of gasoline rationing, passenger traffic on the buses and trolleys of the DSR, already on the increase, rose still further. By September, 1944, 1,960,000 persons jammed the DSR every weekday, up 59.2 percent from three years before. A British diplomat wrote from Detroit in July, 1943, that "You are jostled in trams by Negroes, fat women, fall over children, have workmen in greasy clothes sit on your lap and their female counterparts hold on to your sleeve to stand up." The system's employees worked long, grueling hours, but dozens of runs still were missed daily. Discourtesy towards passengers increased, and inexperienced drivers became involved in numerous accidents. The DSR attempted to remedy its manpower shortage through public appeals for drivers, recruitment campaigns in other cities, and the decision in the summer of 1943 to hire women operators to complement the system's contingent of "conductorettes," at work since mid-1942. Only a handful of "motorettes" were actually employed, however. Although the necessity of keeping the DSR in service was self-evident, the WMC had barred the company from hiring at the gate. The manpower agency finally yielded to official pleas in February, 1945, to give the DSR a revised priority listing; thanks to the added protection from the draft provided by the new rating, the driver shortage eased. The improvement was only temporary, and by August the manpower deficit was worse than ever.[51]

Beset with difficulties, the total transportation system nevertheless fulfilled its primary wartime function: a survey conducted by the WPB and the Detroit Victory Council in May, 1944, revealed that the average Detroit war worker lost only one day of work each year because of transportation problems. The crisis also presented traffic engineers and transportation officials with an unparalleled opportunity to experiment with the integration of all forms of movement within the city—automobile, bus, streetcar, and foot. Mel Scott observes that "although many of the plans [that traffic engineers] helped to devise embodied measures more appropriate to the emergency than to long-term situations, the wartime experience provided a new understanding of the possibilities of improving the movement of people and goods in urban areas."[52]

Disease and poor health posed a continuing threat to production and community welfare. Preinduction medical examinations uncovered a sizeable reservoir of physical and mental ailments among the general population: the Selective Service system inspected some 709,000 Michigan men between 1940 and 1945 and rejected 216,000 of them, or 30 percent, for such defects as bad eyes, rotten teeth, flat feet, poor posture, syphilis, or for what the draft agency described as "mental disease" and "mental deficiency." The rejection rate for blacks approached 50 percent. The inauguration of the production program and the great migration confronted health officials with a still greater problem—the possibility of epidemics resulting from inadequate sewerage. In addition, many southern newcomers to Michigan were carriers of tuberculosis, diphtheria, and meningitis, and the state Department of Health began to record a rising incidence of these maladies from late 1942 onward. The crowded condition of most war centers encouraged the spread of contagious illness.[53]

Serious shortages of medical personnel hampered the fight against disease. The draft took hundreds of Michigan doctors, from general practitioners to specialists in every field. Despite the need for more doctors, the state medical society adamantly opposed the stationing of United States Public Health Service (USPHS) personnel in shortage areas or the licensing of refugee doctors. Nurses left hospitals at alarming rates, some entering the armed services, others accepting jobs at newly established and high-paying industrial health clinics in war plants. So grave was the shortage of staff and orderlies at the Ypsilanti state mental hospital that a classic seriocomic vision assumed reality there in late 1942—the inmates took over responsibility for running parts of the asylum.[54]

Local and state governments took steps to meet the health crisis, but the demands and activities of a number of federal agencies and programs bulked even larger in the endeavor. By the end of the war, 88.5 percent of Michigan's population was served by health departments in sixty-nine counties, as compared to 74.2 percent of the population served in sixty-one counties in 1940. The enactment of a state occupational disease law during the late 1930s led many industries to begin examinations of their employees for tuberculosis, and the military's insistence upon healthy workers encouraged additional firms to screen their labor force and to set up medical clinics. The FWA constructed a number of main line and trunk sewers and hospital additions in war-impacted communities. Under the federal government's Emergency Maternal and Infant Care (EMIC) program, the wives, children, and relatives of soldiers in the lower service grades received free medical care during the prenatal period and the first year of the infant's life. The plan went into effect in Michigan on May 27, 1943, and through June 30, 1946, the state spent $4,500,000 in federal funds to care for 53,321 soldier wives, children and relatives.[55]

Thanks to new efforts at disease control, including the more general use of sulfa drugs, the danger of a major wartime health disaster was averted. The shadow of polio, of course, continued to haunt the summer of every child and every parent. The death rate per thousand from such diseases as cancer and diabetes increased between 1940 and 1945, but long-term trends, not the short-run effects of the war, were responsible. At the same time, the death rate for pneumonia, syphilis, and nephritis decreased. Because EMIC demanded minimum standards for the care of mothers and infants, the quality of obstetric practice improved. The Army used its power to designate off-limits areas to reduce the danger of venereal disease around Battle Creek and other military installations in the state. Agents of the OCWS brought federal pressure to bear on local law enforcement officials reluctant to close down red-light districts. The health picture in Detroit was particularly encouraging; the overall death rate declined steadily from 1943 to 1945, and maternal and infant mortality fell gratifyingly. The requirements of military and economic mobilization had sparked a small revolution in health care.[56]

The arrival of war worker families created a need not only for larger housing units but for schools for thousands of migrating children. Because many youths quit school to seek war work, total school attendance in some areas actually decreased, but the small education systems of suburban Detroit absorbed staggering increases in pupil load. Inflation meanwhile raised Michigan per-pupil expenditure from $81.94 in 1940 to $109.78 in 1944. The most conservative legislator or school-board member could not deny the need for federal intervention to construct school buildings to alleviate desperate overcrowding. The government had ruled that all schools in a particular area must be filled to 200 percent of capacity before such construction could be authorized, and double sessions and classes conducted in corridors or trailers testified that most Detroit area systems were meeting the requirement. By the end of 1943 the FWA had erected 201 classrooms in the four-county Detroit region at a cost of some two million dollars. The utilitarian, one-story federal schoolhouses eventually made their appearance in sixteen other Michigan communities.[57]

Teachers were in short supply during the war because of the profession's low pay. The federal government took no action to prevent an exodus of teachers into the armed forces or industry. Big-city school systems, however, generally found the means to retain a sufficient teacher supply. With unintended irony, a government report noted in December, 1943, that "salaries [in Detroit area schools] have been increased in most cases near enough to those paid semiskilled labor so that it has been possible to prevent too large an influx from teaching positions into defense factories."[58] The teacher shortage fell most severely upon the rural areas of Michigan: one-sixth of the state's rural school districts closed entirely in 1943 for lack of personnel. The state Department of Public Instruction attempted to fill the gap with the emergency war certificate program. Emergency certificates of teaching qualification had been granted on a limited basis before the war to enable rural systems to continue operations. The number of such certificates increased from 337 in 1939 to more than five thousand in 1944 to meet wartime needs. Emergency certification did not always imply inferiority of instruction since the crisis lured many competent retired teachers back into service.[59]

The garish nighttime appearance of the war centers belied
the fact that recreation was a commodity in short supply for
many adults and most children. The national liquor shortage
forced many bars to close. A six-square-mile area of Warren
Township offered a vastly increased population no more than
one movie theater, one bowling alley, two small school gyms,
and a thin scattering of parks, playgrounds, and dance halls.
Many of the citizens who willingly pitched in to finance and
staff local United Service Organization (USO) chapters scoffed
at the idea that war workers might need a comparable program, and advocates of civilian recreation often approached
the subject with an apologetic mien. Most temporary housing
projects possessed a rudimentary community center, and the
FWA opened three "industrial USOs" in Warren Township in
early 1943. These latter units, however, were no equivalent
of the soldier's USO, which provided friendship and food for
the lonely GI. Many war plants promoted recreational sports
leagues, and the UAW took the lead in sponsoring midnight
dance parties for swing-shift workers. Private initiative, especially on the part of youngsters, remained essential to the production of wholesome forms of diversion.[60]

Recreation was not the only scarce commodity in wartime
Michigan. Detroit officials charged throughout the war that
the city was being shortchanged on food because its OPA
quota had been established on the basis of its 1940 population
and did not take into account migration increases. Detroit
found itself in the midst of a meat famine in the winter of
1942–43, and again in the summer of 1945. Thousands of
people supplemented their food supply by growing fruits and
vegetables in backyard or communal victory gardens. State
residents planted a million such plots in 1944. Winter brought
the threat—and the occasional reality—of insufficient heating
fuel. In March, 1943, the WPB ruled that Michigan Bell could
continue to install telephones but could not connect new units
for the duration. Shortages were only annoying, not disastrous,
but they stimulated popular resentment against Washington
over the government's seeming inability to do anything about

them. In October, 1943, the WPB set up a Civilian Requirements Committee, consisting of representatives from relevant
private, state, and federal bodies, to take concerted action to
deal with Detroit's commodity shortage problems. The committee, however, made only slight headway against the accumulated deficiencies.[61]

The presence of large military installations was a significant
factor in only a few Michigan localities. After the Army's Fifth
Division left Fort Custer for combat in 1942, the complement
at the base dropped sharply, relieving Battle Creek of many
burdens.[62] No portion of the continental United States, however,
was as strategically vital to the war effort as the area immediately around Sault Ste. Marie (1940 population: 15,874). Each
year during the conflict more than a hundred million tons of
iron ore and other cargo destined for the northeastern industrial belt passed through the lock canal at the Soo. Defense
preparations at the canal began as early as September, 1939,
and by mid-1942 a mixed combat force of 7,300 soldiers was
stationed at Fort Brady, a short distance from Sault Ste. Marie.
The Army barred unauthorized persons from venturing near
the locks.

"Each day brought something new," a local newspaper commented in 1942. "People would wake up in the morning and
find a barrage balloon site in their backyard, or a block over
would be a company of soldiers getting up hutment homes."[63]
Serious sanitation and housing problems soon developed, food
and medical care became scarce, and the incidence of juvenile
crime rose. By early 1943, the threat of attack on the canal had
become so improbable that the Army announced plans to reduce the size of the Fort Brady garrison. The entire Upper
Peninsula protested; the region relished its status as the heart
of a globally significant military operation, and the Soo appreciated the boost to its economy provided by the military. The
Army cutback finally took effect in September, 1943. By the
end of the war only a single company of military police guarded
the canal.

Communities faced crises all across Michigan. Medicine had

a phrase for their condition: acute congestion. Too many people were crowded into too few homes, buses, restaurants, schools, and recreation centers. Neither village nor metropolis escaped the effects of the domestic mobilization, yet some towns had little or no industry, lay distant from military bases, and seemed able to ride out the war in relatively quiet backwaters. "Charlotte shows some improvement," lawyer Emerson Boyles commented in an August, 1944, letter to a service friend overseas, describing that farm center of 5,500 persons southwest of Lansing. "I notice a new white stripe in the center of the trunk line on Lawrence Avenue. Frank Higby is washing his house, and I note several new haircuts, including my own. Outside of that, little change."[64]

Charlotte was just seventy-five miles from Willow Run, but the two communities were a world apart. The once clear stream that gave its name to the Willow Run area now flowed foul and stagnant because of inadequate sewerage, and enteritis had reached near-epidemic proportions. Ypsilanti Township offered only a single two-room school to which four rooms were added in 1942 for a student population of several hundred youngsters. Merchants and shoppers alike complained about the shortage of meat and other staples in local stores. The turnover and absenteeism at the bomber plant arising from these and like circumstances were legend and were significant contributors to the slowdown of production. In March, 1943, *Detroit News* writer James Sweinhart expressed discontent over "the apparent inability of the powers that control the plant and its environment to grasp the fact we are at war, and putting other considerations aside, to realize that the great basic purpose of the plant is to help win, perhaps even decide the issue of the war." Sweinhart's principle concern was the effect of community conditions upon production; Agnes Meyer's anxiety focused on the people. "After studying the Willow Run area," she wrote that same month, "it seems to me that the federal government will have to do something about the living conditions . . . or its orators will have to stop talking about the dignity of man."[65]

The federal government eventually paid for or assisted in the provision of most of the amenities at Willow Run, besides its expenditures for housing. FWA-financed sewer projects eliminated the danger of epidemic. The Spencer School district received three new buildings in 1943, and average daily pupil attendance rose from 238 in 1942 to 2,335 in 1945. The USPHS and the FPHA together recommended an addition to Ypsilanti's Beyer Hospital, and the two agencies persuaded additional physicians to locate in the Willow Run area. The FPHA also underwrote the establishment of a substation for the Washtenaw County Sheriff's Department at Willow Lodge in 1943, and prodded the Ypsilanti Council of Social Agencies to set up a one-person social work "outpost" in Willow Village in 1944, for which Bomber Local 50 assumed the cost. Local merchants, however, managed to block the construction of a federally financed bomber plant shopping center until January, 1944, with the result that thousands of persons had to walk or drive long distances to buy necessities.[66]

The action of these local merchants typified the continuing battle for profit and power that wracked the community. Carr and Stermer, who studied Willow Run in detail, concluded that the major question at issue in the area was: "Who would assume the burden of the change at Willow Run, the people in possession or the bomber workers?" The local residents and government of Washtenaw County naturally were reluctant to see their quiet semirural world upset, and they were often unwilling to accommodate to the reality of the bomber plant and the influx of migrants. Natives of all classes despised the newcomers and referred to them as "hillbillies" despite the fact that most of the in-migrants came from Michigan. With the war a distant echo but the war worker an ever-present threat, the natives opposed the interests of the newcomers at almost every turn. What they could not defeat, they delayed; what they could not delay, they received with ill grace. The newcomers were severely handicapped in the political struggle that ensued. They were outnumbered, inchoate, and were as unwilling as the natives to extend the hand of friendship.[67]

In December, 1943, the Washtenaw County Clerk announced that a special state census had counted a total of 11,224 persons residing in the five and one-half square mile area east of Ypsilanti that included most of the major Willow Run housing developments. What kind of community did those thousands shape for themselves? It was an unstable and sometimes anonymous community; turnover at Willow Lodge ran 30 percent per month in 1943, and efforts to establish newspapers and tenant councils failed for want of volunteers. A woman who lived in the Sudbury Court temporary project became lost one day when she could not distinguish her look-alike house because her landmark, a bedspring leaning on a neighboring building, had been removed. The black market flourished, as did gambling and, until the Sheriff's Department cracked down, prostitution.[68]

Life was especially hard for the thousands of trailerites. Even those lucky enough to be in a trailer camp had to compete for overburdened utilities and suffered from lack of space, privacy, ventilation, and an overabundance of dirt. Bad health was a constant worry and a nagging reality. Many mothers became "trailer wacky" after days of being cooped up with small children in confined quarters. Children got along as best they could in dreary surroundings. Mr. and Mrs. John Castle and their young son moved from St. John, Michigan, to Willow Run in 1942, setting up trailer housekeeping in a crowded camp. The Castles tried to make the best of their circumstances, but when they returned to their shoebox-shaped home after dinner one Thanksgiving, Mrs. Castle recalled that "the trailer seemed to have shrunk a little. When I looked around, I felt like asking, 'Do we really live here?'"[69]

Two weeks before the Willow Run census results were disclosed in late 1943, social workers, sociologists, public officials, and unionists met at the townsite to discuss community problems and the spirit of the residents. Said Sister Margaret Frye of the Lutheran Church: "These people are bewildered, lost, maladjusted, with no chance to develop spiritually or physically." Another speaker referred to the community as a "malformation." To be sure, Willow Run had its share—and probably more than its share—of hot tempers, hard drinking, traffic violations, petty thievery, and promiscuity. Carr and Stermer note, however, that from July, 1943, to June, 1945, less than a dozen serious crimes and only one serious case of delinquency were reported to the sheriff's substation at Willow Lodge. "Life is not how you make it, but how you take it," said Mrs. Castle of her experience in a Willow Run trailer camp. The in-migrants took it, and, as Carr and Stermer observe, were able to overcome "the confusion and threats of a culturally disorganized area, do their work . . . and still meet the obligations of decency and fair play."[70]

Inadequate housing, transportation, health and recreation facilities and other shortages—all were symptomatic of congestion. Each could be diagnosed separately, but eventually, government officials had to realize that they faced a single condition that required coordinated treatment to prevent community paralysis. Some fifty-four organizations, ranging from the Red Cross and the Washtenaw County Board of Supervisors to the FWA and the WPB, became involved in one or another aspect of the Willow Run crisis. Not until the autumn of 1942, however, did leaders from the affected areas of Washtenaw and Wayne Counties join together in the Willow Run Community Council to coordinate local efforts. The frequent local refusal to accept war-impelled change naturally hindered efforts to develop overall solutions. Meanwhile the federal government, which everyone expected would play the major role in solving the difficulties, reacted haphazardly. During the spring of 1941 representatives of a number of Washington agencies arrived for consultations in the Willow Run area. But each arm of the bureaucracy mounted an independent effort, surveying and resurveying a situation whose dimensions had become painfully obvious before Pearl Harbor. Derisively nicknamed "parachute jumpers" by the vicinity's inhabitants, the federal personnel only strained local patience without producing action.[71]

Metropolitan Detroit's answer to crisis was the appointment by Washington of a community facilities "czar" empowered to rationalize the four-county area's manifold difficulties. Demand for such a coordinator first had arisen during the summer of 1941, and throughout early 1942 the Detroit city government vainly sought President Roosevelt's aid in the matter. In late 1943 the Detroit area's problems came to the attention of a new federal agency, the President's Committee for Congested Production Areas (CCPA). Roosevelt had created the CCPA by executive order on April 7, 1943, in response to mounting conflict and confusion within the community facilities establishment. An action-oriented organization with a small staff and budget, the CCPA designated appropriate congested production areas (CPAs) and dispatched an area representative to unsnarl whatever confusion of agency relationships existed. In addition, the CCPA could call area problems to the attention of concerned agencies, but it could undertake no projects by itself since it was a coordinating, not an operating, organization. Once conditions in a particular CPA were brought up to "minimum wartime standard"—a phrase that never achieved clear definition—CCPA was to close its local office and retire. After six months of delay, the CCPA approved selection on December 3 of Wayne, Oakland, Macomb, and Washtenaw Counties as a unified congested production area.[72]

Detroit wanted a strong coordinator to take vigorous action to cut red tape, bashing bureaucratic heads together if necessary. In reality, however, CCPA area representative Frank M. McLaury and his successor, Russell S. Hummel, eschewed confrontation with the most powerful federal authorities and deliberately worked behind the scenes to obtain results through persuasion. The committee, for example, convinced the FWA to waive the 200 percent overcrowding rule in a few instances in order to obtain school buildings for suburban towns. But in its nine months of effective operation, from January to September, 1944, the CCPA's setbacks and outright failures outweighed its achievements, and federal agencies refused or sidetracked its requests on several occasions. The entire range of Detroit-Willow Run area facilities had been rated only "fair" by CCPA as of April 30, 1944, and that judgment remained unchanged seven months later. Nor did the agency accomplish much in a similar operation in Muskegon during the spring and summer of 1944. The brief tenure of the CCPA ended after Congress rejected an increased appropriation to carry the committee through mid-1945 and decided instead to order the agency's dissolution by December 31, 1944.[73]

The housing situation eased in several smaller cities in early 1945 and the announcement in mid-April of cutbacks at Willow Run precipitated an exodus from the vicinity of the bomber plant. Out-migration from Washtenaw County rose steadily during the spring and summer, vacant homes were disassembled and shipped to areas still short of housing, and by late August the once booming area resembled a deserted village. But the government's occupancy survey of privately owned homes in the Detroit area during June and July revealed a gross habitable vacancy rate of 0.8 percent, a state of affairs essentially unchanged from 1944. The return of the veterans plunged Detroit once more into a desperate housing shortage. Fewer than three thousand ex-servicemen had been arriving in the area per month prior to V-J Day; by November, however, the figure reached five thousand monthly. Some of the temporary projects were available for occupancy by the most distressed GI families, but the DHC could only suggest to thousands of other returning soldiers and sailors that they double up with relatives or friends. The federal government inadvertently made matters worse in mid-October when it removed all restrictions on the sale and use of construction materials. The already scarce supply of lumber, nails, and pipe promptly disappeared from the low-cost housing market while home prices drastically increased.[74]

The war centers performed their production task despite crowded housing, overburdened transportation, schools full to bursting, and occasional commodity shortages. No failure on the battlefield can be traced to a failure in an American community. There was conflict on the local level and a lack of coordination on the federal level, but there were also numerous examples of community cooperation, especially in the volun-

tary participation programs. The national government, for all
its spectacular mistakes, established a remarkable record of
achievement in the construction of homes, hospitals, and schools
for the war-impacted localities. The successful execution of
federal policy enabled the civilian population to eat well and
to remain healthy, a considerable accomplishment even though
the nation was not under actual threat of attack. Detroit and
the other war centers were unable to keep their heads above
the flood of war-related problems that inundated them, but
they did learn to breathe under water.

Prolonged breathing under water was a dangerous expedient for a community and its people. Material shortages had
further delayed the initiation or completion of vital public
works projects already stalled by depression-era deficits. In Detroit, where municipal buildings and services had been neglected for fifteen years, the city planning department began
work during the spring of 1944 on blueprints for forty long-
overdue civic improvements. Although the war agencies had
erected thousands of homes, schools, and other buildings, much
of what had been constructed would have to be torn down at
war's end because of its inferior quality. The families that lived
in tents and shanties, the workers who daily risked disease for
want of decent sanitation, and the children who spent half-
days in crowded schools were also the victims of that extended
submersion.

In her angry 1944 book, significantly titled *Journey Through
Chaos,* Agnes Meyer asked, "How much do we really care what
happens to human beings as a result of our pell-mell, do-or-
die war effort?" She answered that "the chaos and the human
suffering depicted here should impress every American with
our lack of a sufficiently active social consciousness." The citizenry expected, even welcomed, some forms of wartime sacrifice; a certain degree of governmental mismanagement also
was to be expected during an emergency of world proportion.
It is nevertheless reasonable to inquire whether the gross community disruption at Willow Run and other war centers need
have taken place. Civilian distress cannot always be dismissed

by reference to suffering GIs or by the invocation of the era's standard response to complaints, "Don't you know there's a war on?"[75]

From the perspective of a quarter-century, James M. Burns placed much of the blame for unnecessary civilian privation upon the federal government and Franklin Roosevelt. According to Burns, "Roosevelt failed to provide over-arching social goals for the domestic mobilization," and "was responsible for much of the confusion, for he tried artificially to separate war from postwar, temporary crisis from permanent tasks, means from ends. . . . Roosevelt demanded the authority to mobilize for war, but he disclaimed the responsibility for planning against the social disruptions brought by mobilization. . . ." Roosevelt's policies were not fashioned in a vacuum, but were developed within the President's innate awareness that the American people would endure only so much adverse change in the name of national unity. Given the choice, many citizens would have agreed that a short-run wartime disruption followed by a return to something like the prewar status quo was preferable to a neat solution of wartime problems that portended incalculable dislocation. Such attitudes on the part of large sectors of society had created the "atmosphere of ruthless indifference to human suffering" that Meyer found in too many communities, including Willow Run.[76]

Realtors, merchants, and homeowners' groups were not alone in seeking to avoid the costs of war by forcing others to pay even more. Carr and Stermer took note of the nation's chronic inability to define the onset and dimensions of a social crisis and concluded that individual self-centeredness bore a major share of the responsibility for the havoc in the war centers. "All anybody ever did," they wrote passionately in 1952, "was merely to fight, inwardly, outwardly, psychologically, politically, socially, stubbornly, persistently, and to the end, every impact of the war that threatened their own precious little area of security . . . their neighborhoods, and their privileges for power and profit. All they ever did . . . was to fight actively and passively to keep their own humble ways of life unchanged."[77] Disregarding its fervor, this observation still suggests much about the conduct of community interest groups and the ultimate source of confusion and conflict in the resolution of community problems.

Private interest groups fought off drastic community change in many instances, but neither they, the government, nor the general public could resist all change brought on by the war. Nor would they have wished to, since much of that change was beneficial in nature. The return of prosperity, of course, was the most significant element of that transformation. Prosperity and the wartime housing program produced a dramatic shift in the pattern of Detroit home occupancy, the proportion of home owners in the Detroit area rising from 38.6 percent in 1940 to 50.5 percent in 1945.[78] The war years saw hopeful developments in transportation and in health care, and a revival of interest in the quality of the nation's schools. The experiences of the wartime civilian defense effort convinced government leaders on all levels of the need to be prepared for future natural or man-made disasters.

In December, 1944, a federal official analyzing the war's impact on urban America, commented: "If it was in the national interest to assist workers, industries, and communities to obtain maximum return for effort expended during the war, then is it not equally important that assistance be given during the peace to follow?" This speculation came late in the global conflict, and did not typify the thinking of many in Washington. Burns correctly asserts that "the burning cities of 1967 and 1968 were not wholly unrelated to steps not taken, visions not glimpsed, priorities not established, in the federal agencies of 1943 and 1944."[79]

The emergency had strengthened the federal-urban relationship tentatively begun in the 1930s, but major instrumentalities of that tie were shorn away during or shortly after the war. Congress dismantled the National Resources Planning Board, a productive center of research in community problems, during its 1943 housecleaning of New Deal agencies. The CCPA, which bypassed state government to bring federal authority and the localities into direct contact, was forgotten. The NHA was abolished in 1947. In central cities and suburbs, the war had created new concentrations of people and problems. Congested facilities and strained local finances would not disappear. They would require solutions, but the single-minded preoccupation with victory had simply postponed the reckoning.

Chapter 4

Race: Change and Resistance

The war production program was the catalyst for great change in the lives of black Americans. Neither the requirements of production nor the incantation of wartime slogans, however, was sufficient to end discrimination against blacks in significant areas of life. Many whites perceived the wartime acceleration of black progress as a dangerous development, a march that must be slowed, perhaps even turned back. Blacks could and did justify their case for racial equality in terms of its benefits to war production; but concern for production was also a useful rationale for white resistance to black material and social advance.

Blacks maintained complex and ambivalent attitudes regarding their role in the national war effort. All but a handful were convinced that Allied victory over the Axis was the preferred outcome of the world conflict. They worked to that end, but they hoped that such a demonstration of their loyalty to the national cause would be rewarded both during and after the war by concessions from the white majority. They insisted, moreover, with militant words and actions that the federal government be compelled to fulfill the promise of equality implicit in the American political and social system. Other blacks, in Harvard Sitkoff's phrase, "loudly held their loyalty in check" in the belief that it was up to the government to prove its good faith before demanding sacrifices of them.[1] A large but indeterminable number were completely apathetic toward the war.

Most major black leaders and organizations adopted a policy of militancy within the context of national loyalty. This stance at once satisfied the demands of the black majority for advocacy of the case for justice and equality while assuring whites that they need not fear black disaffection. The pursuit of militance enabled the Detroit chapter of the National Association for the Advancement of Colored People (NAACP) to grow from 2,860 members in 1938 to some 20,500 by early 1944. The Detroit branch had mounted campaigns on specific grievances before the war, but the tempo of its activity markedly increased during the conflict. The NAACP organized picket lines, mass rallies, letter-writing campaigns, and lobbying delegations to protest a variety of issues from housing discrimination to the showing of a movie portraying President Andrew Johnson in a favorable light.[2] At its Emergency War Conference held in Detroit from June 3 to June 6, 1943, the national NAACP reaffirmed its opposition to discrimination in all aspects of American life and its determination to follow a fighting course to achieve legal equality. "We refuse to listen to the weak-kneed of both races who tell us not to raise controversies during the war," the delegates declared at the conclusion of the meeting. "We believe, on the contrary, that we are doing a patriotic duty in raising them."[3]

The black press faithfully mirrored the division within the black mind between fidelity and alienation. In February, 1942, the *Pittsburgh Courier* had inaugurated its "Double V" campaign calling for victory against the Axis abroad and against racism and inequality at home. Detroit's two black newspapers, the *Michigan Chronicle* and the *Detroit Tribune*, mixed features that highlighted black participation in the common effort with stories of white outrages against blacks and the militant response to those outrages. These papers took special aim at mistreatment of black soldiers stationed in the South and at nearby Fort Custer, and the Red Cross policy of separating blood by racial origin. In July, 1943, the *Chronicle* voiced an affirmative view of the war and its relationship to blacks: "The very character of this war, a war for freedom, for democracy, for liberation, has of necessity produced profound changes in our own thinking and has accelerated the hopes of all of us for a new America, and even a new world."[4] A week earlier, the same newspaper had devoted itself to a biting attack on segregated public housing, declaring that "Uncle Tom or Aunt Tom will say that these projects are so much better than the shacks from which they come that the tenants ought not to quibble over a little thing like Jim Crowism. . . . Aunt Tom will say you can't expect the government to do the things the Constitution demands, for that would be too radical. . . ."[5] Black publishers and editors hoped that their simultaneous focus on patriotism and protest would serve as a safety valve for black grievances and a signal to the white community of the nature and depth of black frustration.

American whites received the signal in a distorted fashion. Black demands touched the consciences of many whites, but misunderstanding more commonly typified the white response. In December, 1942, an observer for the Office of War Information (OWI) stationed in Detroit noted local white misinterpretation of black objectives and added one of his own: "Negro leadership, in general, focuses its demands on economic gains during the war, feeling that the social gains will take care of themselves. White people are not conscious of this, and feel that the Negro wants everything all at once."[6] At the same time most whites saw black protest against discrimination as disloyalty to the cause of national unity, a disloyalty the more galling for being premised on the goals for which the nation presumably fought. Until the riot summer of 1943 a great majority of whites did not even believe that blacks had anything to complain about.

The federal government answered the black call for civil rights with a policy of drift and expediency. Paternalistic toward many groups, President Roosevelt was never more the *grand seigneur* than in his attitude toward blacks, whose militant activities he considered offensive and possibly unpatriotic. James MacGregor Burns remarks that the President regarded race relations "more as a problem of efficient industrial mobilization than as a fundamental moral problem. . . ."[7] The mobilization would be more efficient if racial animosity could be softened by appeals for unity. Mindful of its constant need for support from southern Congressional committee chairmen, the executive branch was loath to press for more than gradual improvement in the lot of blacks. Gradualism, at any rate, was the guiding philosophy of the most prominent white allies of the black race, including Eleanor Roosevelt. Where clearcut national policy on race relations was lacking, enlightened local leadership could not be expected. Whatever wartime progress blacks made toward racial equality was granted not by a willing nation but through the unforeseeable and ineluctable demands of the world conflict itself.

The northward and eastward tide of black migration swelled during the war. Hundreds of thousands of blacks flocked to the nation's war centers; Detroit city officials estimated in 1946 that some sixty thousand blacks had moved to the area since 1940. The level of black migration, moreover, remained constant while white migration declined after 1943. Migration fueled the spectacular increase of the black population in the Detroit area, where most of the blacks in Michigan resided. The number of blacks in the four-county metropolitan region rose from 170,552 in March, 1940 (6.9 percent of the total) to 259,490 (9.8 percent of the total) in June, 1944. The white population of the city of Detroit declined absolutely by some 2 percent between 1940 and 1944 while the number of blacks increased by 41.5 percent.[8]

The black migration was a major consequence of the manpower requirements of war production, which dictated a vast increase in the utilization of all forms of labor. The total black labor force in the Detroit labor market area (Wayne County and the most populous townships of Macomb, Oakland, and Washtenaw Counties) rose from 74,500 persons in March, 1940 (7.8 percent of the entire workforce), to 177,700 by November, 1944 (14.5 percent of the total). The number of black workers increased during this period at a rate about three times as fast as that for the entire labor force. Although the Ford River Rouge complex remained the largest single employer of blacks in Detroit, with over fifteen thousand at work in 1944, several large firms surpassed Ford in percentage of black employment. Detroit developments in black defense employment were in line with a national trend that doubled black participation in war industry from 4.2 to 8.6 percent between 1942 and 1945.[9]

The opening of the defense program in 1940, however, brought little increase in black employment. Michigan blacks found most vocational training courses and defense-plant hiring offices closed to them. "We colored Americans feel that it is very unfair and undemocratic to deny a man a job solely because of color," said Dr. James McClendon, Detroit NAACP president, in 1941. "The loyalty and patriotism of colored Americans certainly does not justify such treatment."[10] By early 1941 many blacks had begun to turn away from traditional means of persuasion toward more unconventional techniques of protest against employment bias. A. Philip Randolph, president of the Brotherhood of Sleeping Car Porters, put forth a proposal that ten thousand blacks march on Washington to demand equality in hiring and in the armed forces. Randolph's March on Washington Committee (MOWC) set the date of the protest for July 1, with supporting marches to be held on June 27 in Detroit, Los Angeles, Chicago, New York, and other major cities. As the march gained popularity among the nation's blacks, the Roosevelt administration sought frantically but unsuccessfully to force the black leadership to call off the demonstration. After a tense round of negotiations in Washington and New York, Roosevelt agreed to the major demand of the MOWC and on June 25, 1941, signed Executive Order 8802.

In issuing the order, Roosevelt stated that "there shall be no discrimination in the employment of workers in defense industries or government because of race, creed, color, or national origin and . . . [that] it is the duty of employers and of labor organizations . . . to provide for the full and equitable participation of all workers in defense industries without discrimination because of race, color, creed, or national origin. . . ." To implement Executive Order 8802, Roosevelt ordered all defense agencies to insert a fair hiring clause in contracts. To investigate violations of the order, he also established within the OPM a President's Committee on Fair Employment Practice, which soon became known by the initials FEPC. In return for the executive order, Randolph agreed to call off the march and the subsidiary demonstrations, although insisting that mass action had merely been postponed pending a show of the government's good faith. While no action had been taken on MOWC's demands for integration of the armed services, march leaders felt justified in hailing a great victory. In Detroit, the white press virtually ignored these momentous events of late June, but the black newspapers ran banner headlines and praised the march organizers.[11]

The FEPC subsequently spent an unproductive year as a constituent part of a hostile War Manpower Commission and was transferred in June, 1943, to the Executive Office of the President and reorganized with enlarged powers. The FEPC won occasional victories, such as the near abolition of discriminatory hiring advertisements, but such triumphs were few. Its public hearings, held across the country, informed many whites about racial injustice for the first time. The committee lacked sufficient staff and enforcement capabilities and was constantly harassed by southern congressmen. They saw the beacon of hope FEPC held out to the black as a torch laid against the foundation of white supremacy, and so they combined with other conservatives in Congress in 1945 to mandate the agency's termination. Neither the FEPC nor the WMC's Minority Group Service (MGS), which attempted to settle bias disputes before their referral to the FEPC, compiled an impressive record in Michigan. George Kirshner, a staff member in the Detroit MGS office, noted in 1945 that "a slow uphill process with many futile efforts" had been required to secure compliance in the battle against discrimination.[12] The FEPC's efforts boiled down to a "legalized nuisance," a monotonous pestering that merely forced employers to seek more subtle means of preserving the color bar.

Beyond reliance on the FEPC, black community organizations followed differing courses in their efforts to secure increased black employment. The Detroit Urban League pursued its traditional path of quiet persuasion of employers and emphasized its belief that the accomplishments of stable, efficient black workers would overcome prejudice. The Metropolitan Detroit Fair Employment Practice Committee, founded in 1942 (and no relation to the national FEPC), was composed of representatives of all major black groups in the city. It held public forums on employment problems and made sporadic efforts to adjust discrimination complaints with individual companies. The NAACP's program of demonstrations against job bias climaxed with an April, 1943, rally in Detroit's Cadillac Square attended by some five thousand persons. The principal black groups united in an attempt to convince the Michigan legislature to pass a fair employment practices act. Such legislation was introduced in 1943 and passed the Senate in 1945 but got no further.[13]

Employer resistance to the hiring or promotion of blacks proved tenacious. Stereotypes about black abilities persisted: in June, 1945, William Leininger, a leading Detroit industrialist, while conceding that many blacks had performed excellent work during the war, thought that "the Negro is racially more of an individualist than the white. . . . He does not take his work seriously. He is inclined to idle and indulge in horseplay on the job." Ford slackened its black hiring efforts during 1942 and 1943 in angry response to demands for equal treatment and to the fact that, with the coming of unionization, it could no longer pick and choose among black applicants. Many firms held out against the hiring of more than a negligible number of blacks. As a partial result of such prejudice, the rate of black unemployment in the Detroit labor market area, which fell from roughly 30 percent to 4.4 percent between March, 1940, and November, 1943, still exceeded the average area jobless rate in 1943 by nearly three times. It is true, however, that Detroit auto plants were more fully desegregated during the war than industry facilities elsewhere in the nation.[14]

Although thousands of blacks attained semiskilled or skilled production jobs for the first time, upgrading, the process of promotion through in-plant training, remained a contentious issue. Most blacks had ignored the few chances for upgrading offered them before the defense period, concentrating instead on building seniority. Arms manufacture required increased hiring in skilled and assembly line occupations—positions usually reserved by custom and prejudice for whites—and less emphasis on the menial employment held by black workers. Since the changeover to armament production threatened their traditional jobs, they began to demand upgrading. In August, 1941, a group of blacks at the Dodge foundry struck on two occasions when they learned that white foundrymen with less seniority had been upgraded to production jobs at the Chrysler tank arsenal. Employer and white worker resistance delayed black upgrading at Packard until April, 1942. After Pearl Harbor, discrimination and the manpower shortage combined to further limit upgrading for blacks; those who had accumulated seniority in janitorial or foundry jobs often found themselves frozen in these occupations, since replacements were difficult to find. White workers with less seniority thus continued to receive a disproportionate share of upgrading opportunities.[15]

Employers made no secret of their unwillingness to hire black women, whom management apparently regarded as so many refugees from *Porgy and Bess* or Harlem's Cotton Club. The first major breakthrough in black female hiring in Detroit did not come until the end of 1942, when, following a vigorous protest campaign, token numbers of black women began work at Willow Run, Kelsey-Hayes, and Murray Body. The total black female labor force in the four-county Detroit area rose from 20,170 in 1940 to 50,215 in 1944, a rate of increase triple that of white female workers. Thousands of black domestics abandoned their positions as household servants for more lucrative factory work. Black women eventually constituted between 35 and 75 percent of the workforce in certain small Detroit plants. Black females, however, remained concentrated in such low-wage positions as janitors, sweepers, and material handlers.[16]

Blacks offered a variety of social and economic arguments to justify expanded employment opportunities for their race, but they reverted most frequently to the theme of patriotic necessity. "To a democracy which is being tried before the court of world opinion, racial and religious prejudices among its people are a great liability," the Metropolitan Detroit Committee declared. "Our enemies recognize the vital importance of the color problem to the rest of the world. Our allies and the sections of the world whose support we wish to enlist are watching closely the degree of equality we accord to our own minorities."[17] Some employment opportunities doubtless would have been lost without the protest of black groups or the intervention of the FEPC, but the inescapable need for manpower led to more hiring and promotion of blacks than all the private and public attempts at conciliation or compulsion.

Racial prejudice among white managers was often matched or surpassed by the antiblack feeling of white workers. To be sure, thousands of whites accepted their new black coworkers and racial barriers fell in dozens of plants. But other whites, although disclaiming any objection to increased employment and pay for blacks, insisted that blacks be segregated. "Whites and Negroes don't mix," a Detroit white worker insisted in 1943.[18] White women usually put their case against blacks on personal grounds, insisting that blacks smelled bad and were diseased and asserting that they cared neither to share the plant nor toilet facilities with them. "Blood runs out of their fingers," a white employee at Packard said of his black coworkers. "If you handle the same machine, you'll get syphilis."[19] Employers sometimes argued against the hiring of blacks by contending that war production would be hampered if the prejudices of white workers were unduly stirred.

Although negrophobia knew no geographical limit, the wartime influx of southern whites in Detroit certainly swelled by the thousands the ranks of the prejudiced. The fire of their hatred was fanned by the words of many among the estimated three thousand worker-preachers. These men labored on the assembly lines during the week and held forth from storefront fundamentalist churches on Sunday. Some had pulpits within the plants themselves; various departments of the Dodge Main, Dodge Mound Road, and De Soto plants were among those that supported so-called Pleasant Valley Tabernacles. The worker-preachers' sermons ran a gamut of antiblack, anti-

Semitic, and anti-CIO themes. Evidence exists to link the worker-preachers with certain executives who financed the activities of the reactionary clergy.[20]

The worker-preachers were only one element in the underworld of semifascist activities in Detroit. Shadowy associations known as Mantle or Forrest Clubs had begun to appear within several UAW locals in 1939 and 1940, assuming an ominous power among the workers, especially those of southern origin, at Hudson, Packard, and the Chevrolet Gear and Axle Division. Another mysterious group, the National Workers League (later renamed the Rifleman's Association), also surfaced at this time. These organizations and such others as the Dixie Voters, the Southern Society, and the Mothers of America spread anti-Communist, antiblack, and anti-Semitic propaganda throughout Detroit's war plants. The Detroit branch of the Ku Klux Klan rechristened itself the United Sons of America. Hundreds of worker-preachers took their lead from J. Frank Norris, a Texas minister who shuttled between his home congregation in the Southwest and Detroit's Temple Baptist Church, the largest church of its denomination in the city. Week after week, from the pulpit and over the airwaves, Norris denounced Jews and blacks. He declared racial mixing in factories to be iniquitous and demanded that the great majority of the black population, which he described as consisting of "rapists" and "primitives," be strictly segregated in all walks of life.[21]

Although Norris flourished, the best known of the right-wing religionists had been silenced shortly after Pearl Harbor. Father Coughlin's weekly newspaper, *Social Justice*, had continued diatribes against the government even after American entry into the war. Much in the newspaper's attacks upon bureaucratic bungling in Washington could have been echoed by many Americans, but there was also much material of a defeatist nature in the journal. The publication of *Social Justice* could not have hurt the war effort, but a moment of military defeat created an opportunity for the suppression of both the priest and his paper. In May, 1942, the Postmaster General revoked the second-class mailing privileges of *Social Justice*, and the newspaper ceased publication. A federal grand jury meanwhile was investigating Coughlin and several other right-wing extremists, and fearful of divisive national reaction should the priest be among those indicted for sedition, United States Attorney General Francis Biddle decided to seek the aid of the Catholic hierarchy to silence him. After an intermediary placed the administration's case before a cooperative Detroit Archbishop Edward Mooney, the prelate summoned Coughlin to a conference on May 1 and offered him a barren choice—to abandon all public writing or be defrocked. The priest chose to obey, withdrawing from the public stage. His message was now limited to the faithful who attended his sermons at the Shrine of the Little Flower in Royal Oak.

No sooner had *Social Justice* disappeared then it was replaced on Detroit newsstands by *The Cross and the Flag*, a monthly edited by Gerald L. K. Smith, the forty-four-year-old Huey Long lieutenant. Smith had moved to Detroit in 1939, assuming leadership of the antiunion, isolationist committee of 1,000,000. Smith's paper did not scale the inflammatory heights reached by its predecessor, but it shared many of the same antigovernment themes and added a dollop of racism. Its July, 1943, issue, for example, carried a list of activities of which "most white people" disapproved, including "promiscuous mixing" of the races in theaters, restaurants, streetcars, factories, trains, and housing. Capitalizing on public discontent over rationing, rubber restrictions, and the slow progress of the war, Smith won 31 percent of the vote in the September, 1942, Republican primary for U.S. senator against the frontrunner, Wayne County Circuit Judge Homer Ferguson. Smith then undertook a sticker write-in campaign in the fall election, but received only some 3 percent of the 1,200,000 ballots cast.[22]

Along with their exhortations to racial and religious bigotry, the preacher-demagogues also denounced the Communists, the CIO, President Roosevelt, and the national administration. A Norris sermon of December, 1942, for instance, bore the title, "Bureaucratic Price-Fixing: The Mark of the Beast."[23] The right-wing religionists disseminated their propaganda amid the trappings of a fervent, almost rabid, nationalism. Harvey

Springer, the "cowboy evangelist" who made Detroit a regular stop on the circuit from his headquarters in Denver, brought audiences to paroxysms of applause by trampling on the flags of foreign nations before holding an American flag aloft in triumph. It is difficult to determine the effect of this kind of talk, much of which was extreme but still within the bounds of the nation's free-speech tradition, on the people of Detroit. When Smith ran for president in 1944 on the American First ticket, he won only 1,780 votes, split between Michigan and Texas, hardly a ringing endorsement of either the candidate or his views. Suffice it to say that the religious demagogues had an evident but incalculable potential for mischief-making.[24]

Intolerance flared most fiercely in the war plants when workers struck over racial issues. To protest increased black employment or upgrading, whites staged numerous "hate strikes." Rarely did the hate strikers constitute a majority of the work force in any plant, but their actions might well have expressed a majority attitude. Blacks also stopped work on several occasions to protest some form of employment discrimination. Twelve thousand black workers struck the Rouge steel mill on April 29, 1943, in opposition to segregation. Management and the UAW usually stood together against these outbreaks in their insistence upon the enforcement of Executive Order 8802, and the union acted with far greater severity in opposition to racially motivated walkouts than it did against work stoppages begun for other reasons. After Klan sympathizers closed the Hudson arsenal on June 18–19, 1942, the UAW gave full approval to the Navy's discharge of four ringleaders. Companies learned to stand up to white workers who insisted on the removal of blacks, but generally refused black appeals for an end to job bias. The press and federal officials lumped black demonstrations together with white protests, thus implicitly denying the validity of the black complaints by placing them in the same category with those whites who objected to working alongside blacks.[25]

Hate strikes reached a climax in the early hours of June 3, 1943, when whites began walking off the job at Packard's main Detroit plant following the upgrading of three blacks in the

teardown and buildup division. The plant had experienced racial turmoil since the beginning of the defense period, and
workers of both races had struck earlier. By mid-day on June
3 nearly 90 percent of Packard's twenty-five thousand employees had walked out, and angry pickets circled the plant. Blam-
ing the strike on the Klan and other "fifth-column" elements,
UAW president R. J. Thomas and officers of Packard Local
190 strove to bring the strike to an end. A back-to-work movement began as early as June 4, but the walkout dragged on for
two more days before workers voted to end their protest. Packard resumed full production on June 7. In the aftermath, the
black upgraders continued work, and twenty-seven strike leaders were suspended.[26]

The settlement of the June strike did not relieve racial problems at Packard; black foundrymen struck in February, 1944,
and in December another walkout by blacks threw several
thousand workers into idleness after white polishers had refused to assist black upgraders. The incidence of hate strikes
in Michigan had declined by late 1944 and none of significance seems to have occurred in the state during 1945. With a
few exceptions such as the June, 1943, Packard walkout, hate
strikes characteristically involved a negligible number of man-
hours lost. Hate strikes were depressing to wartime morale,
but since many workers felt little compunction about shutting
down a plant over the discharge of a steward, it is not surprising that they were prepared to strike over the more visceral
issue of race. Robert Weaver placed the hate strike in proper
perspective when he remarked in 1946 that "the significant
development was not the hundred or so conflicts, but the fact
that century-old patterns had been modified in five years without more opposition and more frequent clashes."[27]

The national leadership of the UAW-CIO frequently reaffirmed its belief in equality of employment opportunity for the
approximately one hundred thousand black members of the
union, although not without occasional prodding from those
members. Black protests about upgrading forced the UAW to
establish an International Interracial Committee in September, 1941, under black organizer Walter Hardin and to de-

mand that such committees be established by each local. But many union locals continued to oppose the implementation of antibias policies. "We are fed up with this kind of union," wrote black steward Joseph Wickware of Flint Chevrolet No. 3 plant in July, 1942, complaining about Local 659's disinclination to fight for its black members. "We are going to have our rights if we have to march down to Detroit and get them, and if it has to be done, we will march down to Washington."[28] On the national level, the union's 1943 convention defeated various proposals for the election of a black to the International Executive Board. This action perhaps suggested that the white secondary leadership was not yet prepared for such high-level black participation in union affairs. The UAW took a truly affirmative step in September, 1944, however, when Thomas signed an agreement with FEPC chairman Malcolm Ross for mutual cooperation between the government agency and the union's War Policy Division to investigate hate strikes. The agreement, the first of its kind between a union and the FEPC, may have played a part in the subsidence of racial conflict in the plants during the last year of war.

"The CIO unions were not willing to take great risks, but their record was far in advance of that of the AFL," Philip Foner writes in comparing the wartime racial policies of the two national labor federations.[29] The CIO established a Committee Against Discrimination and spent considerable sums on interracial education while its older rival attempted to hinder the work of the FEPC. For intransigence on racial matters, few AFL affiliates or leaders exceeded Detroit Teamsters Local 299 and its founding president, James R. Hoffa. The Teamsters held a closed shop contract with the several Detroit trucking firms involved in interstate transportation of war material. Using a variety of pretexts, every one of these firms refused to hire black drivers. In a rare action, the United States Employment Service discontinued referrals to some of the firms in 1943 as a penalty for their discriminatory conduct, but the vital nature of their work soon necessitated restoration of service. The trucking case reached the FEPC in August, 1944, and investigation disclosed that, union denials to the contrary, the

color bar had been ordered by Jimmy Hoffa, not the companies. Trucking executives admitted that they faced disaster if
they attempted to cross Hoffa, and some were so frightened of
physical retaliation that they would speak only in elliptical
terms about the boss of Detroit's Teamsters.[30]

Following a fruitless conference with Hoffa during the fall
of 1944, the FEPC filed discrimination charges against ten
trucking firms and Local 299.[31] When the accusations became
public in January, 1945, Hoffa defended Teamster policy:
"I'm getting tired of having war agencies and newspapers
trying to tell me how to run this union."[32] At hearings on the
trucking case, which began in Detroit on June 2, many blacks
testified about their inability to break through Local 299's
prejudice, but representatives of only three of the accused
firms and no Teamster spokesman made appearances.[33] The
war ended before the FEPC could hand down a final decision.

The question of black housing contained even more explosive potential for Detroit than that of increased and upgraded
black employment. Frightened white homeowners saw the issue in sweeping, often apocalyptic terms. The blacks would
bring with them the crime and vice that plagued the central
city, converting well-kept areas into festering, overcrowded
slums. Thousands of blacks lived in just those conditions of
squalor imagined by whites, but sought escape from that environment, not a new location for it. They wanted for themselves and their families the chance for open air, good health,
and a safe life that the white neighborhoods of Detroit seemed
to enjoy. The pattern of neighborhood segregation that had
evolved in Detroit in the 1920s, however, had been perpetuated during the 1930s. The Detroit Housing Commission,
founded in 1933, preserved previously established housing
patterns, and the federal government respected local traditions of racial discrimination in disbursing funds for public
housing.

Although the DHC had plans on the drawing boards for
several large-scale black housing projects, federal surveys in
1941 indicated the need for immediate relief of black housing
congestion. Accordingly, in allocating seven hundred dwelling

units for Detroit's defense workers, the United States Housing Authority (USHA) set aside two hundred units for black occupancy and asked the DHC, as its local agent, to select a site for this racially segregated project. The housing commission proposed an area both predominantly black and industrial. The USHA rejected this site suggestion on June 16, 1941. The FWA, in charge of construction, refused both to pay the higher price demanded for industrial land and to place the black project in a crowded location. The federal authorities instead ordered the project to be built on an eighteen-acre site at the intersection of Nevada and Fenelon streets near Ryan Road on Detroit's northeast side. The DHC later claimed that the newly chosen area was predominantly white, but the thinly populated vicinity was in reality a transitional neighborhood.[34]

The location of the project stirred anger and objections. Middle-class blacks in nearby Conant Gardens, many of whom had fled Paradise Valley, expressed concern about the possible lowering of property values after the construction of the apartment-style project. Their objections failed to move the USHA, which confirmed the new site on June 19. The government urged haste in construction, ignoring a protest made by the Common Council on July 1. On September 4, after the DHC had foot-dragged for ten weeks, the USHA concluded negotiations for the construction contract. The government announced three weeks later that the project would bear the name Sojourner Truth Homes, honoring the black abolitionist and poetess who had resided in Battle Creek. Construction began shortly thereafter.

Black objections to the location, although persistent, died down as the black community came to realize the extent of underlying white opposition. Irate whites, organized in the Seven Mile-Fenelon Neighborhood Improvement Association, deluged newspapers, the DHC, and Congress with protesting letters and petitions. Congressman Rudolph Tenerowicz, whose district included the Sojourner Truth neighborhood, demanded either that the site be moved or that the original project be changed to white occupancy. Pressure apparently had its effect, for in meetings on August 18 and 19, officials of the

FWA and USHA decided that, while construction would proceed as scheduled, the question of racial occupancy would be left open until all units of the project had been completed. The USHA announcement six weeks later that the project would be named for a famous black, seemingly reversing the policy decided upon in August, threw both racial groups into confusion. On December 8 Joseph Buffa, president of the Seven Mile-Fenelon Association, appeared before the DHC to attack Sojourner Truth. The next day some 250 whites packed the Common Council chamber at City Hall to denounce the councilmen, who had disclaimed responsibility for the government's site decision. Ten days later, black community leaders held a meeting to organize efforts in favor of black occupancy at Sojourner Truth.[35]

With silent support from powerful southern committee chairmen, Congressman Tenerowicz finally persuaded the USHA, on January 15, 1942, to redesignate Sojourner Truth for white use. The Detroit Housing Commission endorsed this decision, which was accompanied by the promise that a larger project for blacks would be built on the originally proposed site. A black citizens' committee, led by the Reverend Charles Hill, quickly organized a picket line around the DHC offices. Bearing signs proclaiming such slogans as "Hitler Supports Housing Discrimination," scores of blacks and a few white allies marched around the building from January 23 onward, and the committee dispatched a lobbying delegation to Washington.[36] A rapid survey of the city meanwhile revealed that the original site had been requisitioned by Ford for construction of a war plant and that no other area within Detroit was available for new black housing. Armed with these facts and cognizant of the picketers a few blocks from City Hall, Mayor Jeffries on January 29 induced a reluctant Common Council to ask federal authorities to restore the project to the blacks. The council's appeal and direct solicitation by the black delegation convinced Washington to announce on February 2 that, like pieces on a Monopoly board, the houses at Sojourner Truth once again had been traded to new owners.[37]

The whites now took mass action. Some three hundred persons invaded Common Council chambers on February 3 to demand a hearing on Sojourner Truth. "I never thought this could happen in a democratic country," Joseph Buffa declared as his supporters cheered and waved American flags. "We have nothing against Negroes getting housing, we just don't want them out where we have our homes." As the victorious blacks disbanded their picket line around the DHC, disgruntled whites began to parade around City Hall and continued to do so on a daily basis, their signs reading "A White Project for a White Neighborhood" and "This Neighborhood Was White— Keep It White."[38] A shaken Jeffries began to back away from his commitment to the blacks; he wired Washington on February 10 that Ford would release its option on the original site if the government acted quickly to reverse the latest decree.

The government ignored Jeffries's hint, and FWA administrator Baird Snyder informed a delegation of union leaders, black activists, and white civil rights workers on February 12 that Sojourner Truth would be opened for black occupancy and that the tenants would be moved in on February 16. Behind the scenes, the so-called Black Cabinet, a group of second-echelon government advisors such as Robert Weaver and Judge William Hastie, had brought pressure upon the administration's housing bureaucracy on behalf of Detroit's blacks. The mayor exercised his authority over the DHC to delay the opening of the project for several days in the hope that some way might yet be found to avoid racial confrontation. The DHC announced that the first black families would take up residence at Sojourner Truth on Saturday morning, February 28.[39]

Tension mounted throughout the Nevada-Fenelon neighborhood. Daily shifts of some one hundred white homeowners had picketed the project since February 16, the date first set for occupancy, and mysterious fires had broken out within the development. On February 27, the day before the scheduled move, Tenerowicz rose in the House of Representatives to defend the white protesters as "law-abiding homeowners" and to denounce his opposition as Communist-dominated, "rabble-rousing, publicity seeking, ambitious radicals bent on the destruction of human values and property values alike."[40] On guard, the white picket line increased to about three hundred persons, who maintained an all-night vigil. Unknown persons erected and ignited a twenty-foot high cross in a field just south of the project. Cars sped through the district, their black occupants exchanging taunts with the mostly youthful picketers.

By 8:00 A.M. on February 28, groups of angry blacks and whites had gathered on opposite sides of Ryan Road, about a half-mile from the project. The Police Department deployed only 150 men in the area, a force too small to cope with the mounting disorder. Roving patrols of whites turned away several moving vans, but one truck arrived at the intersection of Ryan and Nevada at 9:30 A.M., and became the focus of a short, intense skirmish between brick-throwing, pipe-wielding rioters. The crowds increased during the morning, and by noon some 1,200 whites and an undetermined number of blacks prowled the district, engaging in numerous small but bloody encounters, heedless of occasional light snowfall and of a temperature that hovered barely above freezing. A young black told a reporter from *Life*: "The Army is going to take me to fight for democracy, but I'd as leif fight for democracy right here. Here we are fighting for our own selves."[41]

Just before midday, the mayor decided to halt the scheduled move into Sojourner Truth until the blacks could be safely escorted into the project. That news did not arrive at the battleground in time to prevent another clash at about 12:15 P.M. A reinforced police detachment, firing volleys of tear gas, finally forced the warring groups apart. Intermittent fighting continued throughout the afternoon and early evening. No one had been killed in the fight for Sojourner Truth, but more than thirty persons had been injured, including several policemen, and 108 people were arrested, all but three of them black.[42] A police horse had been stabbed. The twenty-five families that had planned to make the project their new home had to seek shelter in emergency quarters. An angered black community accused Jeffries of taking insufficient action to disperse the hostile whites at the project. The usually moderate *Detroit Tribune* declared that "the upholding of a white, Klan-led mob, who refused to let Negroes use the streets of this free country, not only has left ... the Detroit Police Department ... and Mayor Jeffries in disgrace but has branded these men as unfit to be classed as believers in law and order."[43]

Save for a brief flareup on March 10, the unrest gradually subsided over the following days, as police kept the area cordoned off. The whites, however, maintained their picket line around the project, while Reverend Hill's committee demonstrated daily around City Hall. Jeffries met with a black delegation on March 2 and, although he reaffirmed his stand in favor of black occupancy, declared that he did not intend to order the transfer of black families to take place until he had consulted with Washington. Four days later he met with John Blandford, who had just assumed the directorship of the newly established National Housing Agency. The housing administrator emphasized the government's support for black retention of Sojourner Truth but advised Jeffries that no move should be undertaken until local emotions had cooled. A federal grand jury meanwhile began deliberations in Detroit to determine if the white rioters had violated the civil rights of the prospective tenants.

Plans went forward to transfer the black families to the housing project. Mayor Jeffries formally requested the governor to provide detachments of the Michigan State Troops, and in the early hours of April 29 some one thousand troopers camped on the same field in which the Klan cross had been raised two months before. As they went to work that morning, the stunned residents of the area encountered soldiers with fixed bayonets at fifty-foot intervals throughout a fourteen-block zone. An additional 1,400 state and city police patrolled warily, and passes were required for exit from or entry to the neighborhood. A few hundred white protestors appeared, many of them women carrying American flags and pushing baby carriages, but no violence occurred. The eight black families scheduled to be moved that day arrived during the morning with police escorts. "We are here now, and let the bad luck happen," said Walter Jackson, a war worker and father of five children whose family was the first to move into the project.

"I have only got one time to die, and I'd just as soon die here."[44] The State Troops remained in place for the next three days while forty more families settled into the hostile district. The Sojourner Truth Homes had been occupied; the battle was at an end.

There was blame enough for the mishandling of the So-journer Truth controversy, from the inception of the project to its abortive occupation. Federal housing officials had shown themselves to be evasive and lacking in courage and had re-fused to help Detroit deal with the social disruption Washing-ton's decisions had engendered. But the mayor, the Common Council, and the DHC deliberately ignored the extent to which their own indecisiveness and poor judgment had contributed to the disaster. Congressman Tenerowicz distorted the facts of the controversy on more than one occasion and served his con-stituents ill by his failure to condemn the threat of white viol-ence that his rhetoric had helped to arouse. The whites of the area found themselves entrapped in a web of fear and hatred, partly of their own creation, but partly the product of the fed-eral policy of red-lining transitional neighborhoods, which deprived potential white homeowners of FHA mortgage guarantees and thus encouraged segregated housing. The blacks of Detroit had little choice but to stand by their demand for Sojourner Truth because of its symbolic importance. In possession of Sojourner Truth, the blacks at least could hope for more aid in the future; if they were denied the project, they would understand clearly that nothing at all could be ex-pected from the white governors of their city and nation.

The two hundred homes at Sojourner Truth were hardly the solution to the black housing crisis. The need to provide housing for black war workers grew increasingly acute as the war continued. To obtain greater housing opportunities for blacks, the NAACP picketed the local office of the Federal Public Housing Authority in early 1943 to protest segregation at Willow Run.[45] In April community and labor groups pe-titioned the Common Council to order the DHC to admit tenants on a nondiscriminatory basis to the seven temporary projects then under construction. The council rejected the proposal on April 29 by a margin of seven to one. Jeffries urged the council to take this position, which formalized a heretofore unwritten practice. During the presentation of their case, black leaders insisted that the war effort would be impaired unless their demands were met. In refusing the demands, the mayor and the DHC reversed the black argument. "It is the opinion of the Commission," the DHC members wrote in defense of their stand, "that any attempt to change the racial pattern of any area will result in violent opposition . . . and could very easily reach a point where the war production efforts of this entire community would be in deadly danger."[46] The commissioners made no allusion to the Sojourner Truth riot but that incident clearly was on their minds.

The DHC did little more about black housing until the fall of the year, when it opened a single segregated project and located hundreds of trailers for blacks on scattered sites throughout the city. Early in July, 1944, five black families moved into a portion of Willow Village, the vanguard of a group that ultimately occupied 360 units in the project. The FPHA had completed only 1,874 black dwelling units by January, 1944, with another two thousand under construction. A backlog of more than eleven thousand black housing applications, some dating from 1937, had accumulated by May, 1944. One woman had been trying to get a new home since 1941 and now faced eviction because her house had been condemned. Statistics revealed that the number of blacks living five persons or more per dwelling unit increased in Detroit between 1940 and 1944, while the number of whites so living declined. The quality of black housing had clearly deteriorated and the degree of segregation had clearly increased. Whites had much more hope than blacks of finding decent housing somewhere—if not in the city, then in a nearby suburb.[47]

Detroit officials began to look toward those suburbs for assistance in solving the black housing problem. The FPHA found a site in Royal Oak Township for six hundred black dwelling units and decided upon Dearborn, the industrial community of some ninety-three thousand persons immediately south and west of the city, as the site for another four hundred segregated units. Dearborn would have been a crowded place in peacetime, but it was relatively underpopulated by wartime standards. The city possessed adequate facilities and a large vacant tract convenient to the Rouge, where some fourteen thousand blacks were employed. But the FPHA had more than convenience in mind when it announced during the late summer of 1944 that Dearborn was under consideration as the site for a new black housing project. Thanks to Dearborn's overt and highly successful policy of racial exclusion and opposition to the erection of any public war housing within its corporate limits, not one of the blacks who worked in the city could live there. "Dearborn is a symbol to the anti-democratic and anti-Negro forces in the Detroit area," an FPHA representative wrote. "It is felt that Dearborn has been able to successfully thumb its nose at the government and that the government is more interested in keeping peace with Dearborn than doing its job." The FPHA hoped to placate Dearborn by building the project in an industrial zone but the agency nevertheless intended to make clear that community race prejudice could not override the obvious requirements of production or the higher goals of the war.[48]

The FPHA did not appreciate the intractable nature of Dearborn's opposition to black housing. After a few weeks of calm during the early fall, the entire community appeared to mobilize at once. Residents spontaneously organized protest meetings against the proposed project. Mayor Orville Hubbard charged that the FPHA meant to incite racial strife by forcing a project on Dearborn, thus impeding rather than assisting the war effort. If there was any support for the project in Dearborn, it was drowned by the tidal wave of negative sentiment. In Detroit, however, the NAACP, UAW, and more than two dozen other organizations met on December 6 to form a committee to lobby with the NHA on behalf of the Dearborn site.[49]

Dearborn's principal hope of avoiding an all-black project lay in the possibility that Detroit might open its own neighborhoods to biracial housing. By December, 1944, the ceaseless influx of black migration, continued housing congestion, and suburban unwillingness to aid the city forced the DHC reluctantly but inevitably toward the adoption of such a policy. The commission formally proposed on February 15, 1945, that the Oakwood area of Southwest Detroit receive a thousand-unit temporary project unrestricted as to occupancy. What decades of segregation had created, war-generated necessity seemed on the verge of destroying. Fierce objection quickly arose in the neighborhood. When the Common Council called a hearing for March 9 to examine the Oakwood project, black leaders, fearful of violent confrontation, warned their followers to stay away. In a reprise of the Sojourner Truth hearing, some six hundred protesting whites packed the council chamber while nearly three thousand supporters milled outside City Hall. On March 20 the council defeated the Oakwood proposal by a vote of five to four. There was no reconsideration.[50]

The council decision was yet another blow to the Dearborn plan, which the FPHA abandoned shortly thereafter. The agency already had begun to waver in the face of the protests from Dearborn and from many congressmen fearful of seeing black projects arise in their own districts. An unexpected upward revision of the entire metropolitan area black housing program required a larger project, too big for the original Dearborn site, which would have to be built on unincorporated land. Such land was available both within and outside the city. No longer able to insist that the original site alone met all requirements, including the most critical one of war necessity, the FPHA could not sustain its underlying ideological case for the Dearborn location.[51]

The agency began to draw up contingency plans for a new attack even before it had retreated from the original site. A startled Dearborn learned on May 14 that the government had obtained a court order for possession of 170 acres owned by Ford in Ecorse Township, across the street from the Dearborn city line, on which to construct a 1,410-unit black development. Ford spokesmen angrily charged that the FPHA was out to avenge itself for its defeat at the company's hands over Bomber City. The NHA bowed to pressure from Michigan Senator Homer Ferguson to delay construction pending an analysis of the project by the Senate Special Investigating Committee, chaired by Senator James Mead. The FPHA began clearing ground on the Ford property, but on August 9, the Mead Committee filed an adverse report on the Ecorse housing plan. A week after Japan surrendered, the FPHA capitulated to Dearborn, announcing on August 22 that no war-related reason now remained to warrant further work on the Ecorse Township site.[52]

Wartime racial discrimination in employment and housing eroded black morale, but prejudice against black GIs was still more dispiriting. Not only were black soldiers segregated and generally restricted to menial duties within the armed forces, but they faced the daily reality of unequal treatment in the small rural towns near which many Army camps were located. Only one black family lived in Sault Ste. Marie before some 1,600 to 1,700 blacks arrived in March, 1942, as part of the Fort Brady garrison. They were forbidden to use the town's YMCA, and many taverns asked to be declared off limits rather than serve blacks. To avoid mixing white and black officers, the fort abandoned a common officer's mess. Consternation swept Oscoda, a hamlet of 650 persons in the northern Lower Peninsula, when the community received word in early 1943 that some two thousand blacks would be stationed at the nearby airbase. The Oscoda town council failed in an attempt to pass an ordinance barring blacks from the village, but racial tension did not ease until segregated USO units were opened near the airfield in late 1943.[53]

Although Michigan avoided the outbreaks of racial violence that punctuated life at most Army camps in the South, the state experienced one military incident shocking not only for its violence but for the disclosures it prompted and its disturbing aftermath. Rumors of gross financial misconduct at Selfridge Field north of Detroit had circulated ever since Colonel William Colman had assumed command of the airbase in the spring of 1942. The scandal erupted in the early hours of May 5, 1943, when a drunken Colman shot Private William McRae, a black airman mistakenly detailed as Colman's driver in contravention of the colonel's standing order for white chauffeurs only.

Colman was relieved of command and dispatched to Percy Jones Hospital in Battle Creek for observation while the Army collected evidence of his malfeasance, which included the sale of privileges to enlisted men and the misappropriation of salaries. McRae survived his wounds to testify at Colman's court-martial, at which the colonel was charged with twenty-nine violations of five articles of war. In September Colman was convicted on four counts but was judged guilty only of careless use of a weapon in his assault on McRae. The court-martial sentenced Colman to reduction in rank to captain and placement at the foot of the promotion list for three years. Roosevelt eventually issued a personal order cashiering Colman from the Army, and the War Department announced on November 9, 1943, that the colonel had been retired. The case was closed.[54]

Their numbers and power enhanced by migration to the major war centers and by high war wages, blacks pressed against the barriers that had kept them from restaurants, theaters, and stores previously patronized primarily or exclusively by whites. Some small Michigan towns were able to maintain rigid segregation: in Buchanan (1940 population: 4,100), a manufacturing city in the southwestern corner of the state, the black population, which increased from a single couple to three hundred persons between 1940 and 1944, was refused service at all local recreation centers, denied seating at the three restaurants, and excluded from most stores. The large number of businesses in Detroit made enforcement of the unofficial color bar more difficult, and blacks began to appear in places where they rarely if ever had ventured before. Unable to alter the new social reality, many whites reacted with open bitterness. A group of white women seated in a Detroit restaurant directed loud and derogatory remarks at a black woman entering the establishment. "My wife always shops in the expensive ladies' shop at J. L. Hudson's [Detroit's leading department store]," an aggrieved reporter told a federal government interviewer in 1943. "Niggers never shopped in there. . . .Now my wife says she sees niggers in there trying on lingerie and all sorts of things. . . .Damn it, they don't have to shop where our women go."[55]

Small racial conflicts ranging from verbal abuse to physical assault became an everyday part of life in wartime Detroit. Rival black and white youth gangs waged petty warfare throughout the city. Following a national pattern, the total of all crimes in Detroit dropped between 1940 and 1945, but interracial friction occured within a context of increases in crime against persons—murder, rape, felonious assault, and robbery. Scores of accidental or intentional momentary clashes occurred each day on Detroit's overcrowded buses and street-cars, where the races mixed freely but unharmoniously, liable at any instant to be physically thrown against each other be-cause of a sudden stop. Some blacks went out of their way to be provocative to whites, and elements of Detroit's black com-munity complained about the boorishness of "ruffian Ne-groes" fresh from the South. In the minds of many angry, frightened whites, accidental contact with or occasional rude-ness from individual blacks was magnified into a vast concealed conspiracy, the best-known manifestation of which was the ru-mor of a "bump club." This mythical organization purportedly enrolled blacks to jostle white persons deliberately. Although it is impossible to determine which race displayed the most ag-gressive behavior, blacks unquestionably were more assertive than ever before.[56]

Here and there, a few signs of racial reconciliation flickered briefly in Detroit. Interracial leaders joined together in March, 1942, to form a committee in the hope of preventing further discord, and Mayor Jeffries later appointed his own unofficial interracial advisory group.[57] But portents of a future racial cata-clysm overshadowed the evidence of amity between black and white. Shortly after the disaster at Sojourner Truth, a govern-ment observer in the city warned Washington: "It now appears that only the direct intervention of the President can prevent not only a violent race riot in Detroit, but a steadily widening fissure that will create havoc in the working force of every Northern industrial city."[58] In "Detroit is Dynamite," an August, 1942, photo essay on the city's many problems, *Life* paid par-ticular attention to race relations, concluding ominously that, "Detroit can either blow up Hitler or it can blow up the U.S."[59]

Eight months later the *Michigan Chronicle* pointed to the rise in racial incidents in Detroit and called for "positive action now that will avert a riot and forestall violence in our community."[60] Jittery whites became prey to and then transmitters of rumors that the black community was planning a riot, allegations that black spokesmen sought unsuccessfully to refute. The growing tension in Detroit was symptomatic of a spreading nationwide incidence of racial conflict that rocked dozens of cities and Army camps during the spring of 1943.

High summer came early to Detroit in June, 1943, the days and nights of record-setting temperature providing the backdrop against which the events of the month were played out. The NAACP held its militant Emergency War Conference in the city from June 4 to June 6, a period that overlapped the great Packard hate strike. One week later a long series of racial confrontations culminated in a brawl between blacks and whites in Inkster, a village north of Detroit that long had been a focus of black settlement. Two nights later a battle broke out at Eastwood Amusement Park in suburban Macomb County after white youths attempted to drive black youngsters from the premises. Sheriff's deputies and police from several localities had to be summoned to quell the disturbance. Four nights later Detroit police quelled a melee between blacks and Italian-American zootsuiters. Wayne County Prosecuting Attorney William Dowling warned that the "rabble rousers" of the NAACP were stirring ignorant black youths into conflict with whites, but his was the only voice among Detroit's white civic leaders that was raised even in suggestion of impending catastrophe.[61]

On Sunday, June 20, the temperature reached the nineties, and a hundred thousand persons of both races streamed across the bridge to Belle Isle Park, a two-square-mile recreation area in the Detroit River. There was precedent for trouble on the island; on July 4, 1940, five hundred blacks had stormed its police station, the assault resulting in an undetermined number of injuries to the police, the rioters, and to some three thousand bystanders. Now, on this afternoon three years later, a gang of black juveniles led by Charles "Little Willy" Lyons roamed the park, starting fights with white picnickers. Evening failed to moderate the intolerable heat, and as thousands of cars crawled across the bridge to the Detroit shore, Lyons and his friends chose the jammed roadway as the spot to pick one more fight. A series of disconnected skirmishes broke out among the more than five thousand persons on the bridge, the encounters quickly merging into a single amorphous conflict. Shortly after 11:00 P.M. the riot spread from its focal point in two directions: onto Belle Isle itself and onto the mainland approaches to the bridge. Although weakened by wartime manpower cutbacks, the Detroit police responded in force to the outbreak and put down the disturbance by 2:00 A.M. without firing a shot, arresting fifty combatants.

But the flames of hatred already had ignited anew in the heart of black Detroit. Sometime after midnight, Leo Tipton, an employee of the Forest Club, a Paradise Valley night spot, jumped on the club's stage to yell out a garbled rumor that whites had thrown a black woman and her baby off the Belle Isle bridge. Incensed blacks stormed out of the club heading for the island. Finding police barricades blocking the bridge approaches, the crowd turned back along Hastings Street, breaking into white-owned stores and looting the merchandise, or dragging unlucky whites out of cars, beating some to death (nine in all were to die). The police fired indiscriminately on blacks, whether looters or bystanders, and were responsible for seventeen of the twenty-five black deaths that resulted from the riot.

Five blocks to the east, a rumor flew among the whites on Woodward Avenue that blacks had raped a white woman on Belle Isle. This rumor was no more true than the one Tipton had voiced. Angry white mobs entered theaters and streetcars, assaulting any blacks they found. Other white gangs, ranging in size from five to a thousand persons, attacked individual blacks on the street. In most cases the police stood by while the white crowds did their fearful work. The rioting grew during the morning and afternoon of June 21, bringing business and transportation to a halt in a 3½-square-mile area of the central city. Small disturbances occurred in several other parts of

Detroit. Police kept the white mobs from the black district throughout the day, but by late evening they coalesced at downtown Cadillac Square into a mass of some ten thousand persons with Paradise Valley as their destination. Against the multitude stood only an increasingly ragged line of police.

All this activity had not gone unnoticed by governments on the local, state, and national levels. At 4:00 A.M. on June 21, Mayor Jeffries reviewed procedures for the mobilization of federal troops with the highest ranking Army officer in the city, Colonel August Krech, with whom he had already held several such discussions. Later that morning Jeffries telephoned Michigan Governor Harry Kelly, who was attending the National Governors' Conference in Columbus, Ohio. As a result of the mayor's call, Kelly ordered state police and militia on alert and phoned the Army's Sixth Service Command headquarters in Chicago to discuss the possible use of federal forces. The governor then left for Detroit, erroneously believing that he had set the machinery for such a deployment in motion. At noon a heavily guarded Jeffries was convoyed into Paradise Valley for an abortive meeting with angry black leaders, who had demanded the entry of federal troops since early morning. The commander of the proposed federal force, General John Guthner, arrived in Detroit in mid-afternoon, throwing local officials into consternation by his assertion that a presidential proclamation would be required before his soldiers, bivouacked in camps surrounding the city, could be mobilized.

Unwilling to admit their inability to control the expanding violence without outside aid, Jeffries and Kelly delayed final decision on the use of federal troops. The governor, hoping to use the Michigan State Troops instead, declared a state of emergency in Wayne, Oakland, and Macomb Counties at 6:00 P.M., banning the sale of liquor and establishing a 10:00 P.M. curfew. Since the state troops could not be mobilized quickly enough, Kelly formally requested Army intervention at 9:20 P.M. To cap the day's confusion the troops were dispatched without the presumably required presidential proclamation, still being drafted in the War Department. Elements of the 701st and 728th Military Police batallions moved out of their

encampments and swept through Paradise Valley and down
Woodward Avenue. Less than a thousand strong, but in full
battle gear with bayonets outthrust, the soldiers confronted
and scattered the mobs and put an end to the riot by 11:30
P.M. President Roosevelt signed the proclamation at 11:55
P.M., providing retroactive authority for the action then under
way and calling upon the already dispersed "insurgents" to
"retire peacefully to their respective abodes. . . ."[62]

The toll of the riot can be reckoned in many ways. There
were thirty-four persons dead, 675 injured, and 1,893 arrested
during or immediately after the outbreak on such charges as
looting, carrying a concealed weapon, or breaking curfew.
Property damage was estimated at two million dollars. Studies
of various groups of arrested rioters, although contradictory
in certain respects, agreed that participants of both races were
primarily young males, many of whom were war workers who
had migrated to the city before the war. (Few women were
arrested in the riot, but many white females played critical
roles as mob lookouts or inciters of violence.) Some black rioters
were soldiers apparently seeking to assert their manhood or
inductees indulging in a grotesque last fling. The loss to war
production was calculated at between a half million and six
million man-hours. The UAW-CIO took credit for the fact
that no war plant closed because of the riot, but disturbances
occurred in front of several plants and the black absentee rate
on June 21–22 reached 90 percent at many companies. And
there was the propaganda loss to the Axis nations, which trum-
peted the story of Detroit as evidence of American decadence
and hypocrisy.[63]

On the morning after the riot, Paradise Valley presented a
spectacle of devastation. Broken glass and abandoned food
and merchandise littered sidewalks and streets. Local residents wandered through the debris in apparent disregard of
the scene before them and of the battle-dressed soldiers who
patrolled in jeeps with weapons at the ready. The federal force
was increased to some five thousand men in the days following
June 21. Throughout the city, the MPs enforced the curfew
far more strictly against blacks than whites despite General

Guthner's insistence upon impartiality and restraint. Under direct orders from Detroit Police Commissioner John Witherspoon, police raided a number of Paradise Valley meeting places and exercised their authority within the black district with heightened brutality. Like the aftershocks of an earthquake, minor racial altercations between individuals continued to break out, and the city seethed with rumors of a new riot. When the bulk of the federal troops pulled out of Detroit on July 9, they left behind a pacified but not a peaceful community; 1,400 soldiers remained at nearby encampments should they be needed again.

The inevitable debate over the handling of the riot was launched on June 23 when R. J. Thomas issued an eight-point program for better race relations in the city. The UAW president criticized the mayor's indecisiveness and demanded a grand jury investigation of police conduct during the riot, with particular regard to the unsolved deaths of several blacks. The attack on Jeffries and the police was joined by local NAACP president McClendon and Walter White, national NAACP secretary, who arrived in Detroit shortly after the June 20 outbreak. The mayor responded to one of Thomas's proposals on June 25 by naming a twelve-person Peace Board to study Detroit's race problems, but in a June 30 report on the riot to the Common Council, he denounced local black leadership and stoutly defended the police. The council endorsed Jeffries's report, in which the mayor stated, "The responsible authorities were greenhorns in the area of race riots. We are greenhorns no longer. We are veterans. I admit we made some mistakes. We will not make the same ones again."[64] Prosecutor Dowling refused all demands for the convening of a special grand jury. The mayor's Peace Board soon sank out of sight.

While Detroiters debated official conduct during the riot, they sought to identify the persons or forces responsible for the outbreak. The white press initially blamed the entire incident on "hoodlum elements" of both races who were best dealt with by the maximum application of armed force. Conservatives condemned the CIO and Eleanor Roosevelt for "stirring up" the blacks. There was a brief vogue, most notable in the black press, for the theory that a fifth column of Nazi sympathizers had incited the riot, but the patent lack of evidence to verify the existence of such a conspiracy disproved the assertion. The idea that an alien influence had been at work in the riot was an attractive one, however, and many Detroiters believed that the influence in question was the host of southern in-migrants, especially the white newcomers. Postriot stories in the white press also discussed black "cockiness and arrogance" and linked an alleged spirit of rebellion among black youths to the militant demands of the black press and the NAACP. Such was the conclusion of the governor's fact-finding committee, appointed shortly after June 21, whose members were all local or state law enforcement officials. The committee neither discussed the racist propaganda of the preacher-demagogues nor seriously considered the store of black grievances.[65]

There was only scattered recognition from the white majority that centuries of racial injustice might lie at the heart of the spring and summer rioting throughout the nation, whatever its immediate cause or causes. "The nation is at war," the *Detroit News* editorialized in late June. "We cannot take time out to conduct local experiments in solution of the race problem."[66] Voices on the left suggested that the nation was hypocritical in fighting for democracy abroad while denying democracy to one-tenth of its citizenry at home. But even many liberals were eager to subordinate the race issue to the war effort. President Roosevelt made no public statement or gesture of conciliation. In a secret July 15 memorandum to the President revealed the following month, Attorney General Biddle argued that wartime race problems could be solved by a halt to further black migration into tense areas. "It should seem pretty clear," Biddle observed, "that no more Negroes should move into Detroit."[67] His suggestion was not accepted, but the government implemented Biddle's additional recommendation that a uniform procedure be established for the use of federal troops against domestic riot or insurrection.

It was inevitable that the entire range of wartime racial problems in Detroit would become an issue in the 1943 mayoral campaign. The son and namesake of a municipal judge much respected by labor and blacks, Edward Jeffries, Jr. had received the support of those groups throughout his tenure on the Common Council from 1933 to 1939 and in his mayoral campaigns of 1939 and 1941. Jeffries vacillated in his attitude toward blacks, and as mayor, had lost the backing of the more militant black leaders and had alienated the CIO by his conservative position on other issues. On September 9 the influential Wayne County CIO Council endorsed Circuit Court Commissioner Frank Fitzgerald as its candidate for mayor. Jeffries and Fitzgerald first faced each other and several additional opponents in a primary election to determine which two would be placed on the November ballot. Although the CIO poured thirty thousand dollars into the Fitzgerald effort, most observers considered Jeffries to be invulnerable. Detroit was therefore all the more shocked when Fitzgerald ran solidly ahead of Jeffries in the preliminary canvass. The black voters abandoned Jeffries, and the CIO succeeded in mobilizing a strong labor vote on behalf of its choice.

Hoping to win without black support by playing to the prejudices of the white majority, Jeffries launched an all-out assault on black militants and the CIO. In pamphlets and radio speeches, he told white Detroit that only a handful of "radical Negro leaders" and "CIO politicians" supported unrestricted housing, a policy too dangerous to be considered when war production depended on the maintenance of civic unity.[68] He defended his conduct and that of the police during the riot and subtly implied that the entire black community had been responsible for the outbreak. Fitzgerald hastily denied any approval of biracial housing and accused the mayor of "invading a white neighborhood" in the Sojourner Truth matter.[69] The CIO and black leaders forced Fitzgerald to moderate his more racist statements, which only made the candidate appear equivocal. Jeffries was supported by Detroit's three major dailies, which devoted much attention to the CIO's funding of Fitzgerald, and by a chain of weekly neighborhood newspapers, which specialized in huge scare headlines such as:

FITZGERALD VICTORY MEANS STRATHMOOR AND
COOLEY HIGH GET NEGRO FLOOD.[70]

Memories of June 21 were revived four days before the election when a recorder's court judge sentenced both "Little Willy" Lyons and Leo Tipton to four to five years imprisonment after their conviction on technical charges of rioting.

The election returns were a complete reversal of the primary results. Jeffries defeated Fitzgerald by 207,799 votes to 175,817, a margin of just over 32,000. Although Fitzgerald retained some solid support among CIO voters on the city's west side, his vote remained the same as in the primary in many precincts while that of Jeffries more than doubled the mayor's October showing. The black vote came in overwhelmingly for Fitzgerald—the returns at Sojourner Truth were 210 to 2 in his favor—but was overcome by the vote of the predominantly white northwest section of the city.[71] A week after the election the NAACP extended an olive branch to the victor when the organization's local officers wrote to pledge "unqualified support . . . in developing a sound and intelligent program for better interracial understanding and harmony in the city of Detroit." Jeffries apparently made no direct reply to this letter, and in an interview with the *Chicago Defender* published in January, 1944, he said of black organizations in general that "all of them demand, but there has been very little cooperative spirit, that is, the desire to sit down and calmly work out problems."[72] Jeffries, however, made an important conciliatory gesture toward the black community at the end of 1943 by replacing police commissioner Witherspoon with former welfare superintendent John Ballenger, a figure more trusted by blacks.

The summer of 1943 was a turning point in the history of black America. Until that time the war-era campaign for racial equality had been greatly influenced by such leaders as A. Philip Randolph, who demanded a militant mass-action movement entirely controlled by blacks. The riots of that summer, however, were a chastening experience. A new strategy for the movement had to be developed, one that still enabled blacks to use "war for democracy" rhetoric on behalf of their goals but avoided confrontation with white authority that might result in violence or hazard economic and social gains. The success of such a strategy, in turn, depended on the broadening of support for the black cause within the white community. Part of the price of that increased white support was the moderation of black demands and the transfer of critical leadership roles from black to white hands. Only in this way could many whites be made comfortable in backing the struggle for racial equality, a crusade still widely unpopular throughout the nation. The retreat to moderation did not preclude occasional fights for specific local demands, such as the Dearborn housing project; in general, however, the new program stressed pursuit of legislative goals such as a permanent FEPC on the national level and the cooling of racial passions on the local level.

These were the general outlines of the new interracial movement that gathered momentum after the riots. Interracial committees were at work throughout the nation by the end of 1944. Such groups, of course, had functioned sporadically and generally unsuccessfully for years. Nearly twenty thousand persons jammed the streets around a Paradise Valley church in January, 1944, to hear Eleanor Roosevelt address an interracial forum. That month the Common Council approved Jeffries's proposal for the formation of a permanent Interracial Committee of eleven members to replace the moribund Peace Board. Composed primarily of city department heads and with an eight-to-three white majority, the new committee was unlikely to demand vigorous action on racial matters because of its close political ties to the conservative Jeffries. One of its principal activities until mid-1945 was the maintenance of the so-called barometer, a system of reports from police, transit officials, and private individuals utilized to determine the level of racial tension in the city. The CIO sponsored many of the interracial organizations. Controlled by whites, they devoted themselves to the study of long-range solutions rather than the advocacy of immediate measures to resolve critical local problems.[73]

Overt racial tension in Detroit diminished during the last

two years of war. Numerous individual altercations between blacks and whites occurred and rumors of black conspiracies continued to abound in the white community, but there were no counterparts to the episodes of mass violence that preceded the 1943 riot. The interracial committees could claim some credit for the improvement of race relations since their existence at least symbolized white concern about black problems. Other causes, however, were more significant. Detroit remained in what one observer described as a "state of shock" during the first year following the June riot.[74] The city police and State Troops extensively publicized their preparations for another major disturbance, a fact that probably weighed heavily with would-be incendiaries of both races. At the same time, police commissioner Ballenger instituted a close liaison with black leaders and established race relations courses as part of police training.

The advent of the 1945 Detroit city elections impelled the black community to seek redress of its many grievances through political action. Housing discrimination and inadequate garbage pickup and rat control in Paradise Valley were among the issues around which an unprecedented community-wide coalition developed. Black organizations ranging from the churches to the NAACP decided early in the year on a consensus black candidate for Common Council, the Reverend Charles Hill, who had led the fight for Sojourner Truth. The Hill forces appealed for assistance to the CIO's Political Action Committee, and the minister's name was included on a slate with two other PAC-backed candidates, incumbent councilman George Edwards and Wayne County CIO leader Tracy Doll. The blacks gave little initial thought to a mayoral candidate since no competent challenger to Jeffries seemed available. When UAW vice-president Richard Frankensteen unexpectedly filed for the nomination in early May, however, the black leaders supported him as an acceptable alternative to Jeffries. Although they wanted to change the city's restrictive housing policy, they urged Frankensteen to play down the issue in his campaign. Aided by a large turnout in black and

CIO precincts, Frankensteen outpolled Jeffries. Hill, Edwards, and Doll were nominated for the Common Council.

Concern about the economic future vied with the political campaign for the attention of black Detroit during the last months of the war. Black workers were discharged much faster than whites as war industry cutbacks began in earnest during the spring of 1945. Since most blacks had been hired by the automobile industry after 1942, they had accumulated little seniority protection against layoffs resulting either from re-conversion or the return of former employees from the armed forces. Black women were especially vulnerable in this regard. One hopeful prospect was that the many black workers long employed in janitorial or foundry occupations would be able to retain their jobs. In its first post–V-J Day editorial, the *Michigan Chronicle* caught black Detroit's mood of uncertainty, determination, and hope, declaring that: "The freedoms for which our boys fought will not come automatically nor will any other gains which have been promised. The end of hostilities will only mean that decks have been cleared for progressive action. . . .We will have to join hands with the little people of America, regardless of color, and work together for a rich and abundant life for all."[75]

The events of the early postwar period confirmed the difficulty of the struggle facing Detroit blacks. The Detroit Urban League estimated that 22,500 black workers had been laid off in the week following V-J Day, and additional thousands of blacks lost their jobs during the next few months. UAW secretary-treasurer George Addes charged in October that the USES had returned to its traditional policy of filling employer orders according to discriminatory racial specifications. Local USES director Edward Cushman denied the accusation but admitted that individual employees of the agency might have reverted to former practices in the confusion following the lifting of manpower controls. "Many of the wartime gains made in the elimination of discrimination in employment were lost in the early stages of reconversion," the Detroit Interracial Committee reported at the end of 1945. In reality, black employment as a percentage of all employment in the Detroit labor market area dropped. Between June, 1945, and March, 1945, the number of black persons employed declined twice as fast as all employment did.[76]

Already suffering from economic setbacks, Detroit's black community was dealt a severe blow in the fall political campaign. As in 1943, important civic issues faded while the contest degenerated into a mudslinging match. One anonymous pro-Jeffries group distributed small cards throughout Detroit's white wards that purportedly came from Frankensteen headquarters and read, "Negroes can live anywhere in any area in any section of Detroit with Frankensteen as Mayor. Negroes, do your duty November 6. . . .Unite with Frankensteen for Mayor."[77] Frankensteen proved even less adept a challenger to Jeffries than Fitzgerald had been two years before. The UAW vice-president's equivocation on the housing issue damaged him with both racial groups. Although the PAC was active in Frankensteen's behalf, the organization was handicapped by a split within CIO ranks over the advisability of his candidacy and could not overcome the mayor's effective redbaiting tactics. In a record turnout, Jeffries defeated his challenger by 274,435 to 216,917 votes. Frankensteen carried some 90 percent of the black vote, but the mayor cut wide swathes through white ethnic CIO districts and won the middle-class northwest area by an overwhelming margin. George Edwards ran first among the council candidates, but the Reverend Hill and Tracy Doll placed fourteenth and fifteenth respectively in the field of eighteen persons seeking the nine available seats.[78]

The war years witnessed a sharp rise in black economic power, the collapse of certain unofficial forms of segregation, a growing unity of objectives within the black community, and the possibility, symbolized by the interracial committees, of at least a favorable hearing for the black case in the future. "The American Negro could no longer be considered a marginal man at the end of the war," Neil Wynn observes. "The war had propelled the blacks into the mainstream of American life." The gains, however, could be maintained and extended only by insistent black pressure on a federal government that would be unwilling to dance to the tune of Jim Crow. Blacks did not relent in their pursuit of equality, but the strength of white resistance was to prove dauntingly great. The 1945 Detroit campaign demonstrated that fact, as did a separate but related incident that fall. Charles Johnson, a black ex-serviceman, applied unsuccessfully to the DHC in September for housing in a nonsegregated area of Detroit. Following his rejection, he wrote the Common Council, "We have won the war . . . and are striving to win a complete peace. Each time Negroes are discriminated against, veterans or otherwise, a nail is driven into the coffin of this peace."[79] No longer willing to endure in silence, the Charles Johnsons in Detroit and throughout the nation awaited the white response.

Chapter 5

"Tennessee and Kentucky Are Now in Michigan"

For the thousands of newcomers to Michigan, migration meant change. Much of that change was beneficial; but for many, especially for rural southerners, migration resulted in dislocation and suffering. Southerners, to be sure, had experienced dislocation ever since the beginning of the great northward movement in the early years of the century. The persistence of such problems belied generalizations about wartime happiness and contentment. The migrants tested the ability of the host community to accept differing attitudes and customs, and the community sometimes failed the test. With less publicity than at Willow Run, individual natives and newcomers elsewhere also struggled to adjust to one another and to their transformed environment. The war effort demanded their cooperation, but no image of unity could disguise the fact that encrusted suspicion often kept them apart.

Many a Michigan native must have wondered who these newcomers were—these strangers who were found moving furniture into the vacant apartment next door or who one day appeared in the factory cafeteria. Large numbers of the migrants had come from Michigan itself. The 1944 sample census of the Detroit-Willow Run district estimated that 51,590 of the 254,485 migrants to the region, or 20.3 percent of the total, had transferred to their new homes from other areas of the state. Most of the migration, however, originated outside the borders of Michigan. According to the Detroit census, the southern states together accounted for 94,710 in-migrants, 47.8 percent of all out-of-state newcomers. The states immediately adjacent to Michigan and those of the Great Plains provided one-third of the 1940–44 Detroit interstate migration, the East and Far West supplying the remainder. Migration to Michigan from Ohio, Illinois, and Indiana had been heavier than that from any other region both during the 1930s and the defense period, but the inflow from these states declined after the conversion of their industry to war production created adequate employment opportunities closer to home. Detroit's mounting manpower requirements after 1942 stimulated an increased recruiting effort within the relatively untapped southern labor market, and migration from the South to Michigan rose rapidly in response.[1]

No popular belief about the wartime migrants was so prevalent—or incorrect—as the notion that most of the newcomers had stepped directly from farm to city. Government surveys as early as 1941 revealed that the extent of rural-to-urban movement induced by the defense boom was not fulfilling predictions. Urbanites possessed both wider access to information and more of the skills required for war jobs than the rural populace did. Renewed agricultural prosperity and the government's policy of granting draft deferments to farmworkers, moreover, reduced, without completely halting, the exodus of men and women from the farms. The Detroit census reported that less than one-fifth of the area's in-migrants claimed to have resided on a farm in 1940; even among southerners, the proportion rose to no more than 25 percent.[2]

The Census Bureau's studies of internal migration in the 1935–40 period and its sample surveys of congested production areas provide ample data for an evaluation of the impact of war on interstate population movement. The sexual balance of the population flow tilted from a 51 percent male majority to a 52.7 percent female predominance, implicit evidence of the number of men drawn off to the military and not counted as migrants and of the number of service wives who followed their husbands to military camps or migrated to seek war work. On the whole, the wartime migrants were younger

than their predecessors. Both prewar and wartime migrants
had similar marriage rates. Nearly ninety thousand of the
254,000 wartime newcomers (39.2 percent) fell between the
ages of twenty and thirty-four, and another fifty-seven thousand (27 percent) were estimated to be nineteen years or
younger. Some 67,430 1940–44 in-migrants, however, were
single, widowed, or divorced, young females predominating.
The most dramatic effects of the war can be seen in regard to
migrant employment and unemployment. The proportion of
persons in the migrant labor force (those fourteen years of age
or older) rose from 57 percent in prewar Michigan to 67 percent in wartime Detroit, but the jobless rate plummeted from
11 percent to less than 3 percent during that time.[3]

Once apprised of who the migrants were, a Michigan native
might have asked, "Why did they come?" That question had
many answers, and Freda Yenney, who conducted a survey
among in-migrant families living at the John R. Fisher housing
project in Detroit, recorded some of the reasons offered by her
respondents: "There's no work in Kentucky"; "Mining work in
Pennsylvania doesn't pay"; "Wanted to get away from mining
in West Virginia for a long time." Many natives would have
pounced on such replies as vindication of the oft-expressed
opinion that the majority of newcomers had journeyed to
Michigan with nothing more than personal enrichment in
mind. Indeed, what failed to surface in most of the responses
of the Fisher families was an overt reference to patriotic
considerations that might have prompted the decision to migrate. Recruitment notices for migrant war workers certainly
pounded away at the patriotic theme:

ASSIST THE WAR EFFORT!
To Win the War Our Boys Need Equipment

began a typical 1942 advertisement of a Michigan employer
published in a Tennessee newspaper. This same ad, however,
proceeded to promise "Plenty of Overtime—Time and a Half
Over Forty Hours." It is entirely possible that many migrants
failed to declare their patriotic motivation because they thought

it pointless to state the obvious. The self-serving and the altruistic reasons for migration were clearly compatible.[4]

And so the migrants came, urged on by a mixture of motives—and by newspaper appeals, radio solicitations, and other forms of advertising. If migrants chose Willow Run as their destination, they might have made that decision at one of the many mass meetings sponsored by Ford in the rural South, where company recruiters made stirring calls to patriotic duty and offered glowing reports of economic rewards waiting at the bomber plant. Southerners also chose their new home because relatives who had previously migrated lived there. Extended family networks, originating in the hills and hollows of Kentucky and Tennessee, had long before stretched to Detroit, Flint, Monroe, and other state production centers, and now guided the newcomers to housing, jobs, and friends, and gave the migrants some sense of continuity with their former life. By bus, train, and car they poured into Michigan. Thousands of people passed through Detroit's two railroad stations and the Greyhound bus terminal each day, sometimes carrying all their possessions in a single battered suitcase or canvas bag.

The journey to Michigan was often difficult for the migrants, as were their first experiences in the state. Irene Watt lived with her husband Donald in a small town in mid-Tennessee. In August, 1943, she boarded a train for Ypsilanti, a place totally unknown to her. The trip took most of a day and was spent in a coach crowded with soldiers. Alone and frightened, she went straight to Willow Run. Once at the plant, she had to endure additional exhausting hours of preemployment procedures before she was finally "hired on." As night approached she had nowhere to sleep and was sent to Willow Lodge, only to find that there were no vacancies. A clerk at the dormitory's main desk suggested that Mrs. Watt get something to eat at the nearby cafeteria, an excellent idea since she had had no food for more than twelve hours. When she reached the door of the dining hall the day's experiences overwhelmed her, and she burst into tears, crying without stopping. When she had recovered and eaten, Mrs. Watt returned to the lodge to learn that, thanks to the high turnover at the facility, a room for the night had become available. She gratefully settled in; another newcomer had arrived in Michigan.[5]

The newcomer to Michigan's industrial centers had to adjust quickly to unaccustomed surroundings and unfamiliar neighbors. Adaptation to a changed environment is never easy for most migrating individuals, no matter how favorable the circumstances. The tension and shortages in wartime Detroit or Muskegon only aggravated the worst aspects of the experience. Migrants versed in urban norms and conventions were most likely to make the transition smoothly. The migrant group that faced the greatest difficulties in adjustment came from the mountain fastnesses of the rural South. The metropolitan Detroit sample census of 1944, listing only 22,935 southerners in the four-county area who had resided on a farm in 1940, suggests that only a relatively small number of these mountain people—or mountaineers, as they called themselves—migrated to Michigan. The survey's simple division of residences between "on farm" and "not on farm," however, lumped together persons from New Orleans and Memphis with those from isolated highland hamlets and valley towns of less than two thousand population.[6] Constituting an important element of the largest regional migration to Michigan, these rural southerners shared the problems of the other newcomers and had unique concerns of their own.

The first major problem that confronted most newcomers, whatever their origin, was finding a place to live. Irene Watt was among thousands of southerners who roomed for a time at Willow Lodge; a reporter visiting the hostel in late 1943 found that "mountain dialects run heavy to the acre."[7] An estimated fifteen thousand Detroit in-migrants resided in dormitories, lodging houses, or hotel rooms in 1944.[8] The severity of the housing shortage probably made it more difficult for rural southerners to maintain the kind of tightly knit neighborhood units many had established in Detroit prior to the war. It has been asserted that project homes represented a considerable improvement over the kind of housing to which many migrants were accustomed, but the generalization cannot be made without qualification. To be sure, a gas range is an improvement over a wood stove, as is a sink over a well and a toilet over a privy. But the cramped, cheerless row houses, the basic dwelling units of the wartime projects, were no quantum leap from the log house. The barren tracts on which so many developments huddled—a dispiriting sight to anyone—must have awakened a special sadness in men and women who recalled vistas of forest, field, mountain, and sky.

There can be no question, however, about the general improvement in wages enjoyed by the migrants. Surveying one hundred families at the Fisher project, Yenney found that their average weekly income had increased more than 50 percent during the war.[9] Still, since many migrants could do little more than unskilled work, they constituted yet another group that did not share fully in the wage boom. Also, although workers from the remotest Appalachian heights knew something about machinery after years of tinkering with recalcitrant car and truck engines, the mountaineers were generally less prepared than other groups for the rigors of industrial routine and discipline.

On the one hand, natives often ascribed the difficulties mountain people experienced with factory life to the alleged inherent laziness of the newcomers. On the other hand, many of the same longtime residents complained about the indefatigability of southerners, some of whom, once trained, could work rapidly and efficiently for hours with only brief interruption.[10] Backwoods life was not as carefree as urbanites imagined, and long hours in mines or fields had prepared mountain folk for stretches of tedious, punishing work. When that stamina was coupled to a desire to make the maximum in wages, the result was a performance that either inspired or embittered fellow workers.

Much of life in urban Michigan disoriented and discouraged the mountain people. They were often perplexed in the face of such commonplace challenges as buying clothes in standard sizes, purchasing food in large grocery stores, or using a dial telephone. When investigators from the Maternal Health League of Michigan entered a tarpaper shack in Warren

Township and asked a young Kentucky mother of three children if she had made preparations for her current and obvious pregnancy, she answered, "No, ma'am, because down home we always have a midwife, and I don't know one here."[11] Michigan winters brought with them a miserable combination of frigidity, dampness, and wind that rendered thin southern clothing next to useless and doubtlessly drove many southerners to question their original decision to migrate.

The city proved at once enormous and confining. One rural Tennessee youth, confused by the conflicting signs and signals of Detroit traffic, rode to work counting the number of trees between home and shop; after ticking off the ninety-fourth oak or elm, he knew he had arrived. At the same time, the city afforded few opportunities for the kind of recreation mountaineers enjoyed—walking or hunting in the forest, or "just settin'" on the porch in the quiet of the evening. The local bar was one of the few urban retreats where rural migrants could sit at their leisure, drinking and listening to the commercialized rhythms of country music on the juke box or over the radio, especially to Saturday night's "Grand Ole Op'ry" from a Nashville now more than geographically distant.[12]

Mountain children suffered some of the most wrenching effects of the migration to Michigan. In 1943 Detroit education officials suddenly became aware of large numbers of tall, raw-boned boys and girls who were beginning the third or fourth grade at ages fourteen to sixteen as a result of the inadequate schooling they had received in the South. These children, often shy and withdrawn, absorbed lessons only with great effort, an effort increased by the discomfiture of sitting at desks meant for youngsters half their age and by the taunts and jeers of their fellow pupils.[13] Children of all backgrounds, of course, adapt more readily to new surroundings than older people, and many a rural child quickly became caught up in the world of comic books, radio serials, and dating customs. As a consequence of that adaptation, parental authority and the structure of family life began to break down. In the South, mountain families had been close, cooperative units, each member of the group—from grandparents to the youngest able child—assigned responsibilities vital to the survival of all. In wartime Detroit, the children were freed of their farm chores, but their role in the family enterprise was diminished as school and work separated them from traditional relationships with their parents. For a disproportionate number of these children, the next step on the path away from home led to their designation as delinquents.

In her 1954 novel *The Dollmaker*, Harriet Arnow portrayed in an almost suffocatingly realistic manner the plight of a family transplanted from the rural South to wartime Detroit, with a particularly poignant emphasis upon the desperate lot of the mountain woman. Gertie Nevels, the protagonist in Arnow's grim narrative, is a large, plain, resourceful woman, an artist with knife and whittling block. She lives with her spiritless husband Clovis and their five small children near a settlement in a part of rural eastern Kentucky whose principal crop, in Gertie's words, is "younguns for the wars and them factories."[14] Clovis leaves home to seek a war job in Detroit, and Gertie and the youngsters follow, taking the same nerve-wracking train trip north made by thousands of other migrants. The family settles in a nondescript Detroit housing project much like the Fisher Homes, their neighbors a cross section of social and ethnic types, many of whom are unfriendly to the southern newcomers.

Clovis, a born mechanic, flourishes in his new surroundings, but Gertie withers. Able to cope with almost any challenge that might confront her in a rural environment, she finds urban life incomprehensible and beyond her abilities. To find solace, Gertie begins to carve a Christ figure from a tall cherrywood block. The Nevels family meanwhile has begun to fall apart. Gertie's oldest and best-loved son, twelve-year-old Reuben, runs away to the Kentucky hills he cannot forget. Her daughter, Cassie, lost in memories of the mountain world and of an imaginary playmate, falls under the wheels of a train and dies. Gertie's other children become sullen or preoccupied with the larger world outside the project house in which their mother has become prisoner. The city has taken everything from Gertie and given nothing; Clovis cannot even make enough money in this center of war prosperity to accumulate savings for the postwar period. In a last despairing act, Gertie has the cherrywood Christ, complete but for a face, sawn into boards for the making of dolls that she will attempt to sell—dolls to be produced not by her skilled hands but by Clovis's electric saw.

Many mountain and small-town migrants found in religion an avenue of escape from a daily existence like that lived by the Nevels family. Newspaper ads welcomed salvation-seekers to "Miracle Meetings" to hear "A Fearless Gospel Preacher" or the "Joy Girl of American Evangelism."[15] Sister Ethel Willitts, a latter-day Aimee McPherson, had arrived in Detroit in 1939 with a tent and stayed to preside five years later over the large Everybody's Tabernacle and a $165,000 corporation with a branch in Florida. "Since Pearl Harbor," two journalists wrote in a survey for *Collier's* of the city's white "holiness" churches, "Detroit has become the scene of a greater Armageddon."[16]

Most observers either scoffed at southern rural religious practices as manifestations of Yahoo ignorance or warned that the tabernacles and temples were part of a semifascist conspiracy led by such demagogues as J. Frank Norris and Harvey Springer. Neither supposition, however, dealt with the reality of mountaineer religious attitudes. The majority of the more prosperous southerners attended services at the churches of established denominations in the Detroit area. Many of the less well-off who went to church found their consolation not at the well-publicized political circuses run by the Norrises but in the tiny storefront halls of the worker-preachers. To be sure, the preaching of racial and religious bigotry was the principal business carried on in some of these makeshift houses of worship, but it was not the function of most. In these meeting places, with their exalted names of Pillar of Fire Church and Temple of Spiritual Truth, mountain people, on a weeknight evening or all day on Sunday, could reconstitute the community they had known at home. In such churches, Robert Coles writes, "they [could], for a few minutes, sit down and ponder things, find in life a little structure and a little shape, an answer to isolation, a sense of belonging."[17]

The mountaineers' life in their native environment may

Workers at the Fisher Body plant in Pontiac complete a five-inch naval cannon, a destroyer's main battery. Firing a dozen shells a minute, the gun weighed forty thousand pounds. © *National Geographic Society*.

A B-24 Liberator bomber nears the end of the mile-long assembly line at the Ford Willow Run plant. Midgets worked inside the confined wing space. © *National Geographic Society.*

The Chrysler Tank Arsenal in Warren Township received the armed forces' "E" flag for production excellence in this 1942 ceremony. Scores of Michigan firms were so honored. *Courtesy of the* Detroit News.

The Gar Wood plant in Marysville on Lake Huron converted from the production of speedboats to the construction of towing craft for the Army Transportation Corps. © *National Geographic Society.*

Vital ore cargoes flowed through the lock canal at Sault Ste. Marie in the Upper Peninsula. The army heavily guarded the installation until late 1943. © *National Geographic Society.*

Swingshifters study posters outside a late-evening movie in downtown Detroit. Theaters and bowling alleys remained open all night to accommodate war workers. © *National Geographic Society*.

Dodge UAW workers demonstrating in October, 1942. Signs indicate displeasure with company seniority and production practices, typical fomenters of disputes during the war. *Courtesy of the* Detroit News.

A unit of the Willow Lodge dormitory, opened February, 1943. Thousands of in-migrant workers, including many from the rural South, lived here while employed at the nearby bomber plant. *Courtesy of the* Detroit News.

Detroit police lead a beaten and bloodied black from the Sojourner Truth project during the February, 1942, riot. *Courtesy of the* Detroit News.

A black youth is attacked on Woodward Avenue in downtown Detroit during the June, 1943, race riot. Thirty-four persons, mostly black, were killed during the two-day disturbance. *Courtesy of the* Detroit News.

White pickets formed on February 27, 1942, to prevent blacks from moving into the Sojourner Truth project in northeast Detroit. A riot broke out the following day, postponing the move until April. *Courtesy of the Archives of Labor and Urban Affairs, Wayne State University.*

A real-life Rosie and coworker rivet a center wing section at the Willow Run bomber plant. *Courtesy of the* Detroit News.

Thousands choked Detroit's Cadillac Square to celebrate the war's end on V-J Day, August 14, 1945. *Courtesy of the* Detroit News.

The UAW often placed veterans and their families on picket lines during the 113-day General Motors strike of 1945-46. *Courtesy of the Archives of Labor and Urban Affairs, Wayne State University.*

have been bucolic, but it had not been idyllic. They had known want and oppression, and that reality shaped their very personal and apocalyptic religious view. It was a view that required no modification to account for their trials in a city, nation, and world at war. Their church was a bond with the past, a balm for the present, and a hope for the future. In the little storefront tabernacles, the men and women from the hills could communicate directly with their stern yet understanding God as they always had, using every part of their bodies— head, neck, hands, arms, legs, and, most important, the voice. They could shout, babble in glossolalia (the "speaking in tongues") and sing the old songs—"Shall We Gather at the River," "Amazing Grace," "Throw Out the Lifeline," and "Jesus is a Rock in the Weary Land."[18]

Native hostility made adjustment even more difficult for the newcomers. Occasionally, the enmity of the longtime resident was directed indiscriminately at almost all migrants; but the most frequent target of abuse was the southerner. The antipathy toward this migrant group arose in large part from class, rather than ethnic biases, since the southerners' alleged poverty was a key element in the native stereotype. Because of their marked regional accent, few southerners, regardless of cultural or economic level, could escape the jibes and insults that were sometimes meant in fun but were often meant to wound. To the natives, the southerners were "Kaintucks," "Arkansawans," "Briarhoppers," and, of course, "hillbillies." Seen through the eyes of the native, the mountaineer's urban misadventures must, at times, have appeared comic indeed. To such true stories as that of the tree-counting boy, oldtimers added tall tales about southerners who came to Detroit without shoes or who mailed letters in fire alarm boxes. "How many states are there in the Union?" one person asked another in a joke that circulated in wartime Detroit. "Forty-six," came the answer. "Tennessee and Kentucky are now in Michigan."[19]

The Office of War Information summarized Detroit folklore about the southerner as follows: "He is clannish, dirty, careless, gregarious in his living habits. He lives on biscuits and beans, never buys more than the most basic necessities of life, saves his money, is illiterate and yokelish."[20] These words and phrases have a familiar ring; many of them had been applied to the prewar southern white migration, to the European immigrants of earlier decades, and to black newcomers of all eras. Advertisements for vacant homes occasionally appeared in Detroit newspapers with the restriction, "No Southerners."[21] Local labor leaders taxed the migrants for a supposed willingness to work at any job even at wages that depressed a plant's pay scale, and for their lack of interest in union affairs. The only major difference between these wartime attacks on southern migrants and the earlier aspersions cast upon other minority groups was that enough years had passed so that some of the formerly despised could now demonstrate toward others the same bigotry once directed against them.

The native's most damning accusation against southerners was that they had played a central role in the exacerbation of race tension that ultimately ignited the Detroit riot in the summer of 1943. Whether rural or urban in origin, many southerners had come to Michigan with their vitriolic race prejudice intact. Sporadic incidents between blacks and whites broke out at the Fisher Homes throughout the year following the 1943 turmoil.[22] But Raymond Hatcher, an official of the Detroit Urban League, told an interviewer in September, 1943, that "new arrivals from the South, both black and white, should not exclusively nor particularly be blamed for current racial practice in Detroit. These conflicts existed long before the latest influx of southern labor arrived."[23] A mountaineer made the point more pungently in *The Dollmaker*: "They're always talkin' about Klan-lovin', nigger-hatin' Southerners, but I'm tellin' the truth, there are more nigger-haters and Klan-lovers up here than ever I did know back home."[24]

The host community only infrequently extended a hand of welcome to the newcomers. The Detroit Council of Churches mobilized its resources to send missionaries into the Willow Run trailer camps, and by 1944 twenty-three new churches had been opened in the Detroit area. The DHC made some effort to interview prospective in-migrant project tenants and provided the newcomers with a booklet containing homemaking advice and a map of the project area. Asked during a March, 1943, radio broadcast to name his most serious housing concern, DHC director Charles Edgecomb replied, "Getting across the idea that these migrant war workers coming here to man our war plants at the express wish and request of our government are a good, solid, dependable type of citizen, exactly the same kind of people that the old Detroiters thirty years ago were looking [at] askance when the automobile factories first began to draw waves of workers from all over the country." Edgecomb, however, assured his listeners that the temporary projects that housed many southern families would be torn down as promised at war's end.[25]

Southerners resented the many slights they experienced at the hands of unthinking natives. Yet all the fault did not lie on one side. There were always enough southerners in Detroit whose mannerisms and lifestyle seemed to validate the stereotype. If many natives regarded the migrants—especially the southerners—as a foreign element in the civic body, some southerners also regarded themselves as estranged. Southerners occasionally thought northerners cool and reserved, and Michigan natives were baffled and angered by the aloof pride and arrogance—what some called clannishness—that seemed to characterize the demeanor of numerous mountain men and women. Such mountaineer attitudes, to some extent, derived from the fact that many migrants had owned farms in the South with which they always had done pretty much as they pleased. Coles observes that ideas about land could be translated by rural southerners into a posture toward people: "The moral then is to stand on one's mountain territory . . . and guard it, and not suffer entry into it lightly."[26]

The rural southerners pined for their native hills and valleys. Unlike the wartime migrants to California, they did not establish elaborate state and county societies to perpetuate the memory of home. They had their churches, and fifteen or twenty dollars would buy them a round-trip bus ticket for a weekend visit to Kentucky or Tennessee. Still, they longed for the mountains, no matter how wretched a life they once had lived there. One day during the war, a Willow Run area school

held a group singing session at which the children, mostly
from southern families, were told to sing "Michigan, My
Michigan," the state anthem. They refused; to none of them
was Michigan their real home. The story is perhaps apocry-
phal, but it has the ring of truth. When the burden of urban
life or native hostility became too great to bear, a mountaineer
might simply clear out. In a letter to a local newspaper, David
Crockett Lee announced his leavetaking from Detroit in 1942
after three years in the city. "We found Detroit a cold city, a
city without a heart or a soul," he wrote. "So we are going back
to Tennessee . . . where men and women are neighborly, and
where even the stranger is welcome."[27]

To explain the gulf between natives and southern newcomers, some observers resurrected the notion that inhabitants of
North and South constituted two separate peoples. On a more
sophisticated level, Erdmann D. Beynon had suggested in 1938
that the similar problems of southern migrants and the undif-
ferentiated stereotype the host society had developed about
them were creating a group consciousness that united in mutual defense the entire company of newcomers. Southerners,
of course, constituted no more monolithic a bloc than any
other social group. Occasional letters published in Detroit
newspapers during the war indicate that not all southerners
found the city to be as inhospitable as David Lee had. The
balance of the evidence, however, points to a considerable degree of hostility between a significant number of natives and
newcomers that could not be overcome by the war's larger demand for social unity.[28]

"In this war we are exhibiting curiously little hatred for the
enemy," observed Dr. Edouard Lindman of the New York
School of Social Work, speaking at the 1943 conference on the
problems of Willow Run. "Instead, we are turning to the persecution of minorities."[29] The degree to which southern alienation resulted from general environmental conditions rather
than specific native hostility cannot be determined. Nor can
the effect of native-migrant dissension on Detroit's war effort
be ascertained, although the conflict probably contributed in
some small degree to manpower instability. A large number of

southern white migrants, however, stood with the blacks out-side the mainstream of society; and since southerners did not threaten traditional patterns of life in the same manner that blacks did, society felt itself even less obliged to deal with the group problems of these white newcomers.

From the earliest stages of the war, Michigan natives voiced concern about the postwar status of the migrants. The OWI's 1942 survey of Detroit attitudes, for example, noted a firm belief that the newcomers must leave after the war so that suf-ficient jobs and housing would be available for returning ser-vicemen. Disturbing to the natives was the fact that substantial numbers of migrants had no intention of leaving Michigan after V-J Day. A Gallup Poll of five war production centers published in May, 1943, revealed that fully 48 percent of the in-migrant families questioned in the Michigan-northern In-diana region expressed a desire to remain there after the ces-sation of hostilities. Economic considerations naturally bulked large in the plans of many newcomers. "We don't know what we're going to do," admitted a southern woman resident at the Fisher project. "We like it here. As long as my husband has work, we'll stay."[30]

The effort persisted to limit in-migration and to encourage out-of-state migrants to leave Michigan. On June 3, 1945, the *Detroit News* reported the *Louisville Courier-Journal*'s dismay over the wartime depopulation of Kentucky and painted a glowing picture of postwar economic possibilities in the Bluegrass State. "It is wrong," said the *News*, which had scorned southerners in the past, "to deplete a state of its enterprising stock, the kind that goes away to war and the war factories." The article caused one presumed migrant to reply, "All right, hillbillies, get your suitcases packed. After luring us here by telling us what a won-derful future Detroit offered, the newspapers now say that no place is so amazingly flush with opportunities as Kentucky. I don't know if we can adjust our appetites back to cornpone bread after eating all the beefsteak and pork loins we have had here."[31]

To speed the migrant exodus, the Detroit office of the United States Employment Service offered to advertise jobs available in the South, and the Michigan Unemployment Compensation Commission promised assistance to migrants who encountered difficulties in receiving unemployment benefits upon return- ing home. Whether in response to such gestures or not, out- migration from Michigan increased during early 1945. So closely was the outflow from Detroit balanced by the influx of returning veterans, however, that the city's population re- mained virtually unchanged. Neither editorials nor proffers of government aid, moreover, shook the resolution of the thou- sands of migrants who desired to stay. An analysis of migrant attitudes in the first week of August, 1945, indicated that, if anything, the proportion of those wishing to stay had in- creased and their determination had hardened.[32]

Into a Detroit bus terminal strode a young man sporting high-heeled boots and a cowboy hat. "Give me a ticket to Texas!" he shouted at no one in particular, waving a fifty- dollar bill. "I want to git and git fast. I've had enough of this place." A few miles away near the fast-emptying Willow Run housing projects, a man from Arkansas mused, "My wife likes it here. Says there's more going on all the time. Seems to me like a place to get ahead." Some migrants would leave, and others would stay. Many newcomers already had so faded into the general surroundings that few natives would ever know they had migrated to Michigan. Others, especially the southern mountain people, had distinctive characteristics and problems. Many of those problems had been created or worsened by a war that had brought enormous social benefit to millions of others in Michigan. Before the war, Beynon had pointed out that scattered housing and the public school system were pow- erful forces for assimilation of the southern whites into the larger society. "It seems likely," he had written, "that the social problems of the white migrant laborers in Michigan's cities will be in a short time indistinguishable from those of the northern white laboring class in general." There was no way to know, however, whether migrant and native would be reconciled with one another.[33]

Chapter 6

Women, Youth, and the Limits of Wartime Change

★ 1 ★

When America entered the war, leaders of prominent women's organizations expressed cautious optimism that the nation would respond to the female contribution to victory with the grant of full equality. As V-J Day dawned, however, it was difficult to determine the actual extent of change. The volume of female employment had risen, but women's status had not. The national government, so generous in its praise of female America, still evinced no willingness to award women an effective voice in political or economic decision making. Neither business, labor, nor any other major organized segment of society supported a significant change in women's role based on wartime accomplishments.

Female emancipation had received a severe setback during the 1930s when massive unemployment lent new emphasis to the long-cherished belief that the woman's place was in the home, not in the office or on the assembly line, where her presence might deny work to a man supporting a family. The proportion of women in the Michigan labor force rose slightly between 1930 and 1940, but females remained clustered in the occupations traditionally reserved for them—storeclerk, stenographer, maid, and so forth.[1] The notion of additional female employment in industry had been discussed at the outset of the defense program but had not been implemented to any great extent. Few women entered defense training courses.

Interest in female employment, however, quickened with the
coming of war.

The rapid growth and restructuring of the American female labor force is one of the most frequently noted of wartime
developments. The number of working women in the United
States increased from 14,600,000 in 1941 to 19,370,000 in
1944. The rise of female employment in Michigan was still
more striking: from 391,600 in March, 1940 (24.8 percent of
the nonfarm workforce), the number of employed women in
the state more than doubled by the war peak in November,
1943, to 799,100 (34.8 percent of the nonfarm workers). Examining Detroit war plants in March, 1943, investigators for
the UAW found that women comprised more than a quarter
of the workforce at Briggs, Bendix's Wayne division, and Willow Run.[2]

A Women's Bureau survey disclosed that fully 51 percent of
the 387,000 women at work in Detroit during late 1944 and
early 1945 had been employed before Pearl Harbor. They had
shifted from jobs as waitresses, sales clerks, and maids into
manufacturing and, to a lesser extent, into government work.
The war years also witnessed the emergence of a new type of
female worker: the same study reported that 28 percent of the
Detroit female labor force were housewives, and 18 percent
had been students prior to the declaration of war. The demographic balance of the female labor force altered radically with
the entrance of these new workers in vast numbers. Once dominated by single women under thirty years of age, the female
labor force now contained substantially larger proportions of
older and married women. The Women's Bureau found Detroit's female workers evenly divided 45 percent to 45 percent
between single and married women, the remaining 10 percent
being widowed or divorced. Only 44 percent of the women
were in the prime employment age group of twenty to twenty-
nine years, in contrast to the 41 percent of women workers
over thirty.[3]

A complex set of trends and demands dictated the shape of
the wartime women's workforce. Long-term demographic ten-
dencies within the national female population resulted in a

reduction of the age at marriage and an increase in the number of older women in relation to all women. The coming of war provided a further stimulus to marriages; the number of Michigan weddings performed in December, 1941, set a state record for a single month. The marriage rate declined during the next four years, but rose sharply again with the coming of peace. At the same time, the economic sectors that traditionally employed large numbers of women, such as the federal government, were precisely the areas that expanded most from 1940 to 1945. Seeking a perspective on wartime changes in female employment, William Chafe notes: "At the turn of the century, the young, the single and the poor had dominated the female labor force. Fifty years later, the majority of women workers were married and middle-aged, and a substantial minority came from the middle class. In the story of that dramatic change, World War II represented a watershed event."[4]

Government manpower policy also influenced the nature of the female labor force, but that policy left much to be desired both in conception and execution. At no time did the WMC give women more than an advisory voice in decision making, and usually the commission ignored proffered advice. At first paying little attention to the potential of women workers, the WMC—moved to action by a growing manpower shortage—plunged into an unproductive round of female recruitment drives at the end of 1942, nowhere more fruitlessly than in Detroit. On August 10, mailmen delivered some 650,000 postcards to households in the four-county Detroit area, asking resident women to reply by return mail to the local USES office stating whether or not they were interested in factory work. Although 265,009 cards were returned, only 1,742 women were placed in factories by January, 1943. At the time, many women had not yet realized the seriousness of the manpower crisis, and private industry's unwillingness to utilize the USES further hampered the drive. During 1943 the WMC largely failed in its efforts to persuade Michigan women to take vital, but low paying, civilian service jobs in stores and other businesses. Throughout the war, the Michigan state government refused to allow substantial changes in the regulations governing hours of employment and working conditions for female labor.[5]

The government directed toward women most of the same recruitment appeals that it used to lure other groups into war industry. But some propaganda surrounded war work with an aura of glamor supposedly appealing to women; other publicity, eschewing fantasies about factory life, reminded women of the link between their jobs and the lives of their men in combat. "Since I have found the place where I can serve my country best, I should feel as if there were blood on my hands—his blood—if there were no oil on my hands today," a begrimed woman worker proclaimed from a 1943 recruiting advertisement in Detroit newspapers.[6] Women took jobs out of patriotism or as a way of escape from the tedium of separation from husband or fiancé. Like the migrants, women workers sought to enlarge their economic opportunities, but in many instances, women worked simply to maintain a standard of living equivalent to or even lower than that to which they had become accustomed before the war. Service wives often experienced long delays in receiving government allotment checks or found that the monthly stipend did not stretch far enough. The majority of the women worked to live, not to acquire luxuries.

Despite the declared manpower emergency, Michigan industry welcomed women with something less than enthusiasm. Manufacturers insisted that women simply were not the equal of men in factory work. Employers complained of the added costs of adjusting equipment used by women and of providing such facilities as separate washrooms. Once the women arrived, however, recalcitrant employers discovered that the necessary accommodations did not bring on bankruptcy and often promoted productivity. Observers noted that women's absentee rate was generally lower than that of men and that female motivation was generally higher. Briggs and Packard were among the many firms that hired women as counselors to the female workers. The counselor's mandate varied from plant to plant, but her duties usually included advising women of company policy and assisting them with personal or work-related problems. Management realized that women, after all, could learn quickly and well. Much was made of the ability of tiny feminine hands to deal with intricate components and of women's presumed aptitude for dull, repetitive tasks. Not infrequently, of course, the praise bestowed by management on women workers carried a condescending undertone implying that women still would never match men in industrial competition.[7]

Women workers faced a variety of discriminatory practices after they were admitted to the shop floor. Industry upgraded and promoted women much more slowly than men. Separate seniority lists often confined a woman's upward occupational mobility within a single all-female department. It was the wage issue, however, that caused the most controversy. Manufacturers customarily placed women in the lowest paying jobs and paid them less for the performance of work traditionally done by men. Michigan state law guaranteed women equal pay for "similar" work, but the statute was so vague that it was virtually unenforceable.[8] In September, 1942, the War Labor Board ruled against GM in an equal-pay case brought by the UAW and the United Electrical Workers (UE), and WLB General Order 16, issued in November, permitted companies to equalize male and female pay on a voluntary basis without reference to Washington.

The voluntary clauses of the WLB's order, together with qualifications later placed on the original GM decision, vitiated the Board's original initiative. Organized labor failed to mount a sustained campaign on the equal-pay issue. Employers proved adept in maintaining the sexual pay differential by such means as giving different titles to similar jobs or by changing job classifications from skilled to semiskilled. Despite government laxity, union indifference, and employer evasion, women's average weekly wages in Michigan rose $14.40 between October, 1942, and August, 1944, while male wages increased only an average of $9.90 per week.[9] By August, 1944, women in the state's engine turbine industry earned 94.3 percent as much as men, and females in the automobile industry had closed to within

89 percent of the male wage average. But the weekly wage gap at that time favored males by \$15.22, or more than seven hundred dollars a year.

Male workers and union leaders did not go out of their way to welcome women employees. Men vociferously protested and sometimes went on strike against policies favorable to women, such as the movement of women to better shifts that they were not entitled to by strict seniority.[10] Many women, however, undoubtedly agreed with May McKernan, a delegate to the 1942 UAW convention from a Detroit Plymouth local, who told her fellow unionists: "I should [not] like for the brothers to forget that when the subject of women comes up, they shouldn't say, 'Well, that's the woman's problem.' We are getting tired of men saying, 'Well, that's the woman's problem.'"[11] Women who sought union office usually found that men preferred them in their roles as coffee makers or volunteer typists. Belatedly, the UAW took steps to bring itself into closer touch with its estimated 250,000 dues-paying female workers. In early 1944 the union established a Women's Bureau within its War Policy Division to offer counseling and other forms of aid. Mildred Jeffrey, an experienced organizer in the clothing industry serving at the time on the staff of the War Production Board in Washington, was chosen to head the new department.[12] The union sponsored its first Women's Conference in Detroit that December, where the UAW women, among other actions, supported the CIO stand in opposition to the Equal Rights Amendment then pending in Congress. The extent to which the UAW accepted women, however, may be indicated by the fact that R. J. Thomas began his 1944 annual report to a union one-fifth female in membership with the customary salutation, "Dear Sirs and Brothers."[13]

The woman worker may not have been the beloved of labor and management, but she was the undoubted darling of the press and public. According to a typically gushing newspaper report of mid-1943, every Rosie who riveted at Detroit's N.A. Woodworth Company looked "like a cross between a campus queen and a Hollywood starlet."[14] The press closely scrutinized "the girls," their parties, and their late night meetings with male coworkers at local bars. Such glamorization may have served a useful purpose insofar as it attracted women to war work by assuring them it would not cost them their "feminine" qualities. But the publicity, with its constant emphasis on beauty and sexual innuendo, only reinforced traditional stereotypes.

Much of the excitement surrounding women workers was created by their special wearing apparel. For safety, industry forbade most female production workers to wear jewelry, nail polish, makeup, dresses, or Veronica Lake hairstyles. Snoods, low-heeled shoes, and slacks were "in." In the early 1940s, however, slacks were still garments to be worn only by a Marlene Dietrich or by the most chic of society trendsetters. In 1941 the *Detroit News*'s fashion writer cautiously suggested to her readers: "If you have a truly adventurous spirit, you might pioneer in introducing slacks on city streets. Try wearing them around your neighborhood. . . .Report to us how the neighbors take to the idea." On the right figure, a pair of slacks could cause a sensation; supervision at the Ford Highland Park plant docked a woman a half-hour's pay for wearing a pair of red slacks. The article of clothing in question, management insisted, created safety and production hazards because of its potential for distracting male workers. The case ultimately reached Harry Shulman, the umpire of grievances under the Ford-UAW contract, who decided in favor of the woman in June, 1944. Noting the absence of a company rule against vividly colored garments, Shulman opined, "It is common knowledge that wolves, unlike bulls, may be attracted by colors other than red and by various other enticements in the art and fit of female attire."[15]

Management often feared that the introduction of women workers would set off a sexual explosion. General Motors adopted a strict policy of firing any male supervisor and female employee who were discovered to be "fraternizing." The company justified its position on the grounds that improper sexual conduct by either party could impair labor-management relations and might expose the policy of hiring women to unfair criticism.[16] Unions sometimes proved as puritanical as management on the subject of sex; Flint UAW Local 599 voted in

April, 1943, to instruct committeemen to ignore grievances brought by any woman "indecent in her wearing apparel or actions."[17] The minutes of the meeting offer no clue as to how the female members of the local divided on the issue. Here and there, a woman might have gained a nickel an hour more with a sultry glance, and a foreman may have conditioned the promotion of a woman on her sexual favors, but despite rumors of illicit affairs and illegitimate pregnancies, moral standards in war industry remained remarkably impervious to propinquity.

The working woman of World War II was concerned with far more than the decency of her dress. An employee in plant or office, she was, in many instances, also the manager of a household. She shared with other citizens the discomforts of crowded housing and transportation, but the manpower and supply shortages particularly frustrated her efforts to maintain a home. Too often, she found empty shelves or locked doors at neighborhood groceries. A WPB study of August, 1943, estimated that 75 percent of female absenteeism in one plant could be attributed to inadequate laundry service. The Detroit WPB office announced in February, 1943, the appointment of local socialite and presidential in-law Dorothy Kemp Roosevelt as special coordinator for both female recruitment and for women's out-of-plant problems; little, however, was ever heard from her. In seeking to solve war-related community problems, the federal government rarely distinguished between matters of concern to the entire community and those that impinged especially upon women.[18]

The sudden entrance of thousands of women into industrial life raised many issues, and none carried more far-reaching social implications than the question of whether mothers should work, and the subsidiary problem of care for their children. Some mothers had always worked outside the home, but *Detroit News* women's advisor Nancy Brown stated the prevalent opinion about the practice in a 1940 reply to a woman undecided about seeking a job. "Your children are still of school age," Brown wrote. "It would not be possible for you to carry on two jobs, one outside your home and one inside."[19] Throughout the war, government agencies, social workers, educators, and politicians echoed this sentiment in varying words. Mothers who worked, it was maintained, might do enormous psychic harm to their young children and irreparable damage to the family. The WMC released its first official statement on the working-mother question during the spring of 1942: "The first responsibility of women with young children in war, as in peace, is to give suitable care in their own homes to their children."[20]

Among the arguments mustered on behalf of working mothers was the contention that their employment in war industry might reduce the migration into congested areas. There is no evidence, however, that such a relationship actually developed. The economic imperative certainly weighed heavily upon the woman who had to support her family while her husband was in the service. Even the 1942 WMC directive cited above insisted that no bar to employment be placed in the way of mothers with young children and that "the decision as to gainful employment should, in all cases, be an individual decision made by the woman herself. . . ."[21] When certain Michigan factories attempted to exclude younger mothers, management invariably discovered that many women lied about their family status rather than lose the chance for work.[22] Since women workers were being recruited and since an increasingly large number of mothers intended to work in spite of pleas to the contrary, something had to be done about their children, from whom they would be separated for a large part of each working day.

A few isolated schools had pioneered the concept of day care. Detroit's Merrill-Palmer School, founded in 1920 to instruct young women in home management and child development, opened the state's first nursery school in 1922. During the depression the Federal Emergency Relief Administration and the Works Progress (later the Work Projects) Administration (WPA) introduced day care on a nationwide basis by opening centers for the children of mothers receiving government assistance. The WPA centers were closed to regularly employed women. With the onset of the defense boom in the spring of 1941, officials in the Michigan Department of Social

Welfare (DSW) grew anxious about the "haphazard and un-desirable day nurseries" that were springing up. State welfare officials began to plan for the establishment of a committee to coordinate day-care service in hard hit Wayne County. Such a committee began work in Detroit in January, 1942, its leader-ship and expertise supplied in large part by Irene Murphy, a social worker and lecturer at Wayne University, and Dr. Edna Noble White, for twenty years the director of Merrill-Palmer. Thirty-seven communities across the state eventually orga-nized more or less active counterparts of the Wayne County body. In November, 1942, the Michigan government asked Dr. White to chair a State Day Care Committee (SDCC) under the sponsorship of the Michigan Council of Defense.[23]

Although Michigan took the initiative in setting up an ad-ministrative structure for day care, no network of nursery cen-ters could be organized without federal assistance. Various government agencies, including the United States Children's Bureau (USCB) and the Federal Works Agency, examined the day-care question throughout 1941, and in February, 1942, the FWA received permission to use Lanham Act funds for the construction and maintenance of child-care centers for the children of working mothers. Washington eventually spent nearly fifty-three million dollars for hundreds of day-care cen-ters established primarily in major production areas. Shortly after Pearl Harbor, the WPA opened its centers to children of working mothers and to youngsters with a parent in the armed forces, and this expanded program continued until the agency's demise in mid-1943.

By January, 1945, twenty-eight Michigan communities, most of them in the four-county Detroit area, were sponsoring 179 child-care centers at an estimated cost for the first six months of the year of $1,694,828, of which 60 percent was provided by the FWA. The most popular facility was the day nursery for two- to five-year olds. Practices varied from area to area, but most centers operated continuously for twelve hours, from six-thirty or seven o'clock in the morning onward. They served three meals a day, offered organized recreation directed by nursery teachers and volunteers, and provided cots or beds for afternoon naps. Extended school services allowed mothers to leave children six to fourteen years of age for care immediately before and after school. These centers or "canteens" usually were located within the school building itself. A program for night care proved unsuccessful in Detroit, but similar services apparently worked well in Ypsilanti and Saginaw. Several communities sought to obtain care for infants by encouraging nonworking women to become foster mothers, taking as many as three or four infants into their homes for more individualized attention. Four Michigan cities ran counseling services to guide mothers to the best available child care, and the Wayne County committee organized an elaborate information clearinghouse, the Children's War Service, in April, 1943.[24]

Day-care advocates supported their demands with a flood of statistics suggesting a great unmet need. The Wayne County committee estimated in early 1943 that local war plants and civilian industry employed some sixty thousand mothers, who had forty-five thousand children in need of care. The friends of day care also noted many pathetic instances of individual deprivation. Thousands of children roamed the streets of industrial communities unable to enter homes locked for the day by their war-worker parents. More fortunate youngsters carried the housekey on a string fastened around the neck. Yet those in need responded to day care in disappointingly small numbers. Nationally, Lanham Act programs served a mere hundred thousand children, perhaps a tenth of those eligible, and far fewer than the total of youngsters sheltered by Great Britain's more elaborate system of child care. To be sure, the number of day-care children in Michigan steadily increased, reaching 6,024 in early 1945, while the number of employed women steadily declined. But the same surveys that seemed to affirm the necessity for day care consistently reported that no more than 5 to 10 percent of the presumably needy youngsters were actually enrolled in nursery school programs.[25]

An analysis of the Michigan day-care failure casts light on the underlying forces in society that actively or unwittingly placed limits on wartime change. Bureaucratic in-fighting and political opposition at the national level hobbled the day-care

program from the outset. Neither the Lanham Act nor its supplementary titles mentioned day care, and the entire nursery
program, redolent as it was with overtones of New Deal exper-
imentation, was generally unpopular on Capitol Hill. A bill
revamping and expanding federally sponsored day care died
in Congress in 1943. In several Michigan communities, the
local Council of Social Agencies, which favored day care, fought
with a county MCD committee that did not. In 1944 the state
legislature defeated a program sponsored by the State Day
Care Committee to establish counseling centers and to provide
state funded child-care services in war-impacted areas wher-
ever local initiative failed to do so. Other newly enacted laws
brought private day-care centers under state licensing authority, but represented no fundamental state commitment to
day care. Charged with the major responsibility for the financing and operation of day-care centers, local school boards, usually strapped for cash, objected to paying for a program so
costly and so socially questionable.[26]

Administrative and legal problems also dogged day care in
Michigan. A federal regulation prohibited school districts from
asking for Lanham Act funds until school buildings reached
200 percent of capacity, by which time most such schools no
longer had room for a day-care center. Once a locality applied
for government assistance, it had to surmount seven separate
state and federal reviews before approval was granted. A 1943
study of Detroit day-care needs revealed that many of the centers were poorly located, improperly staffed, and inadequately
administered. The statistics of need the day-care defenders
cited were subject to wild fluctuations: the Census Bureau's
sample survey of the Detroit-Willow Run area in 1944 counted
only half as many children eligible for day care as previous
compilations had indicated. Reflecting on the vicissitudes that
beset the state's child-care effort, the supervisor of the DSW's
Children's Division, Gunnar Dybwad, concluded in November,
1945, that "Michigan has no reason to be particularly proud
of its day care program."[27]

Michigan industry did little to accommodate the working
mother. Hudson established a center for the children of moth-

ers employed in all three of its Detroit plants, but nowhere in Michigan were there day-care centers equal to the highly publicized programs in the west coast shipbuilding industry.[28] Although Michigan labor generally supported day care and Irene Murphy credited the UAW as the driving force behind her Wayne County committee, the unions apparently allowed their female members to carry on alone the battle for expanded child-care services, the struggle being seen as only another "woman's problem." Neither labor nor management seemed eager to take the steps, admittedly complex, required to assign working mothers with young children to convenient shifts.

Day-care specialists spent most of the war years attempting to explain the evident lack of maternal interest in nursery programs. The UAW claimed, with much justification, that many women could not afford day-care fees. Weekly costs in Detroit varied from six dollars at a city-run center to sixteen dollars for a foster home, no small sums for that majority of working women who made less than the average of $47 per week earned by Detroit female employees in 1943. Other observers emphasized the apathy of working mothers as well as their lack of knowledge of programs available to them. Women often resented having to deal with social workers and counselors; middle-class mothers especially perceived day care, with its WPA antecedents, to be a welfare measure and shied away from mixing their children with youngsters from the lower classes.[29]

At base, most women rejected day-care services because they preferred to have their children cared for by relatives, neighbors, or friends—or not at all—rather than by strangers in a nursery or a canteen. When an interviewer asked a group of Detroit working mothers why they did not avail themselves of the local day-care program, she received such replies as the following: "I wouldn't have a stranger"; "No one could be better than my mother"; and, "The baby might catch a disease in a nursery."[30] Such comments in part reflected their knowledge of the deficiencies of the Detroit day-care program, and perhaps a more adequate service might have been better patronized. With the exception of a handful of activists, it was the child-welfare professional, not the mother, who demanded day care in World War II. Social workers and psychologists were convinced that many children suffered grave emotional harm because mothers provided insufficient nurture on the spurious grounds that self-care was "good experience" and that young-sters could "fend for themselves." Yet the child-care experts probably confused and distressed some mothers by constantly arguing over such issues as the desirability of foster care as opposed to group care or the merits and deficiencies of the Lanham Act program. Day-care advocates, moreover, under-cut their case by agreeing with opponents that the working mother could pose a threat to the child.[31]

The Michigan day-care program faced termination with the approach of victory. Lanham Act authorizations were sched-uled to expire on June 30, 1945. During the summer and fall the FWA granted several reprieves, agreeing in October to fi-nance a curtailed operation through July, 1946. A group of two hundred mothers led by Irene Murphy petitioned the De-troit Board of Education in late August to maintain a skeleton system of twenty-five centers, and on September 26, after the Common Council guaranteed the necessary funding, the Board approved the mothers' proposal. Although the State Day Care Committee lingered on, the Wayne County panel, the most vigorous proponent of child care in Michigan, wound up its affairs on November 30, 1945.[32]

Day-care centers constituted what might have been, in Eleanor Straub's words, "the most significant social experiment of the war years."[33] Child-welfare specialists learned through their wartime experience much about the aims and realities of day care. A sufficient number of Detroit mothers became in-terested in the service to support a small program into the late 1940s.[34] Limited, well-run nursery schools gained a measure of acceptance among the postwar middle class, but the concept of large-scale day care for the children of working mothers never caught on. Nothing happened during World War II to war-rant abandonment of the belief that the mother—and the mother alone—bore the principal responsibility for the up-bringing of her children.

The failure of working mothers to make sufficient use of nursery facilities eventually relegated the question of day care to a position of secondary importance. A problem of greater import, and one that could not be swept aside, was the postwar status of working women. In August, 1942, the author of a letter to the *Detroit News* mused: "We have quite a number of intelligent men devising ways and means of getting women in on all the factory and war jobs so we boys can go knock off a Jap and a Heinie, but I really want to meet the chap who is intelligent enough to get them out again when we boys come back." Evidence accumulated to document female intentions of remaining at work. The Women's Bureau reported in May, 1945, that 75 percent of all Detroit working women desired some form of postwar employment. The proportion rose to 80 percent among women employed before Pearl Harbor and fell to no less than 60 percent among former housewives.[35]

Such surveys, of course, indicated what women thought they might do, not what they actually would do, after V-J Day. A large number of women declared against future employment if their husbands could support them or if men were in need of work. A national consensus, moreover, developed rapidly and strongly in support of the contention that women should not remain at work in their wartime numbers once peace returned. The federal government took pains to emphasize the temporary nature of war work and did nothing to encourage women in their aspirations for peacetime jobs. A spate of books and articles appeared, increasing in volume as victory neared, picturing a happy future for women in wedded bliss and in homes chock-a-block with long unavailable consumer goods. Betty Allie, chairwoman of the Michigan Unemployment Compensation Commission, spoke for the majority when she said in November, 1943: "When the period of postwar adjustment comes, and their men come home . . . you will see women returning naturally to their homes. A woman's first interests are her home, her husband and their children. . . ." Women without family ties or who had lost husbands during the war were entitled to employment, Allie continued, "but there need be no fear that all [women] will compete for the postwar job.

They will look on this period in their lives as an interlude. . . . Women will always be women."[36]

When production cutbacks accelerated during the spring and summer of 1945, women were severed from employment at a rate approximately double that of men. Women composed one of the largest elements in the low-seniority pool ordinarily laid off first, but management had other ways of ridding itself of unwanted females. A government survey of conditions in Michigan as of September noted that some employers were shuffling work assignments to give women the sort of heavy lifting jobs that they were either legally barred from performing or that they might not want. By November, 1945, Michigan's nonfarm female workforce stood at 525,000, a quarter of a million less than the wartime peak. Female manufacturing employment in Detroit fell to one-fourth of its wartime high, a mere twenty thousand more than in 1940. Although many women acquiesced in this treatment, others protested. In September a delegation of UAW women confronted the union's International Executive Board with charges of discrimination by management and organized labor alike. Local unions, indeed, sometimes suppressed female grievances and appeals. Preoccupied with assimilating returning veterans and with its forthcoming struggle with GM, the UAW gave little comfort to those women who turned to it for help.[37]

No woman could avoid the war. It sat in her kitchen each day, an unwelcome guest, while she prepared meals that lacked once abundant staples and now featured such oddities as sweetbreads. The war awaited her at the grocery store, where she struggled to keep straight her red and blue ration stamps. Advertisers attempted to win the homemaker's patronage by linking the most mundane of household products to the global conflict. "Commandeer every empty inch of shelf space you can find to store that precious wartime food you've been putting up so patriotically. But don't forget the greatest help in keeping those shelves spotless and sanitary—Royledge Paper Shelving."[38] The government exhorted her to give freely of her kitchen fat, silk hose (for parachutes and ammunition bags), and her time. Women rolled bandages, kept the files at draft boards, sorted gas ration coupons, learned fire fighting and gunhandling techniques, and served as hostesses at USO centers. Although complete statistics are not available, it is certain that several thousand Michigan women undertook the ultimate in wartime volunteer duty available to their sex by joining the Women's Army Auxiliary Corps and its comparable female counterparts in the several military services.

Every woman having a relative in the armed forces came to know pride, doubt, anxiety, or grief in some measure. An abrupt increase in female drunkenness in Detroit signaled the rising need to drown anxiety in alcoholic forgetfulness. No group of women suffered more day-to-day tension than the wives of servicemen. Phyllis Aronson interviewed eighty-six Detroit service wives in 1943–1944, most of whom were in their twenties and had given birth to their first children following their husbands' inductions. About one-third of the women worked, generally in poorly paid employment that, together with the monthly allotment, provided a comfortable standard of living, albeit one reduced in quality from the prewar years. For economic reasons or because they could not otherwise cope with child and home on their own, some women returned to their parents, often regressing to the role of immature daughter. Although they frequently complained of difficulties in securing adequate food and clothing for their babies, most of the women refused to ask for assistance from service agencies, including the Red Cross. None of the women, however, had allowed their children to suffer, and most of the wives maintained a cheerful front, determinedly declaring that others had it far worse than they. But the mask slipped occasionally to reveal the desperation underneath. "It's a lonesome life," said one wife. "You don't live, you just get along."[39]

The agony of wartime separation strengthened the resolve of many marriage partners to hold fast to their relationships, but in countless instances the war heightened the centrifugal forces already tearing individual marriages apart. The military's summons provided couples with the chance to dissolve marriages long dead except in name. At the same time, thousands of hasty marriages were contracted before boyfriends or fiancés shipped out; later, alone and frightened, many women abruptly realized that they had wed almost total strangers. Once separated from a woman he might barely know, the GI found his wedding ring an encumbrance rather than a token of shared love; and for all the happily married wives who waited patiently at home, there were other women who understood that a terrible mistake had been made, a mistake too often compounded by childbirth. Infidelity represented one way out for men and women seeking simple sexual gratification, a deeper sense of closeness, or both. But since the public regarded a service wife's unfaithfulness as a form of moral sabotage against her husband, women—especially war workers—received far more criticism than males for such conduct. Since soldiers could not be divorced until they could appear in court, many women issued informal decrees in "Dear John" letters. Michigan divorces meanwhile climbed from 12,054 in 1940 to 29,158 in 1946.[40] Service separations alone did not account for the increasing rupture of marriages. Prosperity afforded many women the economic security to strike out on their own, ending financially dependent relationships.

The genteel clubleaders and lady college presidents who functioned as national wartime spokeswomen for their sex submitted, with more or less grace, to male notions of women's traditional place. Even if these women had taken a militantly feminist stand on such issues as participation in manpower planning or the achievement of equal pay for equal work, they would have been generals without an army, since the mass of American women did not grasp at the opportunities for liberation that war offered. It was during the war that the apotheosis of the unliberated female, Miss America, became a figure of national prominence and respect. At times it seemed that every nubile young woman was competing for a spot in the pin-up parade. As Eleanor Straub observes: "the average woman held an essentially negative view of the conflict and saw it as a matter of production and military strategy rather than a contest of values and ideas."[41] In other words, women perceived World War II very much as men did.

The war nonetheless induced profound changes in the lives

of millions of individual women. Not all of these changes were for the good. The war took from some wives and mothers their cherished husbands or sons, and, too frequently, never gave them back. Some women ventured into the marketplace only to retreat confused and defeated by the industrial environment. Others found the strength with which to face lonely years of separation. "I have learned—in three difficult lessons—to take a dead vacuum cleaner apart and make it run again," a Detroit service wife exulted in 1943.[42] Many married women found in work a path to a renewed self-worth that did not require rejection of established family ties. For them, the war years were ones of exhilaration and achievement. "I no longer stooge for my family," one woman wrote. "Everyone has to look after themselves. I am once again a person."[43] For the women of Michigan, the war years had been filled with ambiguity.

★ 2 ★

The nation conscripted its youth in both a figurative and a real sense. The child became one of the chief symbols of wartime propaganda. "We are fighting again for human freedom, and especially for the future of our children in a free world," the USCB's Advisory Committee on Children in Wartime wrote to introduce its 1942 "Children's Charter."[44] Youngsters from first grader to high school senior were designated as "home-front soldiers," the shock troops of myriad bond campaigns and scrap drives. Young men between the ages of eighteen and twenty-one, spoken of so often and so glibly as "the leaders of tomorrow," were suddenly perceived as the soldiers of today. The war focused new attention on the problems of young people, but heightened public interest would lead to no important changes in attitudes toward youth or their concerns.

Children were as engrossed in the war as their parents, although the youngsters understood little about more complex issues of the conflict. "Instead of drawing steamboats," a Detroit day-care teacher said of her two- to five-year-old charges, "they draw submarines and battleships. Instead of playing Indians, they play soldiers fighting the war."[45] Besides engaging in such patterns of play, youngsters immersed themselves in war-saturated comic books, radio serials, and Saturday matinees. Children were in a constant state of excitation, a condition that often produced deeply disturbing side effects. Some boys and girls cowered under beds in fear of enemy attack, and children with fathers in the armed forces were the prey of conflicting and frequently frightening emotions—pride, fear, guilt, hatred, and love—all directed at the absent parent. Boys approaching military age confronted a special fear that they often sought to cover with an air of aggressiveness and assertive masculinity. The young girl, too, faced a perilous future as she sought womanhood in a world filled with new dangers and attractions.

Like businessmen, workers, farmers, and blacks, youngsters were expected to obey relevant wartime restrictions and to enlist in patriotic programs open to or especially designed for them. Washington, however, did not feel compelled to offer compensating commitments or to grant substantial rewards to children in return for their sacrifices or for their acquiescence in government policies. To be sure, government handed out countless inexpensive armbands, badges, and certificates of commendation to the millions of children who performed menial but vital chores in the collection of salvage and the vending of war stamps. Children received direct assistance in the form of new schools, recreation halls, and health centers, usually financed and constructed with federal funds. But such facilities typically were built not with the needs of children in mind but as a means of encouraging their parents either to remain in or to move to a critical production area. Federal authorities, moreover, were not behindhand in requiring children to make equal or greater sacrifices than adults; the government never ordered homeowners to double the occupancy of their dwellings, but insisted that schools be jammed to two hundred percent of capacity whenever possible.

Government found children to be the only social group that did not use the war emergency to obtain—or to extort—increased advantage for itself. Children, of course, had no way to organize themselves into a pressure group and necessarily relied on adult spokesmen to state youth's case. The national authority, through parents, teachers, and scout leaders, simply told the children what to do, and—by and large—they did it, with little complaint and generally with unrestrained enthusiasm. For example, twenty-one Ann Arbor youngsters, age three to fifteen, organized themselves under adult supervision in 1943 as the "Junior Commandos" to sell bonds and to do good deeds around their neighborhood. Youths frequently demanded to know what more they might do to help, and adults often were unable to provide an adequate answer.[46]

The Michigan public education system was, for all practical purposes, completely subordinated to and reshaped by wartime demands. Elementary schools encouraged their pupils to assist in government conservation programs, to stay patriotically healthy, and to study the meaning and progress of the war (although teachers avoided discussion of harsher realities such as death in battle). High schools emphasized science, mathematics, and military instruction. Induction-bound seniors could take courses in aerial navigation and preflight mechanics. The teaching of American history entered something of a golden age, for knowledge of the past supposedly buttressed an understanding of why the nation was at war. The participation of girls in war activities was generally confined to instruction in first aid and home economics courses revamped to stress nutrition and consumer education. ROTC drill or volunteer service in the High School Victory Corps was available to those students not already surfeited with war-related pursuits.

"Every school during this war period should consider itself a subsidiary of West Point, Annapolis, or some other military school," said Michigan Superintendent of Public Instruction Eugene Elliott in 1944.[47] The state's colleges and universities most closely approximated Elliott's ideal. Thousands of uniformed men poured onto campus, the soldiers or sailors passing through the Army Specialized Training Program or the Navy's V-12 courses. School administrators introduced trimester or quarter systems to enable students to earn a degree more rapidly. Female enrollment at the university level began to overtake and exceed that of males. Football was abandoned for the duration at East Lansing for lack of talent and coaches, but continued at Ann Arbor. The federal Office of Scientific Research and Development placed millions of dollars in secret war research contracts with the state's larger universities for projects that included radar and the atomic bomb.

Deciding that wartime education was both emotionally and financially unrewarding, thousands of restless young people left school to seek work. Before the war the use of child labor in Michigan had been slowly declining; by 1943 state education officials estimated that 120,000 children had dropped out of school to take jobs. Draft-eligible seniors were particularly likely to leave school, often displaying a familiar pattern of anxiety by rapidly taking and then quitting several jobs in a row. Most children remained in personal service or retail occupations (hourly wages for young store help rose from thirty-five cents in peacetime to fifty or sixty-five cents by 1944), but increasing numbers of teenagers went into war industry, where they made as much as $1.50 per hour. After-school employment became so prevalent that the Detroit Board of Education devised a plan to allow students to count work experience for as much as one-fifth of each semester's total class credit. Some children sought jobs to make a greater contribution to the war effort, but patriotism generally ranked low as a motivating force in their decisions, the desire for spending money or the need to contribute to family income counting as the most important considerations.[48]

State education officials naturally voiced concern at the rise of child labor. At the end of the 1944 vacation season, Superintendent Elliott joined with school officials around the nation in a concerted campaign to persuade youngsters to return to class.[49] Such appeals had some effect, but if a child presented evidence, legal or forged, that he or she was sixteen, the local school board was obliged to issue a work permit. To cope with the manpower shortage and the reality of youthful jobseeking, the state Department of Labor and Industry gradually relaxed many restrictions surrounding the employment of minors. It is not clear to what extent employers violated state child labor laws or the degree to which children connived in such violations but human nature and inadequate state supervision guaranteed a certain amount of malfeasance.

To parents, educators, and politicians alike, the wartime rise of juvenile delinquency seemed a far greater threat to young people and to society in general than the increase of child labor. Juvenile authorities predicted that involvement in the war would incite a rise in deviant behavior, and juvenile delinquency statistics bore them out. Truancy rates shot upward, and Detroit authorities noted a 113 percent increase in apprehensions of youthful runaways, who came to the city from other parts of Michigan or from other states between 1940 and 1943. Delinquency mounted most steeply in war industry areas and declined slightly in rural districts. Children under the age of ten began to account for a greater share of youthful crime than they had before the war. Female delinquency rates shot up some two to three times faster than male rates (girls constituted between 20 and 25 percent of all youthful Detroit offenders) and the crime rate among youthful blacks rose higher than that for white juveniles (young blacks composed about one quarter of all delinquents in Detroit). Theft, property destruction, truancy, "ungovernableness," and various types of sexual misconduct were the principal offenses committed by delinquents.[50]

Everywhere the average citizen looked, young people seemed to be publicly and defiantly up to no good. In November, 1942, a youth gang war erupted in Detroit, bringing local authorities face to face with the magnitude of the wartime delinquency problem for the first time. Waves of vandalism hit several Michigan cities during the summer of 1943, and the race riot of that June produced a disturbingly large crop of young arrestees. It hardly seemed to matter that the total number of youthful malefactors represented only a handful of the state's children. Both during and after the war, moreover, observers declared that it was the awareness of delinquency on the part of press, public, and officials that had increased, not actual delinquency. This heightened awareness stemmed from a compassionate concern for child welfare as well as from the elevation of juvenile crime from its prewar status as simple antisocial behavior to the level of unpatriotic activity.[51]

Female sexual delinquency attracted more public attention than any other form of youthful misconduct. Under the heady influence of wartime excitement and lured by the glamor of a uniform, girls as young as thirteen and fourteen became romantically involved and sometimes had sexual intercourse with soldiers several years older than they. Many young females felt it their patriotic duty to provide sexual relief for presumably combat-bound GIs. The number of these "V girls" and the incidence of venereal disease increased together. Detroit plain-clothes policewomen scoured the city's bus terminals and bars in search of underage girls headed for or already in trouble. Those apprehended routinely underwent an often humiliating examination for VD; boys received such tests far less frequently. The soldier, moreover, often escaped any brush with the law and so evaded responsibility for an act to which he was, at least, an equal contributor. First offenses in Detroit did not establish criminal records, but habitual offenders were eventually judged delinquent.[52]

Everyone seemed to have an opinion regarding the cause or causes of the wartime increase in delinquency. Many experts attributed the rise to a lowering of barriers against expressions of hatred and aggressive impulses and to the disregard of moral standards typified by the tacit approval of sexual license for soldiers. Other authorities emphasized the disruption of the life of children because of migration and the unsettled atmosphere of fatherless homes. The manpower shortage also deprived communities of needed police and social workers. Paul Wiers found that the revival of economic prosperity correlated most highly with the increased occurrence of delinquency and that youth crime per capita was no higher in the 1940–43 period than it was during the boom years 1926–29. Prosperity, Wiers noted, made more money and property available to be stolen, and the absence from home of mothers and fathers reduced parents' ability to control the conduct of their children.[53] Parental neglect came in for a major share of the blame for the youth crisis.

Wartime conditions added a few new considerations to the ongoing discussion of the causes of delinquency, but the debate generally continued along lines established during the previous four decades. On the one hand, psychoanalytic proponents saw delinquency as an individualized phenomenon, best dealt with by personal guidance and therapy. On the other hand, many social workers and their sociologist allies perceived youth crime to be the result of a bad environment, a problem susceptible to community-oriented solutions. The environmentalists temporarily had secured the upper hand in the argument by 1940, when the White House Conference on Children in Democracy came down largely on the side of community action to prevent delinquency.

Most of the solutions for delinquency proposed or adopted during the war bore the earmark of the environmental approach. Judge George Martin of the Dearborn Municipal Court created a stir in October, 1943, when he found Alonzo and Nora Ansell guilty of child neglect for allowing their fifteen-year-old daughter Annis to secure a forged birth certificate for employment purposes and for leaving their younger children without supervision. Martin sentenced the father to a fifty-dollar fine and five weekends in jail and threatened the mother with a ninety-day jail term if she did not quit her job immediately, which she did. Although Martin won praise, few judges followed his example, since a neglected child remained neglected if his parents were incarcerated. Several communities enacted or revived curfew ordinances to control nocturnal youth activities, and since the provision of recreation appeared to be a way of getting children off the streets, many towns and cities set up teenage centers, canteens, or "hang-outs." Young people themselves often took the initiative in developing the centers, and by mid-1945 some 216 facilities were in operation around the state. They varied considerably in quality and size,

but most centers offered a jukebox, dance floor, food, nonal-
coholic drinks, and a lounge, perhaps equipped with a ping-
pong or pool table.[54]

Governor Harry Kelly placed himself at the head of the
forces combating delinquency in Michigan. A former Boy Scout
executive and father of six children, Kelly came to office in
January, 1943, pledged to overhaul the state's juvenile affairs
bureaucracy, in which some thirty-six agencies shared overlap-
ping responsibility for youth. Kelly's principal goal was the reform of the antiquated county agent system, established by
state law in 1873. Appointed until 1939 solely by county pro-
bate judges (and thereafter by the governor with the advice of
those judges) to supervise delinquent youngsters, most county
agents were political hacks who cared little about their jobs or
the children for whom they were responsible.[55] Outside of the
four most populous counties in the state, no county in Michigan employed a skilled, full-time child-welfare worker. To focus public attention on delinquency, Kelly sponsored a statewide
conference that met in Lansing in September and appointed
a committee to make recommendations for legislative action.
"The problem demands an immediate and realistic approach,"
Kelly said. "I want to make it plain that this is no spasmodic
gesture, but an attempt to organize a new approach to the delinquency problem."[56]

The legislature avoided the enactment of harsh legal penalties for "parental delinquency," probably fearing retaliation by
angry mothers and fathers at the polls that November. Since
the various "courthouse gangs" opposed the certification of
county agents, the lawmakers buried the bill. Still, Kelly could
claim a significant achievement; the legislature enacted a revised juvenile court code and made school attendance compul-
sory until the age of sixteen, parents being charged with
responsibility for their children's attendance. A visiting teacher
(school social worker) program was approved, more child-
guidance clinics were funded, and county agents in all counties of more than thirty thousand population were placed on
salary instead of per diem expenses. In 1945 the legislature
created a statewide network for the reporting of uniform and

accurate delinquency statistics and established a Michigan Youth
Guidance Commission. These measures put Michigan in the
forefront of those states that attempted to meet the wartime
delinquency crisis. Most counties and many communities organized youth guidance committees, marking the first time
that some counties had faced up to their youth problem.
Michigan's accomplishments had been achieved with only minimal assistance from federal agencies and federal power.[57]

Even before the first major Kelly proposals became law, police and education authorities began to notice an apparent decline in delinquency.[58] Local and state officials were quick to
credit the establishment of recreation centers or the passage of
the governor's program for the downturn, but other factors,
largely beyond the control of Michigan authorities, were more
significant. Youthful employment steadily increased throughout 1943 and 1944, the draft removed substantial numbers of
eighteen- and nineteen-year-olds from the scene, and the extent of migration decreased. Also, if it was true that it was public perception of delinquency that had increased rather than
the rate of delinquency itself, the public's perception that
something was being done may have induced the belief that
the problem was nearing solution.

Although both the concern about wartime delinquency and
the desire to do something about it were sincere, Michigan's
approach to the youth question, at least in retrospect, seems to
have been that superficial, "spasmodic gesture" Governor Kelly
hoped to avoid. In a 1951 study of the youth guidance movement, Ralph Daniel noted that the various gubernatorial committees and study groups dealing with delinquency were either
entirely composed of or dominated by state agency heads, each
with his own interest to protect, while substantial participation
by private nongovernment groups, concerned citizens, and—
needless to say—young people, was not actively encouraged.
Despite all the talk about parental responsibility and the need
to bolster the home, the state neither supported child study
groups nor instituted altered case work procedures that might
have raised questions about parental care of children. The
provision of more recreation, although undoubtedly a sound

idea, briefly took the child away from the home environment that was presumably to blame for his or her delinquent behavior without in any way changing that environment. The recreation program generated impressive statistics—numbers of centers opened, numbers of youths served, and so forth—that were politically useful but socially meaningless.

"The results show," Daniel writes, "that instead of a new well-rounded approach, the Commission promoted . . . accepted approaches each independent of the other." The governor, of course, had stressed the need for immediate action rather than for innovation, and the meager results of his program may simply reflect the bankruptcy of "old approaches." The Michigan Youth Guidance Commission held a few perfunctory meetings and then ceased to function when its legislative mandate expired in 1947. Stimulated by the wartime experience, public awareness of delinquency continued at a high level in the postwar years, but awareness did not necessarily imply understanding. "The general attitude of the tax-paying public toward [delinquency] is a pitiful sight to behold," psychiatrist Fritz Redl and social worker David Wineman, both active in Detroit's wartime delinquency programs, wrote in 1951. "We either get 'tough' . . . or we become sentimental and delusional. . . .On two issues . . . both camps are agreed: first, that somebody ought to give us a solution soon . . . ; second, that such a solution has to be simple and inexpensive."[59]

Both the general public and political leaders often expressed consternation at an apparent overturn of traditional values brought on by the war. In some undefined but ominous fashion, the war appeared to threaten the future of the American family. There were observers, however, who maintained a more optimistic outlook. "The family is in for a hard time ahead," Ray Baber, a specialist in the field of family relations, warned in 1943, "but it is in no danger of eclipse, even under the extreme test of total war. The immediate outlook is not bright, but the long-term view is encouraging."[60] After their examination of Willow Run, certainly one of the more chaotic of wartime boomtowns, Lowell Carr and James Stermer concluded that, although the new community handled some social problems poorly, families experienced no more disruption than if they had lived in more settled surroundings. For every family shattered by war in some manner, another family achieved economic security as the result of wartime prosperity. None of the major wartime phenomena affecting the family—migration, the employment of women, and the separation from fathers—was new to American life. Their combined force, from 1939 to 1945, simply accelerated the continuing disintegration of the family unit, which had been underway for decades.

Chapter 7

End and Beginning: Victory and Reconversion

★ 1 ★

At last it was over. Americans had experienced shock, grief, and anger at the news from Pearl Harbor, followed by frustration while the production machinery geared up at home and the military staved off defeat in the Pacific. Then the people had worked and waited through the long slow push against enemies on fronts half a world apart. The factory whistles blew and the church bells rang for a delirious moment on D Day and eleven months later Adolf Hitler and his Reich were gone. The celebration on V-E Day was subdued because the people knew that Japan still must be defeated and because they had not yet recovered from the death of President Roosevelt in mid-April. The casualties of that summer's island campaigns were the worst of the entire war, and everyone expected a desperate struggle to the end. And then, in two stunning atomic flashes, it was over.

A false peace alert on August 13 precipitated short-lived horn-honking demonstrations in Detroit. The next morning war plants and stores began to close on rumors of Japanese capitulation. Truman, the new president, confirmed the news in a White House broadcast at seven that evening. The jubilant throng in downtown Detroit stretched nearly a mile from the river to Grand Circus Park. Fifty thousand persons jammed downtown Lansing to watch fireworks. In Hastings, a small community in the southwestern corner of the state, a proces-

214

sion of cars drove back and forth through the town's three-block business section. All across Michigan the air throbbed to the sound of whistles, bells, horns, sirens, and shouts. There were few reports of disorderly behavior; the people danced, waved flags, and tossed confetti, and the soldiers and sailors kissed every girl they could find. Thankful worshippers filled the churches. But those who passed Thompson's Restaurant in Flint were reminded that the day was not glorious for all. Inside a young woman sobbed hysterically. That morning she had learned of her fiance's death in combat.[1]

To the average person the single most consequential result of victory was the return of the GIs. Many Detroit women toasted one another on V-J night with a heartfelt, "Drink up, sister, the men are coming back!" In reality, the men had been coming back since the fall of 1943 when wounded vets and servicemen released for dependency reasons began arriving in the state at a rate of seventy-five to one hundred a day. The bulk of the discharges naturally came after the cessation of hostilities; 245,000 low-point Michigan servicemen awaited discharge well into 1946. More than 50 percent of the half million discharged Michigan GIs made the four-county Detroit metropolitan area their destination.[2]

After reunion with families and friends, most veterans turned their thoughts toward resuming their old jobs or seeking new occupations. The issue of reemployment rights for returning servicemen was first raised in 1939 when the UAW sought the inclusion of a "war clause" in its contract with Chrysler. The Selective Service Act of 1940 guaranteed reemployment to any honorably discharged and physically sound veteran who applied to his former employer within forty (later ninety) days of separation from the armed forces. The law excluded temporary employees, however, and thus sharply restricted its application. Michigan state government assigned reemployment committeemen to each local draft board in 1941 and again from 1943 onward to assist men mustered out of the service. Because of the wartime manpower shortage in Michigan industry, returning servicemen required no aid in securing jobs, but thousands of vets received help from branch offices of the United States Employment Service during the early months of reconversion.[3]

The original conscription law was murky on the relationship of reemployment rights to seniority, but in May, 1944, Selective Service advised its local boards that eligible veterans enjoyed an absolute claim on their old jobs regardless of seniority and, once rehired, were immune from layoff for a year except for good cause or unless their plant closed completely. That October, in an effort to modify the ruling, the UAW's International Executive Board approved a model contract clause that awarded seniority to GI autoworkers on a month-per-month basis for time in the military, and authorized a similar seniority grant to veterans not employed at the time of induction, following the six-month probation period as new employees. The reemployment-versus-seniority issue was not definitively decided until the Supreme Court declared the draft agency's policy regarding veteran reemployment unconstitutional in 1946. The UAW won the inclusion of the model clause in its Chrysler contract the same year but was compelled to settle with Ford and General Motors for vague language or further negotiations on the subject. The reemployment question ultimately faded in significance since, as Davis R. B. Ross points out, only a small number of veterans—perhaps 20 percent— were entitled to reemployment rights, and both labor and management wished to be fair to these men.[4]

The Servicemen's Readjustment Act of June, 1944, provided unprecedented benefits for the returning veteran. The law entitled the qualified vet to receive low-interest loans, a year's unemployment compensation if necessary, and payment of room, board, tuition, and books for education or job training, together with a monthly assistance allowance while in school. No section of the GI Bill of Rights more profoundly affected the nation's future than did the act's educational provisions. Thousands of veterans flocked to colleges and universities in Michigan; in September, 1946, forty-seven thousand ex-servicemen were enrolled at thirty-five state institutions of higher learning. Each campus spawned its "Vetville," a motley collection of trailers, Quonset huts, and temporary housing units.

(The University of Michigan housed its student veterans in homes acquired from Willow Run projects.) The veterans who graduated from college on the GI Bill in the immediate postwar years eventually comprised a considerable portion of the American business and political elite.[5]

The legislature created an Office of Veterans' Affairs (OVA) to coordinate the various services offered the ex-GI. Under OVA auspices counseling centers were established throughout the state to assist former servicemen to obtain state or federal benefits to which they were entitled. A million-dollar Veterans' Trust Fund financed an emergency hospitalization program, initiated in June, 1945, that paid surgical and other medical bills for thousands of veterans. The state set up a network of veterans' clinics, a psychological readjustment center in Ann Arbor, and a vocational retraining school near Battle Creek. Dozens of veterans' institutes in local high schools offered education and job training below the college level. The state granted veterans additional perquisites that ranged from employment preference to liberalized licensing requirements. Never before in American history had state or nation done so much to secure the future well-being of a particular group of citizens.[6]

Although the end of the war and the return of the veterans occasioned an outpouring of unbounded joy, fear and uncertainty soon returned to cloud the thoughts of many of the happiest celebrants of V-J Day. Millions feared that wartime prosperity was only temporary and wondered whether the nation's postwar economy could provide sufficient employment with adequate wages or would slip once again into the slough of depression. That question gripped the popular mind from the earliest days of the defense period. A few were optimistic; more typical, however, was the conviction expressed in July, 1943, by Michigan WPA director Abner E. Larned that "when this war ends, we will have such an avalanche of unemployment as to tax all our resources." From the president and his chief advisers to the men and women in the war plants, there had developed by 1945 a national economic concensus that was guardedly optimistic about long-term prospects but pessimistic

about the reconversion period. With three-tenths of the nation's labor force—and three-fifths of Michigan's—expected to
be demobilized at the end of the war, observers did not doubt
that a postwar downturn would occur, throwing millions into
prolonged joblessness.[7]

The fear of postwar depression shaped wartime attitudes in
various ways. Critics constantly accused war workers of insufficient productivity and a propensity to loaf on the job. When
Senator Homer Ferguson made a surprise visit to the Detroit
Packard plant in March, 1945, he discovered, alongside the
many men and women who were actually working, some employees playing checkers, sleeping, or reading. The Packard
workers were surprised at Ferguson's outrage. For many reasons, a minority of workers did their jobs indifferently or attempted to stretch out the work. They resented management's
labor hoarding that resulted in the provision of three men for
every job in some plants, and they were suspicious of anything
that suggested a speed-up. They hardly felt it necessary to play
Stakhanovite as war production surpassed the military's needs.
But they also sought to make the work last to mitigate future
unemployment. Workers derided as "job-killers" any of their
number who produced or inspected an unusually large quan-
tity of pieces. The wish to stretch out the work sometimes went
hand in hand with a desire that the war be prolonged.[8]

Production cutbacks were the most visible portent of postwar
economic crisis. Because of Michigan's thoroughgoing conversion to war production, the state was bound to experience severe industrial dislocations as the war came to an end. "Cutback
jitters" periodically swept Detroit during 1944 in the wake of
rumors that one or another contract would be cancelled. The
psychological impact of cutbacks was accentuated because the
military failed to devise a method of informing management
and labor of its intentions sufficiently in advance of a planned
reduction. Many workers panicked when their plant stopped
production of a particular item only to see output resumed on
another product. A flurry of armament contracts awarded to
Detroit industry in January, 1945, momentarily heartened the

city, but it had become clear by spring that major cutbacks impended.[9]

Willow Run symbolized the decline. To spread work and avoid layoffs the bomber plant began a five-day, forty-five-hour schedule in September, 1944. During May, 1945, the plant reduced output to a single eight-hour shift and laid off half of its twenty thousand employees. The last of 8,685 Liberators rolled off the factory's mile-long assembly line on June 28, by which time there remained only a few hundred workers of a labor force that once had numbered in excess of forty thousand. By midyear the military had cancelled more than a billion dollars in contracts in Detroit, Flint, and other Michigan production centers. Looking ahead to the end of the year, R. J. Thomas declared that if preventive action were not taken, half a million persons would be unemployed in Detroit and environs.[10]

Lansing began to plan against postwar vicissitudes even before Pearl Harbor. In June, 1941, the Michigan Council of Defense established an advisory postwar planning committee, and three months later Governor Murray Van Wagoner called on all state departments, federal agencies, and communities to compile a six-year inventory of necessary civic improvements. Construction of projects in this public works reserve was intended to cushion the shock of a sudden end to the defense boom. In 1944 the legislature, at Governor Kelly's bidding, created a five-million-dollar revolving fund that provided localities with aid on a matching basis for the preparation of planning studies. By the end of the year various levels of local government had applied for aid in planning $303,000,000 worth of new roads, sewers, parks, bridges, and other undertakings. Sixty of the state's eighty-three counties formed planning commissions, as did numerous cities and townships. Michigan's state and local postwar planning was characterized, as Mel Scott observes of the nation as a whole, by uncoordinated efforts to lessen reconversion unemployment rather than by systematic long-term designs. Only a few Michigan municipalities, moreover, had the ability to finance the construction of their inventories of projects. They could pay for their depression-fighting enterprises only if there was no depression.[11]

Franklin Roosevelt spoke to the nation's postwar hopes and fears in his State of the Union message of January 11, 1944. The adoption of the Bill of Rights had secured political liberty he declared, and the fulfillment of a second, an economic bill of rights, would guarantee the security without which liberty stood imperiled. First among the new rights Roosevelt placed "the right to a useful and remunerative job." He affirmed the right to decent housing, medical care, education, protection for the elderly, maintenance of adequate farm incomes, and freedom from monopolistic control of business. "All of these rights spell security," he concluded, "and after this war is won we must be prepared to move forward in the implementation of these rights to new goals of human happiness and well-being." In his fourth-term campaign Roosevelt stressed the "economic bill of rights," pledging the creation of "close to sixty million jobs" and a future economy of abundance. The critical phrase in that message, however, turned out to be "after this war is won," since the president took no concrete measures to realize his postwar vision.[12]

Congress previously had provided postwar assistance for farmers, veterans, and businessmen, but it balked at the extension of unemployment compensation, continued federalization of the USES, and passage of other measures devised to ease war workers and federal employees through the transition to peace. So great was the animus of Capital Hill toward organized labor and the Washington bureaucracy that no form of direct aid to either institution could pass both houses. The final reconversion legislation, adopted in October, 1944, provided assistance to workers only through such indirect means as federal underwriting of state unemployment funds. Throughout 1945 President Truman urged Congress to pass war-worker aid legislation, to no avail. Nor did the federal lawmakers enact any form of specific help to states and cities struggling with reconversion problems.

The people of Michigan believed that their postwar destiny

lay as much in the hands of the automobile industry as in those of Congress or the president. In June, 1944, the UAW-CIO announced a reconversion program calling for, among other things, the immediate undertaking of postwar planning and the coordination of war production and reconversion in a single, civilian-dominated government agency. But the union readily bowed to the economic leadership of business. *"We do not question the central role of free—really free—private enterprise,"* said R. J. Thomas, outlining the program. His chief concern was that industry might attempt to curtail production. "What has made American industry great has been the initiative displayed in developing new products and improved methods, with resulting large national output."[13] General Motors board chairman Alfred P. Sloan had given his industry's answer to such fears in a December, 1943, address to the National Association of Manufacturers. He urged his fellow executives to disregard talk of a postwar economic slump. Accumulated savings and pent-up demand for consumer durables, he insisted, would fuel a healthy economic boom. And GM would be ready to take advantage: Sloan detailed the firm's plans for modernization and expansion, a project which would ultimately cost more than half a billion dollars.[14]

The pace of automotive reconversion was determined by policies set by the War Production Board in conjunction with the industry. An April, 1944, conference of automakers and WPB officials in Washington discussed the projected changeover to civilian prodution. The Big Three wanted all automotive production to commence simultaneously, with each firm's output restricted to a fixed proportion of its pre-Pearl Harbor share. Maintenance of the "historical pattern" would negate temporary advantages of timing, enable all firms to keep their supplier and dealer networks intact, and, most importantly, hobble new entrants into the automotive field. The smaller producers held out for adjustments that would give them a competitive edge during the initial phase of civilian output by manufacturing vehicles without reference to prewar production patterns. Donald Nelson opposed strict adherence to the historical pattern. Preservation of the pattern, however, seemed to offer the only hope of avoiding postwar competitive chaos.[15]

The auto industry worked on reconversion in piecemeal fashion while awaiting an acceptable allocation plan from the WPB. Under Nelson's general reconversion program announced in mid-June the industry won permission to build experimental models and received priority assistance for the purchase of automotive machine tools (although there was virtually no hope of securing such tools). Some firms pressed for approval of civilian plant construction. Cadillac, for instance, proposed to use its light-tank priorities to obtain material for the construction of a new passenger car assembly plant. The WPB vetoed all such applications; before any further steps could be taken, reconversion planning abruptly halted.[16]

Donald Nelson and other WPB officials had believed that some reconversion to civilian production should begin before the end of the war to provide an employment cushion and that, if necessary, smaller firms should receive competitive advantages to facilitate such production. The big-business element within the WPB, led by C. E. Wilson and Lemuel Bulware of General Electric, wished to impose the historical production pattern on all mass-production industries, thus confining the small competitors to their accustomed place on the margin of the economy and throttling prospective rivals. Even though the major auto manufacturers favored speedy reconversion, they could endure a protraction of the process as long as the government's transition policy ultimately met their demands. Concerned about manpower needs, the War Manpower Commission opposed the initiation of reconversion in wartime. Military leaders insisted that no thought be given to reconversion lest workers drift away from war jobs, placing production schedules in jeopardy. Although business and military elements were aiming at different targets, each was comfortable in its support of the other's case for reconversion delay.

These pressures slowed but did not deter Nelson, who pushed through in June, 1944, an order that allowed regional WPB directors to grant "spot authorization" to producers wishing to manufacture civilian goods, provided that area war contracts were on schedule and sufficient manpower was available. Office of War Mobilization director James Byrnes intervened in response to military and business pleas to delay implementation of the Nelson plan. A revised spot authorization system finally went into effect on August 4, and eleven days later a harassed Nelson accepted President Roosevelt's suggestion that he undertake a special mission to China. Wilson shortly thereafter resigned as WPB executive vice-chairman, and on August 24 the President named Julius Krug to head the WPB. Krug, who favored advanced planning for reconversion, nevertheless bowed to Byrnes and an increasingly shrill military opposition and ordered the rollback of spot authorization in early December. Allied reverses during the Battle of the Bulge ended all reconversion talk for the moment, and in January, 1945, the government tightened rationing and blackout regulations and placed other restrictions on the civilian economy.

The collapse of German arms after the Ardennes surge led to new thought about reconversion. On April 5, 1945, Krug told a Washington meeting of the industry advisory group that the automakers could begin reconversion, although still subject to military priorities. Spot authorization resumed on April 27. A week after V-E Day, the motorcar manufacturers met with the WPB Automotive Division to set interim production quotas, and on May 25 controls were relaxed to allow the production of 215,000 autos during the July 1–December 31, 1945, period, and a total output of 2,146,000 cars in fiscal 1946. Each manufacturer was granted a quota based on his share of the domestic market during August–November, 1941. The total industry allocation was based on estimates of available carbon steel, and the manufacturers had to obtain supplies as best they could. Knowledgeable government and industry officials understood that the automakers were in a much stronger bidding position to secure steel and other materials than were other industries and small firms generally.[17]

The automakers accepted the WPB quotas reluctantly, believing the assigned production totals unduly restrictive. To the large producers, a more welcome feature of the schedule was the provision of only negligible quotas for the smaller manufacturers and of only two thousand units for any new automotive venture. Krug, however, insisted that the smaller shares be adjusted upward and resisted counterarguments from the Big Three, whose representatives met with him on July 19. The WPB subsequently granted eight-thousand-unit July-to-December quotas to Packard, Nash, Hudson, Crossley, Willys, and any new firm that might enter the competitive lists.[18]

As it happened, two men described by *Fortune* as "bald and baggy knights-to-the-rescue" were ready to undertake the joust. Henry Kaiser had accumulated his prewar wealth in construction and added to his millions in wartime as the wizard of west coast shipbuilding. Joseph Frazer was the entrepreneur-president of Graham-Paige, a Detroit automotive supplier that once had produced motorcars. Each man decided independently during the war to enter the postwar auto industry, and in July, 1945, they joined to create the Kaiser-Frazer Corporation. At the outset neither possessed an adequate assembly plant. In September they secured a lease from the Reconstruction Finance Corporation for the Willow Run plant, which the elder Henry Ford had decided to relinquish. "The venture has appealed to one of the main roots of the American nature—the gambling instinct," *Fortune* commented in early 1946. "This instinct has been dormant or repressed for more than a decade of industrial stultification and war. . . .Worries over politics and tactics made cautious conservatism the dominant industrial way of life. . . . Now suddenly the lid is off."[19]

Kaiser-Frazer had the public's good will, but the established automakers had the proven ability and the plants. The new company did not move into Willow Run until November and made not a single car in 1945. Instead, the first civilian passenger automobile manufactured in the United States since 1942 rolled off the assembly line at River Rouge on the morning of July 3, 1945, an ebullient Henry Ford II behind the wheel. Ford called the car a 1946 model, but it was built with the same tools and dies as its 1942 predecessor. Few additional units were expected to follow since the supply of critical materials remained tight.[20]

Americans had accepted an active federal role in national economic management to sustain prosperity; the principle was embodied in the Murray bill, introduced in Congress in 1945 and passed in modified form a year later as the Employment Act of 1946. Yet the government could no more plan for prosperity without the cooperation of the major manufacturers than it could have orchestrated war production without reliance on those manufacturers. Thus the auto industry was again crucial to national hopes. Four weeks after V-J Day, a *New York Times* reporter wrote: "The sprawling automobile plants that dot the outskirts [of Detroit] may easily foretell the future of America."[21] Krug gave the automakers preferential treatment in early 1945 because he believed in the industry's potential as a market for materials and a provider of jobs.[22] Save for this action, however, little was accomplished during the year to prepare the industry—or, for that matter, the nation—for the return to peace. The deliberate pace of reconversion planning was in large part the product of the widely shared assumption that Japan would fight on into 1946.

★ 2 ★

Within hours of the Japanese surrender the government cancelled billions of dollars in armament contracts, including $1,500,000,000 of Detroit area war production. On August 30 the WPB lifted all restrictions on passenger car output. Thanks to accumulated delays, often abetted by big business, production based on a carefully controlled historical pattern went by the board. A mad competitive scramble now ensued among the automakers, one in which the Big Three held the major advantages since they possessed the greatest amounts of working capital and stood to benefit most from the carry-back provisions of the federal excess-profits tax. Within the first few weeks of peace, the government eliminated most important controls, including rationing regulations. The Office of Price Administration, however, maintained its system of price ceilings—evidence of the dawning realization that inflation might ultimately loom larger than depression as a postwar danger.[23]

On Monday, August 20, following a special two-day national holiday and the weekend, laid-off workers gathered in long lines before USES offices across Michigan. If the agency could not refer them to jobs—and most offices had only a handful of skilled vacancies available—the workers were sent to the local branch of the Michigan Unemployment Compensation Commission (MUCC) to register for unemployment payments, which ranged upward to a maximum of twenty dollars weekly for twenty weeks. There were perhaps fifteen thousand in line in Detroit, five thousand in Flint, and additional thousands in other cities, a chilling reminder in the late August heat of the grimmest days of the 1930s. The workers called it "Black Monday," and the following day the lines increased, to seven blocks in length before some Detroit MUCC offices. The press featured optimistic comments from the people waiting in line: "I'm registering, and then I'm going to find another job until the plant is reconverted," said Stanley Larkins, a veteran of seventeen years at Briggs. "But don't worry, we'll all be working before long." The lines of the jobless indeed subsided by noon on Wednesday. Unemployment mounted, however, and compensation claims, which had reached 163,000 statewide during "Black Monday" week, climbed to 237,000 by September 15.[24]

Although Michigan manufacturing employment dropped by nearly 300,000 persons between May and September, the reduction was due as much to retirement from the workforce as to unemployment. Many youngsters, the elderly, and white collar workers left the war plants voluntarily and had no desire to remain in postwar industry. Thousands of women and blacks were involuntarily laid off and had little hope of retaining their wartime occupations. As expected, about half of the southern in-migrants began returning to their homes. Between 100,000 and 150,000 persons left the state between V-E Day and mid-September, many of them heading for southern destinations. The *Detroit News*, which had little good to say of the migrants during the war, marked their leave-taking with a tribute to their services and an unspoken but heartfelt prayer of thanks for their exodus: "They are to be congratulated now on their prudence in returning to the places where their savings can be put to better account than supporting them through idleness. . . ."[25]

Despite rising unemployment, Michigan had reasons for optimism quite apart from a mass out-migration. Many persons taking off for long vacations after grueling years of war work artificially inflated the jobless statistics. Had actual unemployment persisted, the $250,000,000 MUCC fund could have carried several hundred thousand claimants for up to five months. Against the possibility of privation, Michigan citizens had accumulated $3,600,000,000 in savings. Municipal and county governments counted $403,000,000 in postwar public works projects in the blueprint stage. The problems of veterans promised to be alleviated by the generous range of benefits accorded ex-servicemen. To these cheering facts was added the intangible lift of the spirit felt by sports-mad Detroit that fall when, strengthened by the return of Hank Greenberg, the Tigers defeated the Chicago Cubs in the World Series.[26]

The most hopeful sign for the future was the visible rapidity of reconversion throughout Michigan. Many large auto firms recalled considerable portions of their labor forces within a week after V-J Day. Repeating the dramatic scenes of 1942 in reverse, workers tore war production machinery from factory floors, uncrated and installed long unused or new civilian tools, reconstituted the former automotive assembly lines, and cleared huge stocks of partially complete or finished matériel from the plants. Dozens of large firms required little or no reconversion work at all. Typical was Gar Wood Industries of Detroit, a prewar maker of boats and construction machinery, which quadrupled its business during the war but manufactured essentially the same products. After a week's postvictory layoff for inventory, Gar Wood recalled most of its employees to begin filling a backlog of civilian orders for its cranes and winches.[27] The consumer sector of the economy required no reconversion, and groceries, banks, retail stores, and other commercial establishments, severely understaffed during wartime, were eager to employ the now jobless.

Business revived and unemployment declined during the fall of 1945. National unemployment totaled less than two million persons, not the six million projected by most forecasters. In December, however, the upturn abruptly ceased. Although the registered unemployed in Michigan numbered only 139,000 at the end of the year, the USES placed the actual figure at 390,000 persons. Despite the ahead-of-schedule clearance of plants, many concerns still lacked space to store their output before shipping. Parts shortages crippled every firm, causing delays in assembly and occasional factory shutdowns. Automotive output for 1945 totalled not the half million cars the manufacturers hoped to produce after the lifting of controls but a mere 69,532 passenger units.[28]

Labor unrest lay at the heart of Michigan's economic reverse and the automakers' poor showing. The immediate postwar period witnessed strikes in the steel, oil, rubber, glass, chemical, lumber, and meatpacking industries, to mention only the most important sectors of the economy affected by disputes. Hoping for a continuation of wartime labor-management cooperation, President Truman on August 15 called for the retention of the no-strike, no-lockout pledge and announced the convening in the near future of a White House labor-relations conference. But workers long restive under the restraint of the Little Steel formula and other WLB policies rushed to the picket lines. The WLB dissolved itself in mid-December, moreover, leaving the nation without machinery for high-level conciliation of labor disputes.[29]

The auto industry was expected to set the tone of postwar labor relations, and the outlook following V-J Day was anything but certain. R. J. Thomas unceremoniously cancelled the no-strike pledge on August 15, but he asserted that there need be no industry-wide rash of walkouts and warned all locals that strikes must be sanctioned by the International Executive Board. Although locals deluged the Board with strike requests in the following months, it authorized only two stoppages and crushed a wildcat at Kelsey-Hayes that threatened production at Ford. The UAW-CIO was in no position to mount a major offensive against management. With the closing of war plants, especially in the artificially expanded aircraft industry, auto worker membership began to decline. By the end of the year the union had only a half million dues-paying members, far less than half the wartime peak. The loss of dues placed the UAW in straitened financial circumstances, making it a seemingly weak opponent for auto firms whose reconversion problems were eased by the promise of tax rebates.[30]

The UAW's evolving postwar strategy depended for success not on scatter-shot strikes but a concentrated attack on a single target. The union's leadership calculated that the policy, hammered out at a September 10–18 board meeting, would strengthen discipline over the rank and file, keep the union solvent with a continued inflow of dues, and impel the chosen firm to settle quickly for fear of losing its competitive advantage. By closing Ford, the Kelsey-Hayes dispute crippled a rival of the company selected by the Board as the target, General Motors. On August 18, UAW vice-president and GM department head Walter Reuther had asked the company to reopen its contract and to grant the union a 30 percent wage increase without an increase in prices. He wanted all negotiations to be public, and since the firm's financial soundness would determine its ability to meet the wage demands, Reuther also insisted that General Motors open its accounts to public inspection.

Reuther premised his approach to GM on the belief that industry must pay wages sufficient to enable workers to purchase the goods being manufactured and, perhaps, on the judgment that a successful strike against the auto giant could catapult him into the presidency of the UAW-CIO. When President Truman altered his wage-price policy in mid-October to enable companies to apply for increases if they could not otherwise make a profit within six months, he nonetheless gave tacit support to the UAW position and urged restraint on business. But company spokesmen, supported by nearly every manufacturing and trade association, denounced the "open-the-books" proposal and GM negotiators flatly refused to consider the subject. R. J. Thomas, the other target of Reuther's personal strike strategy, also regarded the idea somewhat dubiously, and cast a generally jaundiced eye on his subordinate's conduct of the dispute.

Reuther spurned General Motors' offer, made without commitment on prices, of a 10 percent wage increase (later raised to 12 percent). He was backed by the results of an NLRB ballot in early November that disclosed broad support for a strike among GM workers. Thomas wished to delay the walkout until reconversion had been completed, but Reuther pressed forward. After GM disregarded his conditional proposal to arbitrate the ability-to-pay issue, the strike began on the morning of November 21. Some 180,000 GM workers left the company's plants, joining 140,000 company employees idled by reconversion. The walkout commenced as President Truman's labor-management conference, convened on November 5, plodded toward ultimate failure and adjournment at month's end. The UAW rejected Truman's request for a return to work; and when the President appointed a fact-finding board in late December to investigate the dispute, GM refused to cooperate because of his support of the ability-to-pay contention.

Despite apocalyptic rhetoric on both sides and warnings of a bloody postwar showdown in the auto industry, the General Motors strike was remarkably peaceful. Since the pickets around GM plants were there primarily for morale purposes, the union made a special effort to staff the lines with veterans in uniform and auto worker wives. Many strikers were prepared to endure the period of idleness on their accumulated savings, and the UAW organized soup kitchens for the less fortunate GM workers. Reuther already had won support for the union's case from a committee of liberal luminaries, and a similar group, whose membership included Eleanor Roosevelt and Wayne Morse, was organized to support the strike. The company and the union devoted considerable effort to influencing the general public on behalf of their respective positions in the dispute. Opinion polls of the day, however, disclosed that neither side won overwhelming backing from the people, although the UAW mustered somewhat more sympathy than GM did.[31]

The President's fact-finding board meanwhile reported on

January 10, 1946, that GM's ability to pay was a relevant issue and that the company could afford a 17.5 percent wage increase, or $0.195 per hour, without a price increase. Management and labor initially rejected the proposal, but Reuther shortly changed his mind and accepted it because he had been overtaken by events. By the winter of 1946 the General Motors strike had become only one dispute in an historic wave of walkouts, including a critical stoppage in the steel industry that convulsed the nation. Presidential boards investigating the most important of these strikes had developed an informal guideline for wage increases of $0.185 per hour, a penny less than the amount suggested by the GM fact-finders. In late January, Ford and Chrysler settled with the UAW for $0.18 and $0.185 respectively, without reference to ability to pay. The Communist-dominated United Electrical Workers undermined its arch-foe Reuther on February 9 by settling with GM for $0.185.

The steel settlement was the most serious blow to Reuther. In order to bring an end to the steel strike, Truman was forced to authorize a five-dollar-per-ton rise in steel prices on February 2. The President had realized too late that major industries were willing to take strikes to obtain price rises even at the risk of halting the production upon which the nation's economic future rested.[32] On February 14, he announced a revised federal wage-price policy that restrained wages and allowed business to apply to the OPA for immediate compensatory price relief. Eager for a settlement, Steel Workers president Philip Murray agreed to $0.185 on February 15. Reuther's stand on pay and profits had been repudiated both by the government and his fellow CIO unionists, and his strike strategy had become untenable.

General Motors subsequently offered the UE wage package to Reuther, who spent the last weeks of the strike in a fruitless effort to win the additional penny the January report had recommended. As they ran out of money, many GM workers demanded an end to the walkout. The UAW finally settled for $0.185 on March 13, bringing the 113-day strike to a close. The union claimed that company concessions on seniority, overtime, and vacation pay were equivalent to the missing cent,

but the ability-to-pay issue was nowhere mentioned in the contract, and GM shortly joined the procession of manufacturers
receiving substantial price increases from the OPA. Reuther
failed in his quest to obtain corporate accountability to the
general public, but the UAW-CIO had survived its first postwar confrontation with the automobile industry successfully.
"In the future," Victor Reuther later wrote, "the corporation
was to show much more respect for the strength, the economic
logic, and the morality of the issues the UAW laid before it."[33]
Although his conduct of the strike had been less than master-
ful, Walter Reuther went on from his "victory" over GM to
defeat Thomas for the union presidency in a closely contested
election at the UAW national convention later that March.

Michigan experienced a slow economic advance after the
GM agreement as other labor disputes were settled and remaining reconversion problems were resolved. Some 290,000
persons were unemployed in March (12.7 percent of the state
labor force), and an additional 114,000 workers (5 percent of
the labor force) were idle through direct involvement in strikes.
By September, however, state manufacturing employment totalled 1,031,000, a level comparable to that attained in the
spring of 1945 or in late 1942. Michigan's jobless rate declined
but continued at double or triple the national average until
July. Thereafter, the state percentage fell steeply to approximately 4.3 percent in December, in comparison to a 3.6 percent
unemployment rate in that month for the United States as a
whole.[34]

Alfred P. Sloan turned out to be the sagest among the tribe
of postwar prophets. Fears of depression subsided as output
and employment mounted. For a season, inflation became the
most persistent problem facing government administrators and
the general public. Detroit food costs, for instance, rose 30 percent in the sixteen months after V-J Day. Darrell Cady rightly
points out that Truman administration policies emphasizing
production were crucial in averting a possible postwar slump.
The people's desire for goods, whetted by depression deprivation and wartime scarcity and supported by wartime savings,
counted heavily, however. "We had saved, conserved . . . made

things last," Curtis Stadtfeld remembered of his small Michigan farm community. "But all at once we were ready to consume. . . . The war changed us from savers to consumers."[35]

It was Armistice Day, and 150,000 Detroiters gathered to mark the occasion. Because November 11, 1945, fell on a Sunday, the big parade down Woodward Avenue was held the following day. The city's skyline was unchanged; no bombs had fallen on Detroit. But along the route where hundreds of mothers had marched in protest against war on Armistice Day, 1939, now hundreds of Gold Star mothers and disabled ex-GIs sat in places of honor on the reviewing stand.[36] The crowd cheered the marching columns of veterans, especially the servicemen of the Second World War, their rows of campaign ribbons gleaming. Many among the onlookers had produced the weaponry that the marchers had employed on a dozen battlefields. The crowd and the parading vets were there to celebrate victory and, all unknowing, to bear witness to the beginning of a new era. The city, the state, the country belonged to the veterans now.

Conclusion

War, Change, and Continuity

No American state experienced the social and economic consequences of World War II more profoundly than Michigan. Arthur Marwick observes that "to talk about a war having consequences, save at the most direct level of so many killed, so many houses destroyed, and so on, is really a wrong use of language. War is, at its very essence, negative and destructive. It cannot of itself create anything new."[1] The domestic consequences of the Second World War arose from the conflict between the forces of continuity and change, those existing within the society and those unleashed by the conflict. Although geographically distant, the war compelled great changes in the social and economic pattern of life in Michigan as well as the rest of the United States. The home-front mobilization, on the other hand, was influenced and shaped by the prewar character of that pattern.

For Michigan and the nation, the most obvious economic consequence of the war was the creation of unprecedented prosperity. By every measure, Michigan not only climbed out of the depression but attained a new and extraordinary level of material well-being. It had become fashionable during the 1930s to observe that the American economy had matured, had reached the limit of its possible growth. The doubling of the gross national product during the war and the roaring demand for consumer goods after 1945 demonstrated forcefully that the expansive potential of the nation's economic ma-

234

chinery had been barely tested. Some, like Eliot Janeway, warned that wartime prosperity had been gained at a perilous price in depleted natural resources, but few listened to such talk, and Janeway himself played down the import of his observation.[2] The pre-1929 American faith in endless vistas of economic growth and material happiness had returned. The renaissance of economic optimism was the critical component in the general wartime resurgence of confidence. That confidence was tinged with uncertainty about the performance of the economy during the reconversion period, but once the first postwar test was successfully passed, there was no turning back to the days of doubt.

Increased consumer spending formed one pillar of the new prosperity, but a strong and active federal government became the economy's more massive buttress. The New Deal had attempted to direct national economic life in a halting manner and had achieved indifferent success. Relatively modest federal spending in the 1930s failed to bring recovery. By comparison, vast federal expenditures, especially after 1941, brought recovery beyond the dreams of the most ardent Keynesian. During the war, moreover, Washington exercised greater control over wages, prices, profits, labor relations, manpower allocation, and the distribution of goods than ever before. Although the theoretical foundation of these wartime developments had been laid in the immediate past, the size and scope of federal economic policy changed dramatically during the war, and the success of that policy left an indelible imprint on government and industrial thought.

In future years the federal government became the guarantor of prosperity. The new orthodoxy held that the nation's continuing affluence could be secured if the economy, the so-called pie, could be made to grow a little larger each year, allowing everyone a slightly larger slice. Using increased revenues derived from the restructured tax system, the government contributed to the expansion through large-scale defense spending, supplemented in the 1960s and 1970s by appropriations for a variety of social welfare programs. The president maintained growth by spending to relieve unemployment at one time, by invoking controls to fight inflation at another point. Private decision makers retained power over key sectors of the economy, but no private determination was now made without reference to the possible role of the federal government.

As it grew, the wartime federal government took on a bewildering number of new functions, most of which were represented in Michigan. As the production program diminished the extent of poverty by creating mass employment and furnishing good wages, so the domestic agencies achieved a great deal of incidental social reform through war-related measures that bettered the lives of people. The war housing program, for instance, provided many Americans with the first decent homes they had occupied, and other federally supported efforts improved public health and nutrition. The achievement was one the legislative sponsors of those agencies never intended and one for which their administrators were generally loath to take credit. The war years, after all, witnessed the defeat of reform legislation and the death of many New Deal agencies responsible for the welfare of the poorest citizens. The greater part of the New Deal agencies survived the war intact, however, and some, such as the Federal Housing Administration, played significant roles in the domestic mobilization. At war's end Americans had become accustomed—if not reconciled—to the federal government's enlargement.

Wartime developments within the automobile industry reflected the growth of American business in size and power. Spurred by the armament program, the automakers vastly expanded their facilities; benefiting from special tax provisions written at the insistence of the industry, the larger manufacturers greatly strengthened their financial position. The flood of war contracts let to the three major automotive producers accelerated the ongoing tendency toward concentration in the industry. The continued strengthening of oligopoly within the auto industry after 1939, however, was overshadowed by the establishment of a new relationship between Washington and Detroit. The automakers had repeatedly skirmished with the New Deal prior to the defense period, and they had demonstrated little eagerness to become involved in arms production before Pearl Harbor, in part because of fear of government control. Once the war began, however, industry leaders relaxed as they saw the production bureaucracy filled with the representatives of business, including some from the executive suites of Detroit itself. By 1944 they had moved into active partnership with the government in an attempt to determine the shape of the postwar market.

The automakers, playing an ambivalent role in the emergence of the wartime military-industrial alliance, were not prominent in the 1944 debate over reconversion. The delay in reconversion planning insisted upon by the military aided the major motorcar producers by frustrating the hopes of the smaller firms for competitive advantages; the big automakers had agreed with the generals on this point, but none of the manufacturers wished to pin his future profits on close ties to the armed services. All of them wanted to resume passenger car production as quickly as possible, and they gratefully shed their war work. Indeed, the shape, if not the size, of Michigan's economy emerged from the war relatively unchanged. The state failed to attract the new aviation and electronics-based industries spawned by the war. Defense contracts constituted only a small fraction of the auto industry's postwar business, and civilian motor vehicles remained the state's principal product. As a result, Michigan continued its boom-or-bust reliance on the automobile market.

The war years brought significant changes to Michigan labor. The nature and import of that change were partially obscured by the persistence to a varying degree of such prewar phenomena as strikes, interunion and factional rivalry, and antagonistic labor-management relations. By 1945, however, the UAW-CIO had entrenched itself within the automobile industry, if not in the heart of automotive management, and R. J. Thomas and Walter Reuther had become nationally recognized and respected spokesmen of labor. Responding to public criticism and their own patriotic instincts, the UAW leadership strengthened central control over unruly militant locals in order to stabilize relations within the plants and maintain production. While retaining a still-considerable degree of internal democracy, the union's top command increased the organization's bargaining power in relation to management, paving the way for the industry's grudging acceptance of unionism. The federal government assisted the adjustment by creating labor relations machinery with which both parties, but especially management, were compelled to cooperate. Although its record of electoral success was spotty, the CIO Political Action Committee, dominated in Michigan by the UAW, helped to establish a new postwar agenda of social and economic issues.

The stability and future success of the UAW were open to sharp question at the outset of the European war. A peacetime auto union led by the vacillating Thomas might have foundered in factional conflict; such had almost happend when Homer Martin had attempted to take dictatorial control of the organization. Engrossed in internecine warfare, union leaders might have wasted energies that could otherwise have been devoted to community service or political action. More important, the union would have been at a critical disadvantage in its relations with management. Since the UAW was one of the most important constituent members of the CIO, disruption of the auto union might have threatened the existence of the national labor organization. In its determination to assure production, the federal government created conditions that encouraged the survival of unions such as the UAW. Factionalism continued, but within limits established by the almost unanimous agreement on victory. Time and energy remained for the UAW's community and political activities. At the end of the war, of course, the radical impulse within the union had all but died, smothered in complex contract agreements and fat pay checks. The extent to which the non-Communist leadership and rank and file of the UAW had been "radical" before the war is, however, open to doubt.

The requirements of war production resulted in the resumption or acceleration of previous trends in Michigan's population distribution and migration patterns. The movement of labor into the state's urban industrial centers ended the depression-era hiatus in north-to-south intrastate migration and led to a resurgence of large-scale southern movement into the state. The construction of many warplants in semirural areas and the shortage of housing in nearby central city districts promoted already ongoing suburbanization. The congested communities, lacking adequate resources to cope with the crisis, turned to Washington for assistance. Their appeals for help strengthened the direct relationship between the federal government and the urban areas that had been evolving since the 1930s. The infusion of federal aid enabled the communities to provide a level of services and facilities sufficient to prevent a breakdown of production. At Willow Run, however, where a relatively small community faced overwhelming in-migration and attendant facilities problems, the combination of poor federal coordination and private selfishness produced conditions markedly disadvantageous to the physical and mental welfare of the community's inhabitants.

The war years also witnessed the continuing deterioration of the urban core, a decline that had been evident in Detroit for some time. To the decade of enforced civic neglect during the money-short 1930s had been added years of wartime scarcity in which repairs and improvements were left incomplete or undone. Changes in local law and procedure that might have eased the wartime urban plight came slowly or were blocked entirely by interest groups—landlords and real estate developers, for instance—that perceived a threat to the prewar structure of their privilege and power. The city's vitality was further sapped by the ceaseless flight to the suburbs, facilitated now by federally constructed expressways that led to federally financed factories. If the wartime experience indicated how desperately the cities needed help, in peace as well as in a time of national emergency, the developing tie between Washington and the urban areas offered hope for the future. It would be decades, however, before that hope was realized. Some federal funds flowed into mostly rural impacted communities during the Cold War in a pale revival of the Lanham Act. The creation of cabinet-level departments on urban affairs and the development of costly programs of urban aid came only as a response to the riots of the 1960s, a turbulence that had resulted in part from the neglect of problems that had their genesis during World War II.

The blacks, who increasingly inhabited those cities, made undeniable progress during the war. It is improbable, for instance, that Detroit plants would have opened their gates to black workers in so short a period without the impetus of the wartime manpower crisis. It is unlikely that black income and living standards would have risen so dramatically between 1939 and 1945 without the spur of wartime prosperity. It is doubtful that blacks could have devised a more effective propaganda technique than the linking of their struggle for justice to the global battle against racist fascism. The heightened racial consciousness that accompanied the nationwide "Double V" campaign, moreover, encouraged the development of programs and tactics that attracted the support of the black masses as well as that of the black bourgeoisie. By the end of the war, blacks, like organized labor, had become a group whose needs and desires had to be taken account of by the federal government, if not necessarily fulfilled immediately.

Against this record of progress must be set the fact that black wartime achievements were only initial steps in the attainment of political, economic, and social equality for the race. The black unemployment rate in Michigan exceeded that for whites before, during, and after the war. Blacks could not live in Dearborn in 1939, and they could not live there in 1945. The war years gave blacks some reason to hope for justice but also confronted them—most violently in the riots of 1943—with the power and intractable quality of white resistance to their demands. They would need all the endurance and resourcefulness acquired during centuries of oppression to "overcome."

The persistence of prejudice against blacks suggests something about the character of wartime national unity. "We Americans will contribute unified production and unified acceptance of sacrifice and of effort," President Roosevelt declared in February, 1942. "That means a national unity that knows no limitations of race or creed or selfish politics."[3] The country was united, however, on only a single issue—the necessity for victory. Social and economic groups rarely if ever abandoned prewar aims for the sake of national solidarity; instead, they devised new arguments that made the attainment of those goals appear a prerequisite to victory. Black leaders were among the most skillful at turning the unity call to the special needs of their constituency, but it was often as easy for the opponents of black demands to use a similar tactic. The opening of increased employment opportunities for blacks was deemed essential to victory; the social acceptance of blacks by the white majority was not so recognized. Many of the southern whites who migrated to Michigan suffered a like exclusion from the circle of unity. The natives who had despised the "hillbilly" before Pearl Harbor saw in the war emergency no reason to modify their prejudices to make the newcomer welcome.

Female Americans were not outsiders in the same sense that blacks and southern whites were, but women entered the war years as the social and economic inferiors of men and were excluded from participation in many areas of national life. The war provided enhanced employment possibilities for women as it did for blacks. In the course of performing a job or coping without their GI husbands, many women gained confidence in themselves and attained a consciousness of self-worth missing in their lives. The war era, however, did not witness a great improvement in the status of women as a sex. Unlike blacks, women were not well organized to take advantage of the opportunities for progress war afforded. The militant feminist groups had the most far-reaching demands and the tiniest followings; the sedate women's clubs possessed the largest membership and the most modest of aspirations. Nor did the war experience lead to effective organization on behalf of feminine economic and political equality since most women were not as yet convinced of the need for such equality.

The nuclear family survived the war in recognizable form: indeed, the immediate postwar period marked the high point of the ideological cult of the family. Yet the war accelerated forces in American life that had been disrupting the family unit for decades. Migration and service separation opened rifts in individual families often impossible to repair. Subur-

banization and the concomitant increased use of the automobile worked against family solidity. The increase in the number
of employed mothers and the rising economic independence
of many married women encouraged by the war also tore at
the roots of family unity. The public paid greater attention
than it had in previous years to juvenile delinquency, one of
the most evident manifestations of family disintegration, but
understood not much more than before about youthful devi-
ance. Some of the consequences of the wartime stress and
strain within the family were clear by 1945; others would not
be identified for years.

The changes in Michigan did not constitute a radical alteration of life in the sense of a root-and-branch upheaval. Many
prewar institutions and patterns of thought emerged from the
war intact or only slightly affected by the years of global strife.
Continuity remained a powerful force. After examining the
society of Japan, a nation subject to the effects of the war's full
and devastating impact, Thomas R. H. Havens concludes that
"it is moot whether total war more greatly ossifies or trans-
forms a people in response to national crisis." In his study of
the 1920s, Roderick Nash discovered the same ambiguous interplay of change and continuity. "Only gradually do men inch
away from the old moorings," he noted. "To say ideas change is
really only to say that one way of thinking loses a little ground
while another makes a small gain." In retrospect, however, the
Michigan and America of 1939 are clearly seen to belong to a
world now vanished, while the state and nation of 1945 are
more nearly recognizable. The outlines are beginning to blur
with age and with the increasing velocity of change in recent
years, but the state and nation are incontestably the modern
Michigan and the modern America.[4]

Production was the catalyst of both change and continuity.
It should be clear by now that many of the significant economic, demographic, and social phenomena of the war years
had their origin in the requirements of the military production
program. That program demanded and created change. But
the American people did not enter the war in hopes of social
transformation or rebirth; rather, they sought victory and,

through it, the vindication of their existing institutions. Their president wished the conflict simply to be known as "the Survival War."[5] The people evinced little interest in sweeping postwar visions; Henry Wallace and Wendell Willkie offered such programs, but their ideas evoked more opposition than support within their respective political parties, and partly because of that hostility, both men lost bids for national office in 1944. The gospel of victory through production filled the ideological void for most Americans.

This narrow conception of the war's objective, shared by president and people alike, facilitated the adoption of the expedient or "necessitarian" attitudes upon which several historians have commented. Insofar as production could be maintained under the social and economic rules of 1939 or 1941, it would be so maintained; insofar as change was required to speed production, that change would be designed with specific and very limited purposes. As the focus of the national production mobilization, Michigan was particularly affected by expedient policies and programs created to block change or to preserve established centers of power. The state was thus the victim of the most corrosive effects of this policy; for the affirmation of old values in these backward looking years often made it possible to ignore or downplay the importance of critical social and economic problems. The decaying cities were not the only areas inadequately examined in a postwar era of American self-satisfaction. Yet necessitarianism was opposed by what Marwick calls "the unguided forces of social change."[6] Among such forces at large in wartime Michigan were money, migration, and the bitter heritage of a decade of industrial depression.

On balance, the war years were good ones for America. The nation's noblest ideals were reaffirmed and some of its most ignoble traditions were challenged. In the mid-1970s many Americans, in deep confusion about the worth of their institutions and the possibilities of their future, began to reach back to World War II to recapture a remembered sense of certainty and security. People flocked to such films as *Summer of '42* and *Class of '44*. Recalling his boyhood in conflict-riven wartime Detroit, the poet L. E. Sissman wrote: "Our faith, our patience, and our tolerance were great. Our unity as a people, although less stringently enforced than that of the British, was patent and wonderful." Geoffrey Perrett reflected a similar nostalgic longing when he declared that "my own conviction is that the war experience was as close as this country has ever come to living the American dream."[7]

Dreams such reflections are, embodying as they do a distorted, simplistic picture of the war years. Too often forgotten are the racial and regional antagonisms, the labor unrest, and the competition for crowded housing and transportation that plagued the era. Hardships faded from memory. What remained was a clear recollection, now purged of its concomitant pain, of a moment of cooperation toward a common goal that made life seem more intense and purposeful. A more valid recollection is that tanks, planes, and soldiers did not then prevail without the dedicated support of millions of men, women, and children on the home front. The World War II experience stands as a constant reminder not that the nation will act and will succeed when its way of life is externally threatened, but that it can act, because it did so once.

Notes

INTRODUCTION

1. Ben D. Zevin, ed., *Nothing to Fear: The Selected Addresses of Franklin D. Roosevelt, 1932–1945* (New York: Popular Library, 1961), p. 268.
2. Marc A. Rose, "Detroit—Million Man Arsenal," *Forbes* XLIX (Apr. 15, 1942), 10.
3. For a recent review of fruitful areas of investigation in the 1939–45 period, see Jim F. Heath, "Domestic America in World War II: Research Opportunities for Historians," *Journal of American History*, LXIII (Sept., 1971), 384–414.
4. Eliot Janeway, *The Struggle for Survival: A Chronicle of Economic Mobilization in World War II* (New Haven: Yale University Press, 1951), pp. 331, 335; Geoffrey Perrett, *Days of Sadness, Years of Triumph: The American People, 1939–1945* (New York: Coward, McCann & Geoghegan Inc., 1973), pp. 10–11, 442.
5. Bruce Catton, *The War Lords of Washington* (New York: Harcourt, Brace and Co., 1948), p. 311; Barton J. Bernstein, "America in Peace and War: The Test of Liberalism," in Barton J. Bernstein, ed., *Toward a New Past: Dissenting Essays in American History* (New York: Random House, 1968), p. 290.
6. John Morton Blum, *V Was for Victory: Politics and American Culture during World War II* (New York: Harcourt Brace Jovanovich, 1976), p. 104.
7. James MacGregor Burns, *Roosevelt: The Soldier of Freedom* (New York: Harcourt Brace Jovanovich, 1970), p. viii.
8. David Brody, "The New Deal and World War II," in John Braeman, Robert H. Bremner, and David Brody, eds., *The New Deal*, vol. 1, *The National Level* (Columbus: Ohio State University Press, 1975), p. 305.
9. Richard S. Kirkendall, *The United States, 1929–1945: Years of Crisis and Change* (New York: McGraw-Hill, 1974), pp. 288–89.
10. Richard Polenberg, *War and Society: The United States, 1941–1945* (Philadelphia: J. B. Lippincott, 1972), pp. 4–5, 130, 244.

11. Robert Duffus, "Detroit: Utopia on Wheels," *Harper's*, CLXII (Dec., 1930), 50; Keith T. Sward, *The Legend of Henry Ford* (1948: reprint ed., New York: Russell & Russell, 1968), p. 42.
12. Work Projects Administration, Federal Writers' Program in the State of Michigan, *Michigan, A Guide to the Wolverine State* (New York: Oxford University Press, 1941), p. 231; Webb Waldron, "Where is America Going?," *Century*, C (May, 1920), 58.
13. Waldron, "Where is America Going?," p. 61.
14. Edmund Wilson, *American Earthquake: A Documentary of the Twenties and Thirties* (New York: Doubleday, 1958), p. 232.
15. Richard Deverall to Clarence Glick, June 28, 1943, Papers of Phileo T. Nash, Harry S. Truman Library, Independence, Missouri.
16. Brody, "New Deal and World War II," in Braeman, Bremner, and Brody, eds., *The New Deal: The National Level*, p. 297.
17. *Christian Science Monitor*, Apr. 12, 1940, clipping, Papers of Edward J. Jeffries, Jr., Burton Historical Collection, Detroit Public Library, Detroit, Box 2 (1940).
18. *Detroit News*, Dec. 7, 1941.
19. *Detroit Free Press*, Dec. 8, 1941; *Social Justice*, Dec. 15, 1941, quoted in Sheldon Marcus, *Father Coughlin: The Tumultuous Life of the Priest of the Little Flower* (Boston: Little, Brown, 1973), p. 204.
20. *Detroit News*, Dec. 26, 1941; *Sault Ste. Marie Evening News*, Jan. 2, 1942.

CHAPTER 1

1. *Detroit News*, July 21, 1940.
2. Ibid., May 17, 1940.
3. Barton J. Bernstein, "The Automobile Industry and the Coming of the Second World War," *Southwestern Social Science Quarterly*, XLVIII (June, 1966), 32.
4. Geoffrey Perrett, *Days of Sadness, Years of Triumph: The American People, 1939–1945* (New York: Coward, McCann & Geoghegan Inc., 1973), p. 179.
5. *Detroit News*, July 4, 13, 21, 1940.
6. Michigan WPA, "Michigan Industrial Activity and the Need for WPA Employment," Apr., 1941, p. 1, Division of Social Research, State Administrators' Reports-Michigan, Records of the Work Projects Administration, Record Group 69, National Archives, Washington, D.C. (cited hereafter as WPA Records, RG 69).
7. *Detroit News*, Jan. 5, 1941.
8. Marvin Hoffman, comp. and ed., *Michigan Statistical Abstract* (East Lansing: Michigan State University Press, 1955), p. 135.
9. David Brody, "The New Deal and World War II," in John Braeman, Robert H. Bremner, and David Brody, eds., *The New Deal*, vol. 1: *The National Level* (Columbus: Ohio State University Press, 1975), p. 287.
10. WPA, "Michigan Industrial Activity," p. 3, WPA Records, RG 69.

11. *Detroit News*, June 15, 1941.
12. Ibid., Oct. 26, 1941.
13. Ibid., Dec. 7, 1941.
14. Ibid., Dec. 4, 1941; WPA, "Priorities Unemployment and Need in Michigan," Sept. 26, 1941, pp. 1–2, WPA Records, RG 69.
15. Andrew Stevenson to James W. Fessler, Feb. 15, 1946, Policy Documentation File 631.001R, Records of the War Production Board, Record Group 179, National Archives (cited hereafter as WPB Records, RG 179); William Duffy, "History of the Automotive Division," 1945, pp. 3–5, File 053.108R, ibid.; Policy Analysis and Records Branch, "The Automotive Industry in War Production," May 10, 1944, pp. 14–15, File 631.001R, ibid.
16. William C. Richards to Executive Officer, Mar. 20, 1942, Division of Field Operations, Records of the Office of Government Reports, Record Group 44, Washington National Records Center, Suitland, Md. (cited hereafter as OGR Records, RG 44).
17. *Detroit Free Press*, Mar. 25, 1942.
18. Office of Facts and Figures, "Attitudes Affecting War Production," 1942, OGR Records, RG 44.
19. A.H. Raskin, "Mass Magic in Detroit," *New York Times Magazine*, Mar. 1, 1942, p. 4.
20. "Battle of Detroit," *Time*, XXXIX (Mar. 23, 1942), 10.
21. William C. Richards, "Effect of the War on the Average Man," Jan. 2, 1942, pp. 2–3, OGR Records, RG 44; *Detroit News*, Feb. 15, 26, June 25, July 1, 1942. The Bureau of Labor Statistics defined the Detroit area as the counties of Wayne, Oakland, Macomb, and Washtenaw. Bureau of Labor Statistics, *Working Notebook on the Economic Impact of the War on Detroit* (Washington, D.C.: Government Printing Office, 1943), p. 71.
22. Automobile Manufacturers Association, *Freedom's Arsenal: The Story of the Automotive Council for War Production* (Detroit: The Association, 1950), pp. 114, 118.
23. Francis Walton, *Miracle of World War II: The Story of American War Production* (New York: Macmillan, 1956), p. 240; U.S. Congress, Senate, Special Committee to Investigate the Problems of American Small Business, *Economic Concentration in World War II*. 79 Cong., 2 sess. (Washington, D.C.: Government Printing Office, 1946), p. 150.
24. *Detroit News*, Nov. 16, 24–26, Dec. 3, 1942.
25. Lowell J. Carr and James E. Stermer, *Willow Run: A Study of Industrialization and Cultural Inadequacy* (New York: Harper Bros., 1952), p. 3.
26. Charles A. Lindbergh, *The Wartime Journals of Charles Lindbergh* (New York: Harcourt Brace Jovanovich, 1970), p. 613.
27. Carr and Stermer, *Willow Run*, p. 161.
28. Glendon Swarthout, *Willow Run, A Novel* (New York: Thomas Y. Crowell, 1943), p. 13.
29. War Production Board, *State Listing of Major War Supply Contracts Active as*

of December 31, 1944 (Washington, D.C.: Government Printing Office, 1945), pp. 347–66; Maury Maverick to Harry F. Kelly, June 15, 1943, Records of the Executive Office, Harry F. Kelly, Governor, 1943–46, Record Group 42, Michigan State Archives, Lansing, Box 7 (cited hereafter as Executive Records, RG 42); *Detroit News*, Aug. 8, 1945.

30. Richards, "Effect of the War," p. 11, OGR Records, RG 44.

31. *Detroit News*, Nov. 4, 1943.

32. Ibid., Mar. 2, 1944.

33. Office of Price Administration, *Corporate Profits, 1936–1944: Industry Stabilized at War Peak. War Profits Studies No. 12* (Washington, D.C.: Government Printing Office, 1945), pp. 21, 25, 41, 49.

34. Richard Polenberg, *War and Society: The United States, 1941–1945* (Philadelphia: J. B. Lippincott, 1972), p. 12.

35. Eliot Roosevelt, *As He Saw It* (New York: Duell, Sloan and Pearce, 1946), p. 196. For an alternate version of the Stalin quotation, see Charles E. Bohlen, *Witness to History* (New York: W.W. Norton, 1973), p. 150.

36. U.S. Department of Commerce, Bureau of the Census, *County Data Book, 1947* (Washington: Government Printing Office, 1947), pp. xii–xiii, 199, 207, 213, 277.

37. David Novik, Melvin Anschin, and W.C. Truppner, *Wartime Production Controls* (New York: Columbia University Press, 1949), p. 6.

38. Walton, *Miracle of World War II*, pp. 544–46.

39. Senate Special Committee Investigating the Problems of American Small Business, *Economic Concentration*, pp. 21, 125, 151.

40. "Industry Avenges Pearl Harbor, Speeds Arms to Every War Front," *Michigan Manufacturer and Financial Record*, LXXI (Apr. 24, 1943), 11.

41. *Detroit News*, Dec. 7, 1942.

42. Bureau of the Census, *Historical Statistics of the United States, 1790 to 1957* (Washington, D.C.: Government Printing Office, 1960), p. 70; U.S. Congress, Senate, Special Committee Investigating the National Defense Program, *Hearings. Manpower Problems in Detroit*, 79 Cong., 1 sess. (Washington, D.C.: Government Printing Office, 1945), Part XXVIII, 13,542–43; *Detroit News*, Dec. 4, 1944.

43. *Detroit News*, Jan. 16, 1943; Harvey Klemmer, "Michigan Fights," *National Geographic*, LXXXVI (Dec., 1944), 701; Thomas Hawley, "The Developement of Vocational Education in Michigan during the Period 1940–1947" (M.A. thesis, Wayne University, 1947), pp. 21–64.

44. *Detroit News*, July 21, Sept. 19, Oct. 7, Nov. 29, 1944.

45. Selective Service System, *Industrial Deferment. Special Monograph No. 6* (Washington, D.C.: Government Printing Office, 1948), III, 99–100.

46. *Detroit News*, Nov. 26, 1943.

47. National War Labor Board, *Termination Report of the National War Labor Board*. 3 vols. (Washington, D.C.: Government Printing Office, 1947), I, 1140.

48. *United Automobile Worker*, Sept. 15, Oct. 1, 1941.

49. Charles A. Buber to Victor Reuther, May 29, 1942, United Automobile Workers War Policy Division Collection, Archives of Labor History and Urban Affairs, Wayne State University, Detroit, Box 30 (cited hereafter as UAW War Policy Collection); Hector Bordeau to Walter Reuther, Jan. 27, 1942, ibid., Box 1; E.L. Keenan to Directors, Region V USES, June 19, 1943, ibid., Box 13; WPB, "Meeting in the Detroit Offices of the War Production Board," Sept. 2, 1942, pp. 19–21, File 550.1, WPB Records, RG 179; *Detroit News*, Mar. 15, 1945.

50. *Detroit News*, Jan. 17, 1943.

51. Ibid., July 29, 1943.

52. Ibid., Jan. 16, Dec. 5, 1944, Apr. 23, 1945; Samuel A. Cascanier to Harold S. Woodsley, Feb. 20, 1943, Michigan File 370.53305, Records of the War Manpower Commission, Record Group 211, National Archives.

53. *Detroit News*, Apr. 19, 1942.

54. Ibid., Nov. 4, Dec. 10, 13, 15, 1942.

55. Ibid., Sept. 29, 1943.

56. Ibid., Apr. 20, 1944, Mar. 1, 1945; John Corson to James Knowlson, May 4, 1942, File 241C, WPB Records, RG 179; Donald M. Nelson to Ernest C. Kanzler, May 9, 1942, File 241.3C, ibid.; Kanzler to Nelson, May 14, 1942, ibid.; Kanzler to Nelson, May 15, 1942, ibid.

57. Leroy Peterson to F.M. McLaury, Mar. 31, 1944, Central File, Records of the President's Committee on Congested Production Areas, Record Group 212, National Archives.

58. For further discussion of Michigan wartime agriculture, see Alan Clive, "The Michigan Farmer in World War II," *Michigan History*, LX (Winter, 1976), 291–314.

59. Bureau of the Census, *Census of Agriculture, 1945* (Washington, D.C.: Government Printing Office, 1946), I, Part VI, 2, 5–8.

60. "Michigan Crop Conditions as of May 27, 1943," Executive Records, RG 42, Box 73; *Detroit News*, Apr. 29, 1945.

61. *Detroit News*, June 26, Aug. 2, 1941, Nov. 16, 1944; "Report on Labor Supply in Michigan," Aug. 19, 1941, p. 1, OGR Records, RG 44.

62. Selective Service System, *Agricultural Deferment. Special Monograph No. 7* (Washington, D.C.: Government Printing Office, 1947), pp. 96, 239.

63. Clarence Prentiss, "Sanilac County," 1943, p. 70, Annual Narrative and Statistical Reports, Records of the United States Department of Agriculture, Federal Extension Service, Record Group 33, National Archives (cited hereafter as FES Records, RG 33).

64. L.R. Walker, "Marquette County," 1943, p. 21, ibid.; Gordon R. Schlubatis, "Branch County," 1944, p. 25, ibid.; Lyle Tompkins, "Oceana County," 1943, p. 31, ibid.; J.F. Hoeksma, "St. Joseph County," 1944, pp. 43–44, ibid.

65. Cary McWilliams, *Ill Fares the Land: Migrants and Migratory Labor in the United States* (Boston: Houghton Mifflin, 1942), p. 156.

66. Ibid., p. 271.

67. Lyle Tompkins, "Oceana County," 1944, p. 92, FES Records, RG 33.
68. Robert C. Jones, *Mexican War Workers in the United States: The Mexico-United States Manpower Recruiting Program and Its Operation* (Washington, D.C.: Pan American Union, 1945), p. 25.
69. *Detroit News*, May 24, 1943; *Ann Arbor News*, Feb. 3, 1943.
70. *Detroit News*, July 22, Oct. 10, 15, 1942, Apr. 18, July 11, 15, Aug. 7, 1943.
71. Tompkins, "Oceana County," 1943, p. 73, FES Records, RG 33.
72. Tompkins, "Oceana County," 1944, p. 72, ibid.
73. *Detroit News*, Sept. 5, 1943.
74. Ibid., May 13, Oct. 4, 1943.
75. Ibid., Aug. 9, 1945.
76. James Mencarelli, "Sitting Out World War II in Michigan," *Detroit Free Press Sunday Magazine*, Jan. 5, 1975, p. 15.
77. Walter W. Wilcox, *The Farmer and the Second World War* (Ames, Iowa: Iowa State College Press, 1947), p. 288; Seymour Harris, *Inflation and the American Economy* (New York: McGraw-Hill, 1945), p. 356; Michigan State Department of Agriculture, *Eleventh Biennial Report, 1943–1944* (Lansing, Michigan: The Department, 1945), p. 48; Michigan Department of Agriculture, *Twelfth Biennial Report, 1945–1946* (Lansing, Michigan: The Department, 1947), p. 25.
78. Bureau of the Census, *Census of Agriculture, 1945*, I, Part VI, 2.
79. *Detroit News*, Nov. 13, 1942.
80. Curtis K. Stadtfeld, *From the Land and Back* (New York: Charles Scribner's Sons, 1972), p. 178.
81. John Morton Blum, "World War II," in C. Vann Woodward, ed., *The Comparative Approach to American History* (New York: Basic Books, 1968), p. 318.
82. William Haber, *How Much Does it Cost? A Report to the Michigan Employment Security Commission on Long-Range Benefit Financing and Fund Solvency in Michigan* (Lansing, Michigan: The Commission, 1951), pp. 70, 291; *Detroit News*, Feb. 22, July 23, Nov. 25, 1943.
83. Haber, *How Much*, pp. 312–13; *Muskegon Chronicle*, Jan. 1, 1943; *Detroit News*, Aug. 20, 1944; U.S. Internal Revenue Service, *Annual Report of the Commissioner of Internal Revenue for the Fiscal Year Ending June 30, 1940* (Washington, D.C.: Government Printing Office, 1941), p. 52; Internal Revenue Service, *Annual Report . . . for the Fiscal Year Ending June 30, 1945* (Washington, D.C.: Government Printing Office, 1946), p. 56.
84. *Detroit News*, Oct. 3, 1943.
85. Ibid., May 21–22, 1942, May 17, Aug. 9–12, 1943, July 30, 1944.
86. *Grand Rapids Press*, Jan. 1, 1941, Jan. 1, Feb. 10–11, 1943, June 15, 1945.
87. William B. Gates, *Michigan Copper and Boston Dollars: An Economic History of the Michigan Copper Mining Industry, 1845–1949* (Cambridge, Massachusetts: Harvard University Press, 1951), pp. 210–11.

88. Eliot Janeway, *The Struggle for Survival: A Chronicle of Economic Mobilization in World War II* (New Haven: Yale University Press, 1951), p. 331; Murray D. Van Wagoner, "Operating the Toolshop of America," *Vital Speeches*, VIII (Aug., 1942), 664.

CHAPTER 2

1. *Detroit News*, Mar. 14, 1943; Jeremy Brecher, *Strike!* (San Francisco: Straight Arrow Books, 1972), p. 226.
2. Irving Bernstein, *Turbulent Years: A History of the American Worker, 1933–1941* (Boston: Houghton Mifflin, 1970), p. 744.
3. Martin Halpern, "The 1941 Strike at the Ford Motor Company," (MS, 1974), pp. 16–22, 32–34, 37–43, in Mr. Halpern's possession.
4. Bernstein, *Turbulent Years*, p. 747.
5. David I. Verway, ed., *Michigan Statistical Abstract*, 9th ed. (East Lansing: Michigan State University Press, 1964), p. 90; *Detroit News*, Jan. 13, Aug. 30, Oct. 24, Nov. 8, 12–14, 1941; *Detroit Free Press*, July 16–17, 1941.
6. *Detroit News*, Sept. 30, 1941.
7. Ibid., Dec. 9, 1941.
8. Bureau of Agricultural Economics, Division of Program Surveys, "The Social Dynamics of Detroit," Dec. 3, 1942, p. 3, Records of the Office of Government Reports, Record Group 44, Washington National Records Center, Suitland, Md. (cited hereafter as OGR Records, RG 44).
9. Baldwin Hawes, "UAW-CIO," People's Song Library Collection, Archives of Labor History and Urban Affairs, Wayne State University, Detroit, Box 17.
10. Eli Chinoy, *Automobile Workers and the American Dream* (Garden City, New York: Doubleday, 1955), p. 133; *Detroit News*, Sept. 24, 1943.
11. U.S. Department of Commerce, Bureau of the Census, *Statistical Abstract of the United States, 1946* (Washington, D.C.: Government Printing Office, 1947), p. 213; *Detroit News*, May 2, 1943, Sept. 23, 1944, Jan. 23, 1945.
12. Seymour Harris, *Inflation and the American Economy* (New York: McGraw-Hill, 1945), p. 287; *Detroit News*, Aug. 22, 1943.
13. Edwin E. Witte to Sam Berger, July 13, 1943, Papers of Edwin E. Witte, State Historical Society of Wisconsin, Madison, Box 8 (cited hereafter as Witte Papers).
14. *Detroit News*, Apr. 7, 1942.
15. Lee Pressman, "Memorandum on Problems Arising under the National War Labor Board," May 31, 1944, pp. 2–3, United Automobile Workers Research Department Collection, Archives of Labor History and Urban Affairs, Wayne State University, Detroit, Box 10 (unprocessed) (cited hereafter as UAW Research Collection).
16. *Detroit News*, Dec. 1, 1943, Aug. 1, 3, 1945.
17. Ibid., Mar. 18, 1945.
18. Ibid., Dec. 23, 1943, Jan. 28, 1944.

19. "Memorandum on Relations of Ford Local 600, UAW-CIO, with U.S. Army Officers Stationed in the Detroit Area," Feb. 9, 1942, United Automobile Workers War Policy Division Collection, Archives of Labor History and Urban Affairs, Box 1 (cited hereafter as UAW War Policy Collection); *Detroit News*, June 8–9, 1942, Jan. 13, 1943; Captain J.A. Mullen, "Materials for Daily Labor Situation Report," Dec. 9, 1943, Records of the State Police, Record Group 65–31, Michigan State Archives, Lansing, Box 8 (cited hereafter as State Police Records, RG 65–31); "Monthly Tabulation of Labor Disputes," June, 1945, ibid., Box 9; "Monthly Geographical Breakdown of Labor Disputes," June, 1945, ibid. For examples of State Police labor intelligence reports, see Detective Charles Lake to Captain Harold Mulbar, June 13, 1944, ibid., Box 8; and "Industrial Intelligence Report," Dec., 1943, ibid.

20. BAE, "Social Dynamics," pp. 14–15, OGR Records, RG 44.

21. Lowell J. Carr and James E. Stermer, *Willow Run: A Study of Industrialization and Cultural Inadequacy* (New York: Harper Brothers, 1952), p. 182.

22. BAE, "Social Dynamics," p. 15, OGR Records, RG 44.

23. Edwin E. Witte to Leon Epstein, Mar. 17, 1943, Witte Papers, Box 8; Strike Reports, July-Aug., 1944, UAW Research Collection, Box 4 (unprocessed).

24. Clarence Boles to Thomas Burns, Jan. 2, 1943, UAW War Policy Collection, Box 13.

25. Anthony Luchek to Philip Garman, July 17, 1943, Policy Documention File 245C, Records of the War Production Board, Record Group 179, National Archives (cited hereafter as WPB Records, RG 179).

26. "Report on Conditions at Willow Run," Feb. 24, 1943, p. 7, UAW War Policy Collection, Box 16.

27. Oral History Interview of Jess Ferrazza, May 26, 1961, p. 12, Michigan Historical Collections, Ann Arbor. For examples of the Taylor-Local 212 warfare, see "On Guard" (a bulletin for shop stewards), Oct. 24, 1944, Local 212 Collection, Archives of Labor History, Box 7; Taylor to Jess Ferrazza, Nov. 24, 1944, ibid.

28. Joel Seidman, *American Labor from Defense to Reconversion* (Chicago: University of Chicago Press, 1953), p. 176; *Detroit News*, Mar. 19, 1945; "Report on Activities of Labor-Management Committee, Local 155," undated, UAW Research Collection, Box 3 (unprocessed); *Detroit News*, Mar. 25, 1942, Dec. 17, 24, 1943.

29. *Detroit News*, Dec. 9–10, 14, 1942.

30. Edwin E. Witte to Harry Brown, July 19, 1943, Witte Papers, Box 8; National War Labor Board, *Termination Report of the National War Labor Board*. 3 vols. (Washington, D.C.: Government Printing Office, 1947), I, 755–58, 1169–73.

31. Edwin E. Witte, memorandum, 1943, Witte Papers, Box 84; *Detroit News*, Aug. 1, 1942, June 28–29, 1945.

32. *Detroit News*, Feb. 7, 1943.

33. Ibid., June 2, 1944.
34. Edwin E. Witte, "Confidential Memorandum on Conference with John Reid," Feb. 22, 1943, Witte Papers, Box 84.
35. "Convention of Automobile Workers (CIO), 1943," *Monthly Labor Review*, LVII (Nov., 1943), 954; Carr and Stermer, *Willow Run*, p. 193; James P. Mitchell, "Report on Investigation of Labor Factors Affecting Production at the Willow Run Bomber Plant of the Ford Motor Company," Feb. 25, 1943, pp. 5–6, Central File, Records of the President's Committee on Congested Production Areas, Record Group 212, National Archives.
36. A.H. Raskin, "Industrial Conflict in Detroit," June 9, 1944, p. 2, File 245C, WPB Records, RG 179.
37. Nelson Lichtenstein, "Industrial Unionism Under the No-Strike Pledge: A Study of the CIO During World War II" (Ph.D. thesis, University of California, Berkeley, 1974), p. 315.
38. Seidman, *American Labor*, p. 107; RWLB Press Releases, Nov. 14, 1943, Mar. 7, 1944, Witte Papers, Box 88.
39. Verway, ed., *Michigan Statistical Abstract*, p. 90; Michigan State Labor Mediation Board, *Third Annual Report, 1944–1945* (Lansing, Michigan: The Board, 1945), p. 11.
40. Rosa Lee Swafford, *Wartime Record of Strikes and Walkouts, 1940–1945. Senate Document No. 136.* 79 Cong., 2 sess. (Washington, D.C.: Government Printing Office, 1946), p. 8.
41. Ed Jennings, "Wildcat! The Wartime Strike Wave in Auto," *Radical America*, IX (July-Aug., 1975), 85, 90.
42. "Hitler or the U.S.?," *Time*, XL (Aug. 24, 1942), 17.
43. *Detroit News*, Feb. 17, 1945.
44. Edwin E. Witte to Harry Brown, July 21, 1943, Witte Papers, Box 8; Oral History Interview of John W. Anderson, Feb. 17–May 21, 1960, p. 105, Michigan Historical Collections; Seidman, *American Labor*, p. 133.
45. Ernest Clark et al to Edward J. Jeffries, Jr., June 9, 1944, Papers of Edward J. Jeffries, Jr., Burton Historical Collection, Detroit Public Library, Detroit, Box 10 (1944). For Michigan reaction to strikes, see *Detroit Times*, May 26, 1944; *Ann Arbor News*, May 28, 1944; *Saginaw News*, May 30, 1944.
46. Lichtenstein, "Industrial Unionism," p. 439.
47. Ibid., p. 619.
48. *Detroit News*, May 28, 1944.
49. United Automobile Workers (CIO), *Proceedings of the Ninth Annual Convention, September 11–17, 1944* (Detroit: UAW, 1945), pp. 154, 175.
50. Alan Clive, "Michigan in the Presidential Election of 1944: A Narrative of American Politics in Action" (MS, 1970), pp. 49–60.
51. Ibid., pp. 60–136.
52. James Caldwell Foster, *The Union Politic: The CIO Political Action Committee* (Columbia, Missouri: University of Missouri Press, 1975), p. 44.
53. "Partial Report, UAW-CIO Referendum Committee," 1945, pp. 71–72,

110–11, UAW Research Collection, Addendum to the Collection, Sept. 5, 1972, Box 1 of 3 (unprocessed).

54. *Detroit News*, Jan. 18, Feb. 17, Mar. 16, 1945.

55. Ibid., Mar. 7, 1945.

56. BAE, "Social Dynamics," p. 24, OGR Records, RG 44; Edwin E. Witte to Sam Berger, July 15, 1943, Witte Papers, Box 8.

57. *Detroit Free Press*, Mar. 10, 1945.

58. *United Automobile Worker*, May 1, 1945.

59. *Detroit News*, Mar. 4, 1945.

60. David Brody, "The New Deal and World War II," in John Braeman, Robert H. Bremner, and David Brody, eds., *The New Deal*, vol. 1: *The National Level* (Columbus: Ohio State University Press, 1975), p. 299.

61. Bureau of Agricultural Economics, Division of Program Surveys, "Factory Workers Typescript," 1943, p. 136, Records of the United States Department of Agriculture, Bureau of Agricultural Economics, Record Group 83, National Archives.

62. Lichtenstein, "Industrial Unionism," pp. iv, 721.

63. *Detroit News*, Dec. 4, 31, 1943.

CHAPTER 3

1. Detroit Office of Civilian Defense, "Your Civilian Defense," script for broadcast of August 20, 1942, p. 3, Papers of Edward J. Jeffries, Jr., Burton Historical Collection, Detroit Public Library, Detroit, Box 7 (1942) (cited hereafter as Mayor's Office Records).

2. William C. Richards, "Effect of the War on the Average Man," Jan. 10, 1942, p. 17, Records of the Office of Government Reports, Record Group 44, Washington National Records Center, Suitland, Md. (cited hereafter as OGR Records, RG 44); Bureau of Agricultural Economics, Division of Program Surveys, "The Social Dynamics of Detroit," Dec. 3, 1942, p. 5, ibid.; *Detroit News*, Jan. 15-Apr. 9, 1942, clippings, *Detroit News* Lansing Bureau Collection, Michigan Historical Collections, Ann Arbor, Box 5; Michigan Office of Civilian Defense, "Summary of Operations for 1944 and Outlook for 1945," Jan., 1945, p. 1, Mayor's Office Records, Box 8 (1945).

3. *Jackson Citizen-Patriot*, Apr. 4, 1944; *Detroit News*, Feb. 1, 1944.

4. *Detroit News*, Apr. 14, 1943.

5. City of Detroit, *Municipal Code, 1945* (Detroit: City of Detroit, 1945), p. 877.

6. Frank Hartung, "A Study in Law and Social Differentiation: As Exemplified in Violations of the Emergency Price Control Act of 1942 and the Second War Powers Act, in the Detroit Wholesale Meat Industry" (Ph.D. thesis, University of Michigan, 1949), p. 215.

7. Richard Polenberg, *War and Society: The United States, 1941–1945* (Philadelphia: J. B. Lippincott, 1972), p. 138; Hope T. Eldridge, "Problems and Methods of Estimating Post Censal Population," *Social Forces*, XXIV (Oct.,

1945), 46; "Estimates of Net Civilian Inter-County Migration, April 1, 1940-November 1, 1943," *The Labor Market* (Apr., 1945), p. 28.

8. U.S. Department of Commerce, Bureau of the Census, *Estimated Civilian Population of the United States by County, November 1, 1943. Population Reports Series P-44, No. 3* (Washington, D.C.: Government Printing Office, 1944), p. 14.

9. Bureau of the Census, *Characteristics of the Population, Labor Force, Families and Housing, Detroit-Willow Run Congested Production Area: June, 1944. Population Special Reports Series CA-3, No. 9* (Washington, D.C.: Government Printing Office, 1944), p. 7; Bureau of the Census, *Characteristics of the Population, Labor Force, Families and Housing, Muskegon Congested Production Area: June, 1944. Population Special Reports Series CA-3, No. 10* (Washington, D.C.: Government Printing Office, 1944), p. 6; *Bureau of the Census, Special Census of Inkster, Michigan, April 14, 1945. Population Special Reports Series PSC No. 59* (Washington, D.C., 1945), p. 1; *Bureau of the Census, Special Census of Gratiot Township, August 17, 1945. Population Special Reports Series PSC No. 80* (Washington, D.C.: Government Printing Office, 1945).

10. *Detroit News*, Sept. 24, 1939, May 27–28, June 2, July 7, 1940, Feb. 16, Mar. 21, June 29, July 10, 1941, Oct. 23, 1942; Robert C. Goodwin to Montague A. Clark, Nov. 21, 1943, File 533.14/1944, Records of the War Manpower Commission, Record Group 211, National Archives, Washington, D.C. (cited hereafter as WMC Records, RG 211); Edward Cushman to Robert C. Goodwin, Feb. 14, 1944, ibid.; Cushman to Goodwin, Aug. 22, 1944, ibid.

11. Robert L. Duffus, "A City That Forges Thunderbolts," *New York Times Magazine*, Jan. 10, 1943, p. 13.

12. Richard R. Lingeman, *Don't You Know There's A War On? The American Home Front, 1941–1945* (New York: G.P. Putnam's Sons, 1970), p. 175.

13. *Battle Creek Enquirer and News*, Jan. 2, 1942; *Detroit News*, Mar. 20, 1941.

14. *Detroit News*, June 25, 1943; Downing E. Proctor to Mark A. McCloskey, Oct. 11, 1943, General Classified Files, Region V-Michigan, Records of the Office of Community War Services, Record Group 215, National Archives (cited hereafter as OCWS Records, RG 215); Harry Grayson to Joseph Wilson, Dec. 26, 1944, Central File, Records of the President's Committee on Congested Production Areas, Record Group 212, National Archives (cited hereafter as CCPA Records, RG 212).

15. *Detroit Free Press*, July 25, 1943; *Detroit News*, Oct. 27, 1943; Edwin E. Witte to Norris Hall, Apr. 8, 1943, Papers of Edwin E. Witte, State Historical Society of Wisconsin, Madison, Box 8; Herbert Hill et al, "Survey of Religious and Racial Conflict Forces in Detroit," Sept. 30, 1943, pp. 2–3, Civil Rights Congress of Michigan Collection, Archives of Labor History and Urban Affairs, Wayne State University, Detroit, Box 71 (cited hereafter as CRC Collection); Agnes E. Meyer, *Journey through Chaos* (New York: Harcourt, Brace & Co., 1944), p. 73.

16. Michigan State Department of Public Administration, *Fifteen Years of State Government Financial Statistics, 1940–1955* (Lansing: The Department, 1955), pp. 1, 5; *Detroit Free Press*, Mar. 6, 1943.

17. U.S. Congress, House, Committee on Public Buildings and Grounds, *Hearings*, 77 Cong., 1 sess. (Washington, D.C.: Government Printing Office, 1941), Part II, 90.

18. Edward J. Jeffries, Jr. to Arthur H. Vandenberg, Nov. 18, 1941, Mayor's Office Records, Box 12 (1941); Jeffries to Frank Knox, Mar. 17, 1941, ibid.; Knox to Jeffries, Mar. 24, 1941, ibid.

19. *Congressional Record*, 76 Cong., 3 sess. (Washington, D.C.: Government Printing Office, 1941), LXXXVI, Part II, 11,872.

20. National Housing Agency, *Fourth Annual Report, 1945* (Washington, D.C.: Government Printing Office, 1946), Part I, 73.

21. James MacGregor Burns, *Roosevelt: The Soldier of Freedom* (New York: Harcourt Brace Jovanovich, 1970), p. 343.

22. *Detroit News*, Nov. 9, 1941.

23. Edward J. Jeffries, Jr. to Prentiss M. Brown, Feb. 3, 1943, Mayor's Office Records, Box 10 (1942).

24. Rudolf Tenerowicz to Edward J. Jeffries, Jan. 30, 1942, ibid.; Louis C. Rabaut to Jeffries, Jan. 26, 1942, ibid.; Prentiss M. Brown to M.E. Gilmour, 194[2], ibid.; Jeffries to Harold D. Smith, Feb. 27, 1942, ibid.; Prentiss M. Brown to Marvin MacIntyre, Mar. 5, 1942, ibid.; Harold D. Smith to Jeffries, Apr. 9, 1942, ibid.

25. Joseph H. Fisher, Harold D. Furlong, and L.A. Fullerton, *Macomb-Oakland Industrial Defense Area of Michigan* (Lansing, Michigan: Michigan Council of Defense, 1941), pp. 1–32, 46–65; *Detroit News*, Feb. 25, Mar. 7, Sept. 16, Nov. 6, 1941, Oct. 10, 1942; Region V, OCWS, "Composite Report on Health, Welfare, and Related Activities in the Detroit, Michigan, War Area," Dec. 22, 1943, p. 80, OCWS Records, RG 215.

26. Bureau of Agricultural Economics, Division of Program Surveys, "Detroit People in Perspective: A Study of Group Attitudes and Aspirations," [1942], p. 3, OGR Records, RG 44.

27. *Ann Arbor News*, July 17, 1941.

28. U.S. Congress, Senate, Special Committee Investigating the National Defense Program, *Hearings. Willow Run Housing*, 77 Cong., 2 sess. (Washington, D.C.: Government Printing Office, 1942), Part XII, 5391.

29. Detroit Housing Commission, *Seventh Annual Report, 1940* (Detroit: The Commission, 1941), pp. 16–17.

30. *Detroit News*, Aug. 17, 1940, May 20, July 15, Dec. 3, 1942; Bureau of the Census, *Survey of Occupancy in Privately-Owned Dwelling Units in Detroit and Adjoining Communities, Michigan* (Washington, D.C.: Government Printing Office, 1944), p. 1; Bureau of the Census, *Report CA-3, No. 9*, pp. 26–27.

31. *Detroit News*, Oct. 4, 8–9, 11, 15, 20, 25, 1942, Dec. 26, 1943; *Detroit Free Press*, Sept. 26, 1943.

32. Bureau of Labor Statistics, *Working Notebook of the Impact of the War on Detroit* (Washington, D.C.: Government Printing Office, 1943), p. 69; *Detroit News*, July 11, 1943, Aug. 1, 1945.

33. Bureau of the Census, *Housing Construction Statistics, 1889–1964* (Washington, D.C.: Government Printing Office, 1966), pp. 22, 153; NHA, *Fourth Annual Report*, IV, 64; "Lanham Act War Housing," 1945, Records of the Executive Office, Harry F. Kelly, Governor, 1943–46, Record Group 42, Michigan State Archives, Lansing, Box 66 (cited hereafter as Executive Records, RG 42).

34. Detroit Housing Commission, *Ninth Annual Report, 1944* (Detroit: The Commission, 1944), p. 35.

35. Freda S. Yenney, "Areas of Tension within the John R. Fisher Homes as Revealed by One Hundred Wives Living on the Project" (M.A. thesis, Wayne University, 1944), pp. 50–60, 98–103; DHC, *Ninth Annual Report*, p. 25.

36. Yenney, "Areas of Tension," pp. 49–50.

37. *Detroit News*, June 29, 1941, July 29–30, 1942; Detroit Housing Commission, *Eighth Annual Report, 1942* (Detroit: The Commission, 1943), p. 9; Maury Maverick to Edward J. Jeffries, Jr., July 10, 1943, Mayor's Office Records, Box 10 (1943).

38. *Detroit News*, Aug. 8, Dec. 16, 1941, Apr. 14, May 16–17, July 8, 10–11, 1942; U.S. Congress, House, Committee on Public Buildings and Grounds, *Hearings on War Housing*, 77 Cong., 2 sess. (Washington, D.C.: Government Printing Office, 1942), p. 135.

39. DHC, *Ninth Annual Report*, p. 16.

40. *Detroit News*, Feb. 1, 1942.

41. Ibid., Apr. 26, 1942; U.S. Congress, Senate, Special Committee Investigating the National Defense Program, *Hearings*, Part XII, 5408.

42. *Ann Arbor News*, May 7, 15, 1942.

43. *Detroit News*, May 13, 1942.

44. Ibid., May 19, 1942.

45. Ibid., June 18, 21, 23–26, July 7, 19, 22–23, 30, 1942.

46. Ibid., Aug. 30, 1942; Meyer, *Journey Through Chaos*, p. 34.

47. *Detroit News*, Feb. 14, Aug. 30, 1943, Feb. 16, 1944; Region V OCWS, "Composite Report," p. 37, OCWS Records, RG 215; Lowell J. Carr and James E. Stermer, *Willow Run: A Study of Industrialization and Cultural Inadequacy* (New York: Harper Brothers, 1952), p. 62.

48. *Detroit News*, Dec. 24, 1941, Jan. 2, Mar. 11, Sept. 10, 12, 1942, Jan. 31, 1943.

49. Del A. Smith to Victor Reuther, Mar. 23, 1943, United Automobile Workers War Policy Division Collection, Archives of Labor History and Urban Affairs, Wayne State University, Detroit, Box 11; *Detroit News*, Feb. 14, 1943.

50. *Detroit News*, Nov. 5–30, Dec. 1–3, 1942; David I. Verway, ed., *Michigan*

Statistical Abstract, 9th ed. (East Lansing: Michigan State University Press, 1964), p. 318; Region V OCWS, "Composite Report," p. 39, OCWS Records, RG 215.

51. *Detroit News*, Jan. 25, 28, Feb. 26, Aug. 17, Nov. 22, 1943, Oct. 14, Dec. 19, 1944, Feb. 24–25, Sept. 9, 1945; Thomas E. Hachey, "The Wages of War: A British Commentary on Life in Detroit in July, 1943," *Michigan History*, LIX (Winter, 1975), 234.

52. Civilian Requirements Committee, WPB, and Detroit Victory Council, *Inventory of Goods and Services Shortages in Metropolitan Detroit* (Detroit: Detroit Victory Council, 1944), p. 36; Mel Scott, *American City Planning since 1890* (Berkeley and Los Angeles: University of California Press, 1969), p. 392.

53. Selective Service System, *Special Groups. Special Monograph No. 10* (Washington, D.C.: Government Printing Office, 1953), pp. 122–23, 126; *Detroit News*, Aug. 13, Oct. 5, Dec. 9, 1942, Apr. 27, Dec. 29, 1943, July 1, 1944, Feb. 6, 1945.

54. *Detroit News*, Jan. 22, 25, 1943; L.S. Woodward to Montague A. Clark, Jan. 22, 1943, OCWS Records, RG 215; *Grand Rapids Press*, Dec. 11, 1942.

55. Michigan Department of Health, *Sixty-Eighth Annual Report, 1939–1940* (Lansing, Michigan: The Department, 1941), p. 175; Michigan Department of Health, *Seventy-First Annual Report, 1942–1943* (Lansing, Michigan: The Department, 1944), p. 126; Michigan Department of Health, *Seventy-Fourth Annual Report, 1945–1946* (Lansing, Michigan: The Department, 1946), pp. 38, 45; *Detroit News*, Apr. 18, 1943; Region V OCWS, "Composite Report," pp. 80, 92–95, OCWS Records, RG 215.

56. Michigan Department of Health, *Seventy-Fourth Annual Report*, pp. 126–132; "Excerpts of Reports by State Directors of the Office of Government Reports," Apr., 1942, OCWS Records, RG 215; Spencer Fullerton to Eliot Ness, Oct. 14, 1943, ibid.; Ness to John Williams, Oct. 20, 1943, ibid.; *Detroit News*, May 10, 1945.

57. Harry F. Kelly, *Reports of Heads of State Departments on Emergency Problems from the War* (Lansing, Michigan: n.p., 1946), p. 55; Region V OCWS, "Composite Report," p. 44, OCWS Records, RG 215; "Programs in War-Impacted Areas in Michigan to which FWA Assistance is Being Provided," 1945, p. 2, Executive Records, RG 42, Box 114.

58. Region V OCWS, "Composite Report," p. 52, OCWS Records, RG 215.

59. Michigan Department of Public Instruction, *Rural Michigan: A Handbook for Planning and Action* (Lansing, Michigan: n.p., 1945), p. 13; Donald E. Disbrow, *Schools for an Urban Society* (Lansing, Michigan: Michigan Historical Commission, 1968), p. 154; Kelly, *Reports of Heads*, p. 55.

60. Region V OCWS, "Composite Report," p. 63, OCWS Records, RG 215; *Detroit News*, Feb. 9, Apr. 5, 1943.

61. *Detroit News*, Nov. 6, Dec. 9, 1942, Jan. 7, Mar. 18, Nov. 26, 1943; Chester

Bowles to Edward J. Jeffries, Jr., Aug. 6, 1945, Mayor's Office Records, Box 8 (1945); "Production of Michigan Victory Gardens in 1943," 1944, Executive Records, RG 42, Box 152.

62. *Battle Creek Enquirer and News*, Jan. 1, 1943, Jan. 2, 31, 1944.

63. *Sault Ste. Marie Evening News*, Dec. 31, 1942.

64. Emerson Boiles to B.P. Brown, Aug. 22, 1944, Papers of Emerson Boiles, Michigan Historical Collections, Ann Arbor, Box 3.

65. *Detroit News*, Mar. 22, 1943; Meyer, *Journey Through Chaos*, p. 33.

66. Region V OCWS, "Composite Report," p. 92, OCWS Records, RG 215; "Programs in War-Impacted Areas," 1945, p. 2, Executive Records, RG 42, Box 114; *Ann Arbor News*, Nov. 20, 1943; Alfred Katz, "Counseling Outpost for War Workers," *Family*, XXVI (Apr., 1945), 44; *Detroit News*, Jan. 7, 1944.

67. Carr and Stermer, *Willow Run*, p. 310.

68. *Ann Arbor News*, Dec. 22, 1943; *Detroit Free Press*, Nov. 21, 1943.

69. Carr and Stermer, *Willow Run*, p. 109.

70. *Detroit News*, Dec. 14, 1943; Carr and Stermer, *Willow Run*, pp. 110, 289.

71. Region V OCWS, "Composite Report," pp. 24, 36, OCWS Records, RG 215.

72. Fisher, Furlong, and Fullerton, *Macomb-Oakland Area*, p. 5; Edward J. Jeffries, Jr. to Franklin D. Roosevelt, Mar. 11, 1942, Mayor's Office Records, Box 2 (1942); Jeffries to Roosevelt, Apr. 27, 1942, ibid.; Raymond Clancy to Jeffries, Apr. 22, 1942, ibid.; John H. Blandford to Jeffries, undated, but probably May, 1942, ibid.; President's Committee for Congested Production Areas, *Final Report* (Washington, D.C.: Government Printing Office, 1944), p. 5; Mary E. Woods to Dean Snyder, Dec. 8, 1943, OCWS Records, RG 215.

73. "Summary of Operations of the Detroit-Willow Run Area Office, President's Committee for Congested Production Areas, January-September, 1944," Oct. 14, 1944, pp. 5–18, CCPA Records, RG 212; "Concerning the Rating of Adequacy of Community Facilities and Services in Designated Congested Production Areas," Apr. 30, 1944 and Nov. 30, 1944, transmitted in Russell S. Hummel to Corrington Gill, Dec. 12, 1944, ibid.; Leroy Peterson [?], "Summary of Operations of the Muskegon Office, President's Committee on Congested Production Areas," 1944, pp. 1–3, ibid.; "Rating of Adequacy of Community Facilities and Services in Designated Congested Production Areas," Sept. 2, 1944, ibid.

74. *Detroit News*, Apr. 18, Aug. 5, 26, Sept. 23, 30, Nov. 24, Dec. 11, 15, 28, 1945; Bureau of Labor Statistics, *Survey of Vacancy and Occupancy in Privately-Owned Dwelling Units in Detroit Area* (Washington, D.C.: Government Printing Office, 1945), p. 1.

75. Meyer, *Journey Through Chaos*, pp. xi, 33.

76. Burns, *Roosevelt*, p. 455; Meyer, *Journey Through Chaos*, p. xii.

77. Carr and Stermer, *Willow Run*, p. 312.

78. BLS, *Survey of Vacancy* (1945), p. 1.
79. John Webb, "Observations on Sample Censuses in Ten Congested Production Areas," Dec., 1944, p. 11, File 245.52R, Records of the War Production Board, Record Group 179, National Archives; Burns, *Roosevelt*, p. 455.

CHAPTER 4

1. Harvard Sitkoff, "Racial Militancy and Interracial Violence in the Second World War," *Journal of American History*, LVIII (Dec., 1971), 664.
2. Detroit NAACP, *Forward with Action* (Detroit: Detroit NAACP, 1944), pp. 14, 16, 22–26, 37–40.
3. *Detroit News*, June 6, 1943.
4. *Michigan Chronicle*, July 3, 1943.
5. Ibid., June 26, 1943.
6. Bureau of Agricultural Economics, Division of Program Surveys, "The Social Dynamics of Detroit," Dec. 3, 1942, p. 36, Records of the Office of Government Reports, Record Group 44, Washington National Records Center, Suitland, Md. (cited hereafter as OGR Records, RG 44).
7. James MacGregor Burns, *Roosevelt: The Soldier of Freedom* (New York: Harcourt Brace Jovanovich, 1970), p. 266.
8. *Detroit News*, Feb. 2, 1946; Robert C. Goodwin to Louis Levine, Nov. 15, 1943, File 533.14, Records of the War Manpower Commission, Record Group 211, National Archives, Washington, D.C.; Edward L. Cushman to Victor Reuther, August 17, 1944, United Automobile Workers War Policy Division Collection, Archives of Labor History and Urban Affairs, Wayne State University, Detroit, Box 25 (cited hereafter as UAW War Policy Collection); U.S. Department of Commerce, Bureau of the Census, *Characteristics of the Population, Labor Force, Families and Housing, Detroit-Willow Run Congested Production Area: June, 1944. Population Special Reports CA-3, No. 9* (Washington, D.C.: Government Printing Office, 1944), p. 7.
9. U.S. Congress, Senate, Special Committee Investigating the National Defense Program, *Hearings. Manpower Problems in Detroit*, 79 Cong., 1 sess. (Washington, D.C.: Government Printing Office, 1945), Part XXVIII, 13,541; "Total and Percentage of Nonwhite Employment for November, 1942, November, 1943, November, 1944, March, 1945, and July, 1945, by Twelve Selected Establishments," 1945, General Records of Region V, Records of the President's Committee on Fair Employment Practice, Record Group 228, National Archives (cited hereafter as FEPC Records, RG 228); Robert C. Weaver, *Negro Labor, A National Problem* (New York: Harcourt, Brace & Co., 1946), p. 79.
10. *Detroit News*, June 22, 1941.
11. Gilbert Osofsky, ed., *The Burden of Race: A Documentary History of Negro-White Relations in America* (New York: Harper & Row, 1967), p. 400; *Detroit Tribune*, July 12, 1941.
12. George Kirshner, "Government Agencies in Detroit in the Work of Ov-

ercoming Discrimination against the Negro in Private Employment" (M.A. thesis, Wayne University, 1915), p. 99.

13. Detroit Urban League, "Negroes Beginning to Get Jobs Now: Sixteen Points on How to Make Good," 1942, Papers of the Detroit Urban League, Michigan Historical Collections, Ann Arbor, Box 4 (cited hereafter as DUL Papers); Clarence W. Anderson, "Metropolitan Detroit FEPC: A History of the Organization and Operation of a Citizens' Action Group to Encourage Equality of Opportunity in Employment Practice without Regard to Race, Creed, Color or National Origin" (M.A. thesis, Wayne University, 1947), pp. 46–115; *Detroit Tribune*, Apr. 18, 1943; Anderson, "Metropolitan Detroit FEPC," pp. 116–45.
14. *Detroit News*, Jan. 10, 1945; Victor Reuther, memorandum, Mar. 11, 1943, UAW War Policy Collection, Box 21.
15. Anthony Luchek to Joseph D. Keenan, July 14, 1943, Central File, Records of the President's Committee for Congested Production Areas, Record Group 212, National Archives (cited hereafter as CCPA Records, RG 212).
16. Bureau of the Census, *Report CA-3, No. 9*, p. 11; Catherine Blood, *Negro Women War Workers. Women's Bureau Bulletin No. 205* (Washington, D.C.: Government Printing Office, 1945), p. 7.
17. Anderson, "Metropolitan Detroit FEPC, " p. 76.
18. Seldon Menefee, *Assignment: U.S.A.* (New York: Reynal & Hitchcock, Inc., 1943), p. 151.
19. Alfred McClung Lee and Norman D. Humphrey, *Race Riot* (New York: Dryden Press, 1943), p. 110.
20. Herbert Hill et al, "Survey of Religious and Racial Conflict Forces in Detroit," Sept. 30, 1943, pp. 6–7, 37–39, Civil Rights Congress of Michigan Collection, Archives of Labor History, Box 71 (cited hereafter as CRC Collection).
21. *New York Post*, May 15, 17–19, 22, 24, 26, 1944, clippings, CRC Collection, Box 65; Richard J. Ballou, "Race Riots and Hate Strikes: An Analysis of Racial Conflict within the Automobile Plants of Wartime Detroit, 1939–1943" (MS, 1972), pp. 31, 35–37, in Mr. Ballou's possession; Hill et al, "Survey," p. 35, CRC Collection, Box 71.
22. *The Cross and the Flag*, July, 1943; John White, *Michigan Votes: Election Statistics, 1928–1956. University of Michigan Bureau of Government Research Papers in Public Administration No. 24* (Ann Arbor: Bureau of Government Research, 1958), pp. 62–63.
23. *Detroit News*, July 1, 1943.
24. Hill et al, "Survey," pp. 36, 94–95, 112–15, CRC Collection, Box 71; *Congressional Quarterly*, ed., *Congressional Quarterly's Guide to U.S. Elections* (Washington, D.C.: Congressional Quarterly, 1975), p. 305.
25. "Hate Strikes in Which Services of President's Committee on Fair Employment Practice Have Been Requested," 1943, CRC Collection, Box 64; *Detroit News*, June 18, 20, 1942.

26. *Detroit News*, Mar. 19–20, June 3–7, 1943.
27. "Strikes Occurring over Racial Issues during Period July 1, 1943–December 1, 1944," 1945, FEPC Records, RG 228; "Report from the Tension File," Dec., 1944, ibid.; Weaver, *Negro Labor*, p. 238.
28. Joseph Wickware to Victor Reuther, July 9, 1942, UAW War Policy Collection, Box 14.
29. Philip Foner, *Organized Labor and the Black Worker, 1619–1973* (New York: Praeger Books, 1974), p. 263.
30. Kirshner, "Government Agencies," pp. 64–71.
31. William T. McKnight to Will Maslow, Dec. 27, 1944, FEPC Records, RG 228; McKnight to William Swan, May 8, 1945, ibid.
32. *Detroit Free Press*, Jan. 6, 1945.
33. *Detroit News*, June 2, 1945.
34. Ibid., Mar. 7, 1942.
35. *Congressional Record*, 77 Cong., 2 sess. (Washington, D.C.: Government Printing Office, 1942), LXXXVIII, Part II, 1763–65; *Detroit Tribune*, Nov. 29, 1941; *Detroit News*, Nov. 19, Dec. 16, 23, 1941, Mar. 7, 1942.
36. *Detroit News*, Jan. 23, 1942.
37. *Congressional Record*, LXXXVIII, Part II, 1765.
38. *Detroit News*, Feb. 3, 1942; *Detroit Tribune*, Mar. 7, 1942.
39. *Congressional Record*, LXXXVIII, Part II, 1767–68.
40. *Detroit Free Press*, Feb. 28, 1942.
41. "Detroit Has a Race Riot," *Life*, XII (Mar. 16, 1942), 40.
42. *Detroit News*, Mar. 1, 1942.
43. *Detroit Tribune*, Mar. 7, 1942.
44. *Detroit News*, Apr. 29, 1942.
45. Detroit NAACP, *Forward with Action*, p. 40.
46. *Detroit News*, Apr. 29, 1943.
47. Ibid., Jan. 25, 1944; *Michigan Chronicle*, May 6, 1944; Bureau of the Census, *Report CA-3, No. 9*, p. 27; *Ann Arbor News*, July 10, 1943.
48. *Detroit News*, June 14, 1943; George Schermer[?], "Analysis of Social and Political Factors Pertaining to the Selection of a Site for Unrestricted War Housing Project in Detroit Area," 1944, Papers of the Detroit Citizens' Housing and Planning Council, Burton Historical Collection, Detroit Public Library, Detroit, Box 24 (cited hereafter as CHPC Papers).
49. *Dearborn Independent*, Nov. 17, 1944; Press release, Dec. 6, 1944, CHPC Papers, Box 73.
50. Gloster B. Current, "Negro Participation in the August 7, 1945 Primary in Detroit" (M.A. thesis, Wayne University, 1949), pp. 16–19.
51. "Summary of Meeting in Mr. Klutznick's Office," Feb. 28, 1945, CHPC Papers, Box 41.
52. *Dearborn Press*, May 17, 24, 31, June 14, July 19, 26, Aug. 9, 23, 1945.
53. Irving K. First to Eliot Ness, May 7, 1942, General Classified Files, Region V-Michigan, Records of the Office of Community War Services, Record Group 215, National Archives (cited hereafter as OCWS Rec-

ords, RG 215); Downing N. Proctor, "Sault Ste. Marie, Michigan: Special Report on the Negro Situation," Sept. 23, 1942, ibid.; Michigan State Police, Complaint report, Mar. 17, 1943, Records of the Executive Office, Harry F. Kelly, Governor, 1943–46, Record Group 42, Michigan State Archives, Lansing, Box 12; Mark A. McCloskey, Memorandum, June 2, 1942, OCWS Records, RG 215; Downing N. Proctor to McCloskey, Sept. 1, 1943, ibid.; Proctor to J. Donald Phillips, Oct. 19, 1943, ibid.; *Bay City Times*, Apr. 14, 1943; *Michigan Chronicle*, May 1, 1943.

54. *Detroit Tribune*, May 15, 1943; *Detroit Free Press*, May 7, Sept. 18, 20, 1943.

55. R.A. Hoyer to Sherwood Gates, June 30, 1944, OCWS Records, RG 215; "Conversation with a Group of Newspapermen," June, 1943, Papers of Philleo T. Nash, Harry S. Truman Library, Independence, Missouri (cited hereafter as Nash Papers).

56. Detroit Police Department, *Eightieth Annual Report, 1945* (Detroit: The Department, 1946), pp. 15, 75; Ulysses W. Boykin, *A Handbook on the Detroit Negro* (Detroit: Minority Study Associates, 1943), p. 137; Office of War Information, "Opinions in Detroit 36 Hours after the Riot," June 28, 1943, pp. 7–9, CCPA Records, RG 212.

57. *Detroit News*, Mar. 18, 1942.

58. "Special Report, Detroit, Michigan," Mar., 1942, OGR Records, RG 44.

59. "Detroit Is Dynamite," *Life*, XIII (Aug. 17, 1942), 15.

60. *Michigan Chronicle*, Apr. 10, 1943.

61. Philleo T. Nash to Malcolm Ross, July 1, 1943, Nash Papers.

62. Harvard Sitcoff. "The Detroit Race Riot of 1943," *Michigan History*, LIII (Fall, 1969), 195.

63. Robert Shogan and Tom Craig, *The Detroit Race Riot: A Study in Violence* (Philadelphia: J. B. Lippincott, 1964), p. 108; Office of War Information, Memorandum to Charles Lovett, June 28, 1943, Nash Papers; Ballou, "Race Riots," p. 63.

64. Shogan and Craig, *Detroit Race Riot*, p. 103.

65. *Detroit Free Press*, June 23, 1943; *Detroit News*, July 29, 1943.

66. *Detroit News*, June 23, 1943.

67. Ibid., Aug. 13, 1943.

68. Ibid., Oct. 26, 1943.

69. Ibid.

70. Louis Martin, "Detroit—Still Dynamite," *Crisis*, LI (Jan., 1944), 10.

71. *Detroit News*, Nov. 3, 1943.

72. James J. McClendon and Robert Evans to Edward J. Jeffries, Jr., Nov. 9, 1943, Papers of Edward J. Jeffries, Jr., Burton Historical Collection, Box 9 (1943) (cited hereafter as Mayor's Office Records); *Chicago Defender*, Jan. 15, 1944, clipping, ibid., Box 3 (1944).

73. Edward J. Jeffries, Jr. to Martin S. Hayden, Jan. 31, 1944, ibid., Box 3 (1944); *Detroit News*, Jan. 13, 1944; Helen A. Kulka, "The Barometer of the City of Detroit Interracial Committee: An Attempt to Measure Racial Tension" (M.A. thesis, Wayne University, 1946), pp. 4–22.

74. Kulka, "Barometer of the City," p. 31.
75. *Michigan Chronicle*, Aug. 18, 1945.
76. Ibid., Aug. 25, 1945; *Detroit News*, Oct. 10, 1945; John C. Dancy, *Sand Against the Wind: The Memoirs of John C. Dancy* (Detroit: Wayne State University Press, 1966), p. 205; William Haber, *How Much Does It Cost? A Report to the Michigan Employment Security Commission on Long-Range Benefit Financing and Fund Solvency in Michigan* (Lansing, Michigan: The Commission, 1951), p. 285.
77. Stephen B. Sarasohn and Carl O. Smith, "Hate Propaganda in Detroit in the 1945 Election," *Public Opinion Quarterly*, X (Spring, 1946), 37.
78. *Detroit News*, Nov. 7, 1945.
79. Neil A. Wynn, "The Impact of the Second World War on the American Negro," *Journal of Contemporary History*, VI (1971), 53; Betty Smith Jenkins, "The Racial Policies of the Detroit Housing Commission and Their Administration" (M.A. thesis, Wayne University, 1950), p. 28.

CHAPTER 5

1. United States Department of Commerce, Bureau of the Census, *Characteristics of the Population, Labor Force, Families and Housing, Detroit-Willow Run Congested Production Area: June, 1944. Population Special Reports CA-3, No. 9* (Washington, D.C.: Government Printing Office, 1944), pp. 17–18.
2. Ibid., pp. 17, 19.
3. Ibid., pp. 19, 20, 21; Bureau of the Census, *Sixteenth Census of the United States, Internal Migration 1935 to 1940* (Washington, D.C.: Government Printing Office, 1943–46), I, 166; II, 163; III, 106–7.
4. Freda S. Yenney, "Areas of Tension within the John R. Fisher Homes as Revealed by One Hundred Wives Living on the Project" (M.A. thesis, Wayne University, 1944), pp. 31–32; *Nashville Tennesseean*, July 18, 1942.
5. Irene Watt to author, July 14, 28, 1973.
6. Bureau of the Census, *Report CA-3, No. 9*, p. 19. I have borrowed the phrases "mountain people" and "mountaineers" from Robert Coles, *The South Goes North. Children of Crisis*, vol. 3 (Boston: Atlantic, Little Brown, 1972) p. 373.
7. *Detroit Free Press*, Dec. 21, 1943.
8. Bureau of the Census, *Report CA-3, No. 9*, p. 23.
9. Yenney, "Areas of Tension," p. 32.
10. Bureau of Agricultural Economics, Division of Program Surveys, "Detroit People in Perspective: A Study of Group Attitudes and Aspirations," [1943], Illustrative appendix, p. 28, Records of the United States Department of Agriculture, Bureau of Agricultural Economics, Record Group 83, National Archives, Washington, D.C.
11. Maternal Health League of Michigan, *A Description of Detroit's Defense Area* (n.p., 1941), p. 12.
12. Reba Smellage to author, Nov. 4, 1973; Cleo Y. Boyd, "Detroit's Southern Whites and the Store-Front Churches," (MS, 1958), p. 3, Depart-

ment of Sociology and Economics, Detroit Public Library, Detroit. Detroit radio station WWJ began weekly broadcasts of the "Op'ry" in October, 1943. *Detroit News*, Oct. 9, 1943.

13. *Detroit News*, May 20, 1943.

14. Harriet Arnow, *The Dollmaker* (New York: Macmillan, 1954), p. 23.

15. *Detroit News*, Jan. 31, 1942.

16. Brewster Campbell and James Pooler, "Hallelujah in Boomtown," *Collier's*, CXIII (Apr. 1, 1944), 18.

17. Robert Coles, *Migrants, Sharecroppers, Mountaineers. Children of Crisis*, vol. 1 (Boston: Little Brown, 1967), p. 595.

18. Harriet Arnow to author, 1974, enclosing list of favorite songs of the Kentucky hills.

19. Mrs. Lawrence Blackmon to author, Oct. 29, 1973; Robert L. Duffus, "A City that Forges Thunderbolts," *New York Times Magazine* (Jan. 10, 1943), p..15; Harvey Klemmer, "Michigan Fights," *National Geographic*, LXXXVI (Dec., 1944), 697.

20. Bureau of Agricultural Economics, Division of Program Surveys, "Detroit People in Perspective: A Study of Group Attitudes and Aspirations," [1943], p. 29, Records of the Office of Government Reports, Record Group 44, Washington National Records Center, Suitland, Md. (cited hereafter as OGR Records, RG 44).

21. *Michigan Chronicle*, May 1, 1943.

22. Yenney, "Areas of Tension," p. 61.

23. Herbert Hill et al, "Survey of Religious and Racial Conflict Forces in Detroit," Sept. 30, 1943, p. 48, Civil Rights Congress of Michigan Collection, Archives of Labor History and Urban Affairs, Wayne State University, Detroit, Box 71.

24. Arnow, *Dollmaker*, p. 517.

25. *Detroit News*, Jan. 8, 1944; Detroit Housing Commission, *Ninth Annual Report, 1944* (Detroit: The Commission, 1944), p. 37; Detroit Office of Civilian Defense, "Your Civilian Defense," script for broadcast of Mar. 25, 1943, p. 2, Papers of Edward J. Jeffries, Jr., Burton Historical Collection, Detroit Public Library, Box 7 (1943).

26. Coles, *South Goes North*, p. 393.

27. Richard R. Lingeman, *Don't You Know There's A War On? The American Home Front, 1941–1945* (New York: G.P. Putnam's Sons, 1970), p. 84; *Detroit News*, May 26, 1942.

28. Erdmann D. Beynon, "The Southern White Laborer Migrates to Michigan," *American Sociological Review*, III (June, 1938), 334–35; *Detroit News*, Jan. 4, 1944.

29. *Detroit News*, Dec. 4, 1943.

30. Bureau of Agricultural Economics, Division of Program Surveys, "The Social Dynamics of Detroit," Dec. 3, 1942, p. 9, OGR Records, RG 44; *Detroit News*, May 9, 1943, Sept. 24, 1944.

31. *Detroit News*, June 3, 10, 1945.

32. Ibid., June 7, Aug. 5, 1945.
33. T.E. Murphy, "The Orphans of Willow Run," *Saturday Evening Post*, CCXVIII (Aug. 4, 1945), 109; Beynon, "Southern White Laborer," p. 343.

CHAPTER 6

1. U.S. Department of Commerce, Bureau of the Census, *Sixteenth Census of the United States, 1940 Population* (Washington, D.C.: Government Printing Office, 1943), III, Part III, 593-95.
2. William Henry Chafe, *The American Woman: Her Changing Social, Economic, and Political Roles, 1920–1970* (New York: Oxford University Press, 1972), p. 137; U.S. Congress, Senate, Special Committee Investigating the National Defense Program, *Hearings. Manpower Problems in Detroit*, 79 Cong., 1 sess. (Washington, D.C.: Government Printing Office, 1945), Part XXVIII, 13,528; UAW Research Department, "Notes on Women Workers in UAW-CIO Plants," Mar., 1943, p. 1, United Automobile Workers Research Department Collection (unprocessed), Archives of Labor History and Urban Affairs, Wayne State University, Detroit, Box 14.
3. U.S. Department of Labor, Women's Bureau, *Women Workers in Ten War Production Areas and Their Postwar Employment Plans. Women's Bureau Bulletin No. 209* (Washington, D.C.: Government Printing Office, 1946), pp. 29–30, 35–49; *Detroit News*, Apr. 6, 1942.
4. Michigan Department of Public Health, *Michigan Public Health Statistics* (Lansing, Michigan: The Department, 1951), p. 13; Chafe, *The American Woman*, p. 195.
5. *Detroit News*, Aug. 10, 1942, Feb. 11, Oct. 1, 1943; Michigan USES, "Cumulative Summary Report on Voluntary Registration of Women for War Work," Jan. 9, 1943, Michigan File 533.183, Records of the War Manpower Commission, Record Group 211, National Archives, Washington, D.C. (cited hereafter as WMC Records, RG 211).
6. *Detroit News*, Sept. 8, 1943.
7. War Manpower Commission—Michigan, "Female Counseling," May, 1944, Michigan File 533.18, WMC Records, RG 211; *Detroit News*, Mar. 16, 1943.
8. "Equal Pay: Resolution and Discussion . . . , Chicago, Illinois, August, 1942," p. 1, Acc. 56–850, Records of the Women's Bureau, Record Group 86, Washington National Records Center, Suitland, Md. (cited hereafter as Women's Bureau Records, RG 86).
9. "Hours and Earnings of Men and Women in Factories: Michigan, August, 1944," *Monthly Labor Review*, LX (Aug., 1944), 159–61.
10. *Decisions of the Impartial Umpire under the October 19, 1942 Agreement between General Motors Corporation and International Union, United Automobile, Aircraft, and Agricultural Implement Workers of America, CIO*. 2 vols. (Detroit: n.p., 1945), I, 465–66, 573–76.

11. "Equal Pay," p. 2, Women's Bureau Records, RG 86.
12. *United Automobile Worker*, Mar. 1, 1944.
13. Ibid., Sept. 15, 1944.
14. *Detroit News*, Aug. 17, 1943.
15. Ibid., Apr. 25, 1941; Harry Shulman, *Opinions of the Umpire, Ford Motor Company and UAW-CIO, 1945–1946* (Detroit: n.p., 1946), p. A-117.
16. *Decisions of the Umpire* (GM), I, 735–36.
17. "Minutes of the Meeting, Local 599," Apr. 11, 1943, p. 5, Local 599 Collection, Archives of Labor History, Series 3, Box 2.
18. War Production Board, "Problems of Women War Workers in Detroit," Aug. 20, 1943, pp. 1–2, General Classified Files, Region V—Michigan, Records of the Office of Community War Services, Record Group 215, National Archives (cited hereafter as OCWS Records, RG 215); *Detroit News*, Feb. 25, 1943.
19. *Detroit News*, Apr. 11, 1940.
20. Chafe, *The American Woman*, p. 164.
21. Eleanor Straub, "Government Policy toward Civilian Women during World War II" (Ph.D. thesis, Emory University, 1973), p. 261.
22. Clarence H. Young and William A. Quinn, *Foundation for Living: The Story of Charles Stewart Mott and Flint* (New York: McGraw-Hill, 1963), pp. 161–62.
23. Gladys Cook to Dr. Edna Noble White, June 6, 1941, Administrative Records Relating to Nursery Schools, Record Group 70–49, Michigan State Archives, Lansing, Box 2 (cited hereafter as Nursery School Records, RG 70–49); Irma Unruh to Gladys Cook, Nov. 6, 1941, ibid.; Cook to Unruh, Nov. 13, 1941, ibid.; Irene E. Murphy, "Day Care in Wayne County: Its Past and Future," Nov. 30, 1945, p. 1, ibid.; Michigan Department of Social Welfare, "Proposed State Plan for Day Care in Michigan," Oct. 29, 1942, p. 1, ibid., Box 1; *Detroit News*, Nov. 13, 1942.
24. "Programs in War Impacted Communities to Which FWA Assistance Is Being Provided," 1945, p. 1, Records of the Executive Office, Harry F. Kelly, Governor, 1943–46, Record Group 42, Michigan State Archives, Box 114 (cited hereafter as Executive Records, RG 42); Michigan Department of Social Welfare, "Day Care in Michigan," Feb. 3, 1944, Nursery School Records, RG 70–49, Box 1; Ruth C. Rogers, "Report on Children's War Service," June 16, 1943, ibid.
25. Region V OCWS, "Composite Report on Health, Welfare and Related Activities in the Detroit, Michigan War Area," Dec. 22, 1943, p. 56, OCWS Records, RG 215; Chafe, *The American Woman*, p. 170; "Programs in War-Impacted Communities," p. 1, Executive Records, RG 42, Box 114; Ruth C. Rogers, "Care of Children of Working Mothers in Michigan," Apr. 18, 1944, p. 2, Nursery School Records, RG 70–49, Box 1; DSW, "Day Care Bulletin," Jan. 13, 1944, p. 1, ibid.
26. DSW, "Report on Day Care," (1943), p. 1, ibid.; Gunnar Dybwad to Monica Owen, Nov. 19, 1945, ibid., Box 2; *Day Care News*, Apr. 1945, p. 1,

Lanham Act Records, Records of the U.S. Office of Education, Record Group 12, National Archives (cited hereafter as Education Records, RG 12).

27. Betty Heliker, "The Need for a Day Care Program in Detroit for the Children of Working Mothers" (M.A. thesis, University of Michigan, 1943), pp. 19–22, 40–53; *Day Care News*, Sept. 27, 1944, p. 1, Education Records, RG 12; Dybwad to Owen, Nov. 19, 1945, Nursery School Records, RG 70–49, Box 2.

28. *Detroit News*, Sept. 26, 1943.

29. U.S. Congress, Senate, Committee on Education and Labor, *Hearings. Wartime Care and Protection of Children*, 78 Cong., 1 sess. (Washington, D.C.: Government Printing Office, 1943), I, 91; State Day Care Committee, "Report to Governor Harry F. Kelly on the Need for a State Day Care Program," Dec. 30, 1943, p. 9, Executive Records, RG 42, Box 86.

30. Phyllis Aronson, "The Adequacy of the Family Allowance System as It Affects the Wives and Children of Men Drafted into the Armed Forces" (M.A. thesis, Wayne University, 1944), p. 69.

31. *Day Care News*, Jan., 1945, p. 1, Education Records, RG 12; *Grand Rapids Press*, July 2, 1943.

32. "Minutes of the Meeting of the State Day Care Committee," July 24, 1945, p. 1, Nursery School Records, RG 70–49, Box 2; R.C. Ashton to F.F. Fauri, Oct. 22, 1945, ibid.; Alice May to Gunnar Dybwad, Aug. 26, 1945, ibid.; *Detroit News*, Aug. 28–29, Sept. 26, 1945; Murphy, "Day Care in Wayne County," p. 1, Nursery School Records, RG 70–49, Box 2.

33. Straub, "Government Policy," p. 296.

34. Michigan Social Welfare Commission, *Fourth Biennial Report, July, 1944–June, 1946* (Lansing, Michigan: The Commission, 1946), p. 57.

35. *Detroit News*, Aug. 2, 1942, May 9, 1945.

36. Ibid., Nov. 26, 1943.

37. Straub, "Government Policy," pp. 338–43; William Haber, *How Much Does It Cost? A Report to the Michigan Employment Security Commission on Long-Range Unemployment Insurance Benefit Financing and Fund Solvency in Michigan* (Lansing, Michigan: The Commission, 1951), p. 149. Shortly after V-J Day, a small group of women picketed UAW headquarters in Detroit, demanding that the Women's Bureau be upgraded within the union's structure; an all-woman staff be provided for the Bureau; and female representation be increased on the staff of other UAW dvisions. *Michigan Chronicle*, Aug. 18, 1945; Nancy Gabin, "Women Workers and the UAW after World War II, 1945–1954" (MS, 1978), p. 12, in Ms. Gabin's possession.

38. *Detroit News*, Sept. 12, 1943.

39. *Detroit Free Press*, Dec. 25, 1943; Aronson, "Adequacy of Dependency," pp. 9, 14–18, 29–33, 57, 61, 64–77, 83, 85–86.

40. Department of Public Health, *Health Statistics*, p. 13.

41. Eleanor Straub, "United States Government Policy toward Civilian Women during World War II," *Prologue*, V (Winter, 1973), 254.
42. *Detroit News*, May 28, 1943.
43. Ibid., Mar. 11, 1943.
44. Sidone M. Gruenberg, ed., *The Family in a World at War* (New York: Harper & Bros., 1942), p. 288.
45. *Detroit News*, May 18, 1942.
46. *Ann Arbor News*, Aug. 18, 21, 1943; Violet Garrison Schankin, "War-Effort-Related Opinions and Practices of Detroit Elementary Teachers" (M.A. thesis, Wayne University, 1943), pp. 33–34.
47. *Detroit News*, Aug. 10, 1944.
48. *Ann Arbor News*, Sept. 24, 1943; *Detroit News*, Feb. 29, July 29, 1944.
49. *Detroit News*, Aug. 10, 1944.
50. Paul Wiers, "Wartime Increases in Michigan Delinquency," *American Sociological Review*, X (Aug., 1944), 515; Ralph Carr Fletcher, "Runaway Youth to Detroit during the War," *Social Service Review*, XXII (Sept., 1948), 350; Michigan Youth Guidance Committee [?], *Proceedings of the Governor's Conference on Juvenile Delinquency, September, 1943, and Report of the Governor's Study Committee on Juvenile Delinquency, December, 1943* (n.p., n.d.), pp. 19, 23; Constance Smith, "A Five-Year Study from 1941 to 1945, of Children with Behavior Problems Who Were Brought to the Juvenile Court for the First Time" (M.A. thesis, University of Michigan, 1948), pp. 4, 36.
51. Wayne County Youth Guidance Committee, "Progress Report of the Wayne County Youth Guidance Committee," Nov., 1943, p. 1, Records of the Department of Social Welfare, Record Group 65–57-A, Michigan State Archives, Box 8 (cited hereafter as DSW Records, RG 65–57-A); *Detroit News*, June 16, July 6, 1943; Fletcher, "Runaway Youth," p. 349.
52. Francis J. Weber to H. Allen Moyer, Sept. 29, 1943, Executive Records, RG 42, Box 6; John F. Williams to Eliot Ness, June 5, 1944, OCWS Records, RG 215.
53. Wiers, "Wartime Increases," pp. 522–23.
54. *Detroit News*, Oct. 13–15, 22, 1943; Michigan Youth Guidance Committee, "Development and Achievements of the Michigan Youth Guidance Program from May, 1943 to June, 1945," 1945, p. 8, Executive Records, RG 42, Box 89.
55. Ralph Daniel, "Youth Guidance in Michigan: A Study of the Work of the Michigan Youth Guidance Committee and the Michigan Youth Guidance Commission, 1943 to 1947" (M.A. thesis, University of Michigan, 1951), pp. 7–9.
56. *Detroit News*, June 11, 1943.
57. Ibid., Mar. 6, 1944; MYGC, "Development and Achievements," pp. 3–4, 7–9, Executive Records, RG 42, Box 89.
58. *Detroit News*, Jan. 30, 1944; Wayne County Youth Guidance Committee,

"Progress Report Supplementary to the November, 1943 Report of the Wayne County Youth Guidance Committee," Oct., 1944, p. 58, DSW Records, RG 65–57-A, Box 18.

59. Daniel, "Youth Guidance in Michigan," p. 160; Fritz Redl and David Wineman, *Children Who Hate: The Disorganization and Breakdown of Behavioral Controls* (Glencoe, Illinois: The Free Press, 1951), p. 19.

60. Ray E. Baber, "Marriage and the Family after the War," *Annals of the American Academy of Political and Social Science*, CCXXIX (Sept., 1943), 175.

CHAPTER 7

1. *Detroit News*, Aug. 14–15, 1945; *Lansing State Journal*, Aug. 15, 1945; *Hastings Banner*, Aug. 15, 1945; *Flint Journal*, Aug. 15, 1945.

2. *Detroit News*, Oct. 10, 1943, Aug. 15, 1945; Michigan Office of Veterans' Affairs, *Director's Report* (Lansing, Michigan: OVA, 1946), pp. ii, 50.

3. *Detroit News*, Oct. 15, 1939, Aug. 22, Oct. 10, Nov. 13, 1943.

4. *United Automobile Worker*, Sept. 15, 1944; UAW-CIO Press release, Oct. 18, 1944, United Automobile Workers War Policy Division Collection, Archives of Labor History and Urban Affairs, Wayne State University, Detroit, Box 23 (cited hereafter as UAW War Policy Collection); *United Automobile Worker*, Feb., 1946; *Agreement between International Union, United Automobile, Aircraft, and Agricultural Implement Workers of America, UAW-CIO, and Ford Motor Company, February 26, 1946* (n.p., 1946), pp. 51, 57, 68; *Agreement between General Motors Corporation and UAW-CIO, March 19, 1946* (n.p., 1946), pp. 60–61; Davis R.B. Ross, *Preparing for Ulysses: Politics and Veterans during World War II* (New York: Columbia University Press, 1969), p. 157.

5. OVA, *Director's Report*, p. 200; *Detroit News*, Oct. 8, 1945.

6. OVA, *Director's Report*, pp. 2–56, 99–197.

7. *Detroit News*, July 21, 1943; Seymour Harris, *Inflation and the American Economy* (New York: McGraw-Hill, 1945), p. 514.

8. *Detroit News*, Nov. 21, 26, 1943, Mar. 18, 1945; A. H. Raskin, "Industrial Conflict in Detroit," June 9, 1944, p. 2, Policy Documentation File 245C, Records of the War Production Board, Record Group 179, National Archives, Washington, D.C. (cited hereafter as WPB Records, RG 179).

9. *Detroit News*, Apr. 21, Oct. 1, 1944, Apr. 21, May 2, 26, June 20, 1945.

10. Ibid., Sept. 1, 1944, May 21, 26, 29, June 28, 1945.

11. Ibid., June 4, Sept. 2, 1941, Mar. 15, July 24, 1942, Mar. 18, Apr. 7, Nov. 7, 1944; Mel Scott, *American City Planning since 1890* (Berkeley and Los Angeles: University of California Press, 1969), p. 411.

12. James MacGregor Burns, *Roosevelt: The Soldier of Freedom* (New York: Harcourt Brace Jovanovich, 1970), pp. 425, 528.

13. "UAW Reconversion Program," June 21, 1944, UAW War Policy Collection, Box 20.

14. Alfred P. Sloan, Jr., *My Years with General Motors* (New York: Doubleday, Inc., 1964), p. 206.
15. William Duffy, "History of the Automotive Division," Nov. 1945, pp. 9–13, File 053.108R, WPB Records, RG 179.
16. *Detroit News*, Sept. 18, 1944; Edward L. Cushman to Edward T. Gushee, Oct. 3, 5, 1944, Records of the War Manpower Commission, Record Group 211, National Archives (cited hereafter as WMC Records, RG 211); J. K. Johnson to War Manpower Commission–Washington, D.C., Oct. 7, 1944, ibid.; Duffy, "History," p. 15, File 053.108R, WPB Records, RG 179.
17. Duffy, "History," p. 18–19.
18. Ibid., pp. 19–20.
19. "Adventures of Henry and Joe in Autoland," *Fortune*, XXXIII (Mar., 1946), 96, 97.
20. *Detroit News*, July 3, Nov. 1, 1945. Unable to organize an effective sales network or to persuade skeptical consumers to buy an undistinguished variation of the typical American car, K-F never won more than 5 percent of the domestic market and abandoned passenger car production in the United States in 1955. Kaiser sold the Willow Run plant to GM in 1953. John B. Rae, *The American Automobile, A Brief History* (Chicago: University of Chicago Press, 1965), pp. 168–170.
21. Russell Porter, "Detroit-Reconversion Laboratory," *New York Times Magazine*, Sept. 9, 1945, p. 10.
22. Darrel Robert Cady, "The Truman Administration's Reconversion Policies, 1945–1947" (Ph.D. thesis, University of Kansas, 1974), p. 42.
23. *Detroit News*, Aug. 18, 1945; Duffy, "History," p. 21, File 053.108R, WPB Records, RG 179.
24. *Detroit News*, Aug. 20–21, 22, 29, Sept. 20, 1945; *Flint Journal*, Aug. 20, 1945; *Lansing State Journal*, Aug. 21, 1945.
25. William Haber, *How Much Does It Cost? A Report to the Michigan Employment Security Commission on Long-Range Unemployment Insurance Benefit Financing and Fund Solvency in Michigan* (Lansing, Michigan: The Commission, 1951), pp. 137, 304; *Detroit News*, Aug. 22, Oct. 14, 1945.
26. Ibid., Aug. 11, Aug. 26, Oct. 10, 1945.
27. "Peace Arrives at Gar Wood," *Fortune*, XXXII (Oct., 1945), 153–56, 238–40.
28. Cady, "Reconversion Policies," p. 94; *Detroit News*, Dec. 31, 1945; Rae, *American Automobile*, p. 236.
29. Although Michigan strikes fell from 562 to 478 between 1944 and 1945, man-days idle during the latter year more than tripled, from 1,836,000, to 5,690,000, despite a decline in the number of workers involved. David I. Verway, ed., *Michigan Statistical Abstract*, 9th ed. (East Lansing: Michigan State University Press, 1964), p. 90.
30. *Detroit News*, Aug. 15, 1945; Nelson Lichtenstein, "Industrial Unionism

under the No-Strike Pledge: A Study of the CIO during World War II" (Ph.D. thesis, University of California, Berkeley, 1974), p. 688.

31. Hadley Cantril, ed., *Public Opinion, 1935–1946* (Princeton: Princeton University Press, 1951), p. 825.
32. Cady, "Reconversion Policies," p. 115.
33. Victor G. Reuther, *The Brothers Reuther and the Story of the UAW: A Memoir* (Boston: Houghton Mifflin, 1976), p. 258.
34. Haber, *How Much*, pp. 198, 201, 304.
35. U.S. Department of Labor, Bureau of Labor Statistics, *Handbook of Labor Statistics. Bulletin No. 916* (Washington, D.C.: Government Printing Office, 1948), p. 109; Curtis K. Stadtfeld, *From the Land and Back* (New York: Charles Scribner's Sons, 1972), p. 185.
36. *Detroit Free Press*, Nov. 13, 1945.

CONCLUSION

1. Arthur C. Marwick, *Britain in the Century of Total War: War, Peace, and Social Change, 1900–1967* (Boston: Houghton Mifflin, 1968), p. 12.
2. Eliot Janeway, *The Struggle for Survival: A Chronicle of Economic Mobilization in World War II* (New Haven: Yale University Press, 1951), p. 335.
3. Ben D. Zevin, ed., *Nothing to Fear: The Selected Addresses of Franklin D. Roosevelt, 1932–1945* (New York: Popular Library, 1961), p. 331.
4. Thomas R.H. Havens, "Women and War in Japan, 1937–45," *American Historical Review*, LXXX (Oct., 1975), 914; Roderick Nash, *The Nervous Generation: American Thought, 1917–1930* (Chicago: Rand McNally & Co., 1970), p. viii.
5. Eric F. Goldman, *Rendezvous with Destiny: A History of American Reform* (New York: Random House, 1956), p. 301.
6. Marwick, *Britain*, p. 16.
7. L.E. Sissman, "Missing the Forties," *Atlantic*, CCXXII (Oct., 1973), 35; Geoffrey Perrett, *Days of Sadness, Years of Triumph: The American People, 1939–1945* (New York: Coward, McCann & Geohegan Inc., 1973), p. 442.

Bibliography

MANUSCRIPT COLLECTIONS

Ann Arbor. Michigan Historical Collections.
  National Defense Committee Papers.
  F. Clever Bald Papers.
  Emerson Boiles Papers.
  Prentiss Marsh Brown Scrapbooks.
  Wilbur M. Brucker Papers.
  Detroit News Lansing Bureau Collection.
  Detroit Urban League Collection.
  Harold A. Furlong Papers.
  Francis Kornegay Papers.
  United Automobile Workers Oral History Collection.
  ———. Interview with John W. Anderson, February 17–May 21, 1960.
  ———. Interview with Jess Ferrazza, May 26, 1961.
  ———. Interview with Leonard Woodcock, April 30, 1963.
  Murray D. Van Wagoner Papers.
  Willow Run Public Library Collection.

Detroit. Archives of Labor History and Urban Affairs.
  Civil Rights Congress of Michigan Collection.
  Local 212 Collection.
  Local 599 Collection.
  Michigan AFL-CIO Collection.
  United Automobile Workers War Policy Division Collection.

Detroit. Burton Historical Collection.
  Citizens' Housing and Planning Council of Detroit Papers.
  Papers of Edward J. Jeffries, Jr.

Independence, Missouri. Harry S Truman Library.
  Papers of Philleo T. Nash.

273

Lansing. Michigan State Archives.
Accession 42. Records of the Michigan Council of Defense.
Accession 50. Records of the Executive Office, Murray D. Van Wagoner, Governor, 1941–42.
Record Group 42. Records of the Executive Office, Harry F. Kelly, Governor, 1943–46.
Record Group 65–31. Records of the Michigan State Police.
Record Group 65–57-A. Records of the Michigan Department of Social Welfare.
Record Group 70-49. Administrative Records Relating to Nursery Schools.

Madison, Wisconsin. State Historical Society of Wisconsin.
Papers of Edwin E. Witte.

Suitland, Maryland. Washington National Records Center.
Record Group 44. Records of the Office of Government Reports.
Record Group 86. Records of the U.S. Women's Bureau.

Washington, D.C. National Archives.
Record Group 12. Records of the U.S. Office of Education.
Record Group 33. Records of the U.S. Department of Agriculture, Federal Extension Service.
Record Group 69. Records of the Work Projects Administration.
Record Group 83. Records of the U.S. Department of Agriculture, Bureau of Agricultural Economics.
Record Group 179. Records of the War Production Board.
Record Group 211. Records of the War Manpower Commission.
Record Group 212. Records of the President's Committee for Congested Production Areas.
Record Group 215. Records of the Office of Community War Services.
Record Group 228. Records of the President's Committee on Fair Employment Practice.

NEWSPAPERS

Ann Arbor News
Ann Arbor Washtenaw Post-Tribune
Battle Creek Enquirer and News
Bay City Times
Benton Harbor News-Palladium
Dearborn Independent
Dearborn Press
Detroit Free Press
Detroit Labor News
Detroit News
Detroit Times

Detroit Tribune
Escanaba Daily Press
Flint Journal
Grand Rapids Press
Hastings Banner
Jackson Citizen-Patriot
Kalamazoo Gazette
Lansing State Journal
Michigan Chronicle (Detroit)
Michigan CIO News (Detroit)
Michigan Farmer (Lansing)

Muskegon Chronicle　　　　　　　*United Automobile Worker* (Detroit)
New York Times　　　　　　　　　*Voice of 212* (Detroit)
Saginaw News　　　　　　　　　　*Ypsilanti Press*
Sault Ste. Marie Evening News

GOVERNMENT DOCUMENTS

Blood, Catherine. *Negro Women War Workers. Women's Bureau Bulletin No. 205.* Washington, D.C.: Government Printing Office, 1945.

Buchanan, Margaret Terry. *The Migration of Workers from Tennessee to Michigan.* Nashville: Research and Statistics Section, Tennessee Unemployment Compensation Division, 1940.

Detroit Housing Commission.

———. *Seventh Annual Report, 1941.* Detroit: The Commission, 1942.

———. *Eighth Annual Report, 1942.* Detroit: The Commission, 1943.

———. *Ninth Annual Report, 1943.* Detroit: The Commission, 1944.

———. *Tenth Annual Report, 1944.* Detroit: The Commission, 1945.

———. *Eleventh Annual Report, 1945.* Detroit: The Commission, 1946.

Detroit Police Department. *Eightieth Annual Report, 1945.* Detroit: The Department, 1945.

Fisher, Joseph R.; Furlong, Harold A.; and Fullerton, L.A. *Macomb-Oakland Industrial Defense Area of Michigan.* Lansing, Michigan: Michigan Council of Defense, 1941.

Gill, Corrington. *Administrative History of the President's Committee for Congested Production Areas.* 2 vols. Washington, D.C.: Government Printing Office, 1945.

Haber, William. *How Much Does it Cost? A Report to the Michigan Employment Security Commission on Long-Range Unemployment Insurance Benefit Financing and Fund Solvency in Michigan.* Lansing, Michigan: The Commission, 1951.

Hoffer, Charles. *Adjustments of Michigan Farm Families to War Conditions. Quarterly Bulletin of the Agricultural College Experimental Station, No. 333.* Lansing, Michigan, 1945.

Kelly, Harry F. *Reports of Heads of State Departments on Emergency Problems from the War.* Lansing, Michigan, 1946.

Michigan Council of Defense. *Organization, History, and Fields of Activity of the MCD.* Lansing, Michigan: Michigan Council of Defense, 1942.

Michigan Department of Administration. *Fifteen Years of Michigan State Government Financial Statistics, 1940–1954. Special Report No. 3.* Lansing, Michigan: The Department, 1955.

Michigan Department of Public Instruction. *Rural Michigan: A Workbook for Discussion, Planning, and Action.* Lansing, Michigan, 1945.

Michigan. Governor's Fact-Finding Committee to Investigate the Riot Occurring in Detroit on June 21, 1943. *Factual Report Submitted to Governor Harry F. Kelly.* Detroit, 1943.

Michigan. State Labor Mediation Board. *Third Annual Report, 1943–1944.* Lansing, Michigan: SLMB, 1945.

Michigan Office of Veterans' Affairs. *Director's Report.* Lansing, Michigan: OVA, 1946.

Michigan State Employment Service[?] *Michigan State Conference on Employment Problems of the Negro.* Detroit, 1940.

Michigan Youth Guidance Committee[?] *Proceedings of the Governor's Conference on Juvenile Delinquency, September, 1943, and Report of the Governor's Study Committee on Juvenile Delinquency, December, 1943.* n.p., n.d.

Swafford, Rosa Lee. *Wartime Record of Strikes and Lockouts, 1940–1945.* Senate Document No. 136. 79 Cong., 2 sess. Washington, D.C.: Government Printing Office, 1946.

U.S. Congress. House. Committee on Public Buildings and Grounds. *Hearings on War Housing.* 77 Cong., 2 sess. Washington, D.C.: Government Printing Office, 1942. Part II.

U.S. Congress. House. Select Committee Investigating National Defense Migration. *Hearings. Detroit Industrial Section.* 77 Cong., 1 sess. Washington, D.C.: Government Printing Office, 1941. Part XVIII.

U.S. Congress. Senate. Committee on Education and Labor. *Hearings. Wartime Care and Protection of Children.* 78 Cong., 1 sess. Washington, D.C.: Government Printing Office, 1943. Part I.

U.S. Congress. Senate. Special Committee Investigating the National Defense Program. *Hearings.*

———. *Willow Run Housing.* 77 Cong., 2 sess. Washington, D.C.: Government Printing Office, 1942. Part XII.

———. *Hearings. Manpower Problems in Detroit.* 79 Cong., 1 sess. Washington, D.C.: Government Printing Office, 1945. Part XXVIII.

U.S. Department of Commerce. Bureau of the Census.

———. *Census of Agriculture, 1945.* Washington, D.C.: Government Printing Office, 1946.

———. *Characteristics of the Population, Labor Force, Families, and Housing, Detroit-Willow Run Congested Production Area: June, 1944. Population Special Reports Series CA-3, No. 9.* Washington, D.C.: Government Printing Office, 1944.

———. *County Data Book, 1947.* Washington, D.C.: Government Printing Office, 1947.

———. *Estimated Civilian Population of the United States by County, November 1, 1943. Population Reports Series P-44, no. 3.* Washington, D.C.: Government Printing Office, 1944.

———. *Historical Statistics of the United States, 1790–1957.* Washington, D.C.: Government Printing Office, 1960.

———. *Housing Construction Statistics, 1889–1964.* Washington, D.C.: Government Printing Office, 1966.

U.S. Department of Labor. Bureau of Labor Statistics.

———. *Working Notebook of the Impact of the War on Detroit.* Washington, D.C.: Government Printing Office, 1943.

———. U.S. Employment Service. Technical Service Division. *A Short History of the War Manpower Commission.* Washington, D.C.: Government Printing Office, 1948.

———. U.S. Women's Bureau. *Women Workers in Ten War Production Areas and Their Postwar Employment Plans. Women's Bureau Bulletin No. 209.* Washington, D.C.: Government Printing Office, 1946.

U.S. National Archives. *Federal Records of World War II, Civilian Agencies.* 2 vols. Washington, D.C.: Government Printing Office, 1950.

U.S. National Housing Agency. *Fourth Annual Report.* Washington, D.C.: Government Printing Office, 1946.

U.S. National War Labor Board. *Termination Report of the National War Labor Board.* 3 vols. Washington, D.C.: Government Printing Office, 1947–49.

U.S. Office of Community War Services. *Teamwork in Community Services, 1941–1946.* Washington, D.C.: Government Printing Office, 1946.

U.S. President's Committee for Congested Production Areas. *Final Report.* Washington, D.C.: Government Printing Office, 1944.

U.S. Selective Service System.

———. *Agricultural Deferment. Special Monograph No. 7.* Washington, D.C.: Government Printing Office, 1946.

———. *Industrial Deferment. Special Monograph No. 6.* Washington, D.C.: Government Printing Office, 1948.

Van Wagoner, Murray D. *Message to the Legislature in Extraordinary Session.* Lansing, Michigan, 1942.

UNPUBLISHED MATERIAL

Anderson, Clarence. "Metropolitan Detroit FEPC: A History of the Organization and Operation of a Citizens' Action Group to Encourage Equality of Opportunity in Employment Practice without Regard to Race, Creed, Color or National Origin." Master's thesis, Wayne University, 1947.

Anderson, Karen Sue Tucker. "The Impact of World War II in the Puget Sound Area on the Status of Women and the Family." Ph.D. dissertation, University of Washington, 1975.

Aronson, Phyllis. "The Adequacy of the Family Allowance System as It Affects the Wives and Children of Men Drafted into the Armed Forces." Master's thesis, Wayne University, 1944.

Bailer, Lloyd Harding. "Negro Labor in the Automobile Industry." Ph.D. dissertation, University of Michigan, 1943.

Ballou, Richard J. "Race Riots and Hate Strikes: An Analysis of Racial Conflict within the Automobile Plants of Wartime Detroit, 1939–1943." Seminar paper, University of Michigan, 1972.

Black, Harold. "Restrictive Covenants in Relation to Segregated Negro Housing in Detroit." Master's thesis, Wayne University, 1947.

Blackwood, George D. "The United Automobile Workers of America, 1935–1951." Ph.D. dissertation, University of Chicago, 1951.

Cady, Darrell Robert. "The Truman Administration's Reconversion Policy, 1945–1947." Ph.D. dissertation, University of Kansas, 1974.

Current, Gloster Bryant. "Negro Participation in the August 7, 1945 Primary in Detroit." Master's thesis, Wayne University, 1949.

Daniel, Ralph. "Youth Guidance in Michigan: A Study of the Work of the Michigan Youth Guidance Committee and the Michigan Youth Guidance Commission, 1943–1947." Master's thesis, University of Michigan, 1951.

Gabaccia, Donna. "Legislators, Experts, and Mothers: Day Care in World War II." Seminar paper, University of Michigan, 1974.

Halpern, Martin. "The 1941 Strike at the Ford Motor Company." Seminar paper, University of Michigan, 1973.

Harrison, Harold Jerome. "A Study of the Work of the Coordinating Committee on Democratic Human Relations in the Detroit Public Schools from September, 1943 to June, 1952." Ph.D. dissertation, Wayne University, 1953.

Hartung, Frank E. "A Study in Law and Social Differentation: As Exemplified in Violations of the Emergency Price Control Act of 1942 and the Second War Powers Act, in the Detroit Wholesale Meat Industry." Ph.D. dissertation, University of Michigan, 1949.

Hawley, William B. "Development of Vocational Education in Michigan during the Period 1940–1947." Master's thesis, Wayne University, 1947.

Heliker, Betty. "The Need for a Day Care Program in Detroit for the Children of Working Mothers." Master's thesis, University of Michigan, 1943.

Jenkins, Bette Smith. "The Racial Policies of the Detroit Housing Commission and Their Administration." Master's thesis, Wayne University, 1951.

Kirshner, George. "Government Agencies in Detroit in the Work of Overcoming Discrimination Against the Negro in Private Employment." Master's thesis, Wayne University, 1945.

Koistinen, Paul A.C. "The Hammer and the Sword: Labor, the Military and the Industrial Mobilization, 1920–1945." Ph.D. dissertation, University of California, 1964.

Kulka, Helen A. "The Barometer of the Detroit Mayor's Interracial Committee: An Attempt to Measure Racial Tension." Master's thesis, Wayne University, 1945.

Ledesma, Irene J. "The Committee on Race Relations of the Michigan Council of Churches: A Historical Study, January, 1943–February, 1946." Master's thesis, University of Michigan, 1946.

Levine, David Allan. "Expecting the Barbarians: Social Control and Race Relations, Detroit, 1915 to 1925." Ph.D. dissertation, University of Chicago, 1970.

Lichtenstein, Nelson. "Industrial Unionism under the No-Strike Pledge: A Study of the CIO during the Second World War." Ph.D. dissertation, University of California, Berkeley, 1974.

Middlebrook, Virginia. "An Analysis of Youth Needs in a War Production Area." Master's thesis, Wayne University, 1945.

Postl, Mary. "Detroit Develops an International Conciousness, 1930–1945." Master's thesis, University of Detroit, 1955.

Riker, William H. "The CIO in Politics, 1936 to 1946." Ph.D. dissertation, Harvard University, 1948.

Rupp, Leila J. "A Reappraisal of American Women in A Man's War, 1941–1945." Paper delivered at Second Annual Berkshire Conference on Women's History, Radcliffe College, October, 1974. Mimeographed.

Shankin, Violet Garrison. "War-Effort Related Opinions and Practices of Detroit Elementary School Teachers." Master's thesis, Wayne University, 1943.

Skeels, Jack William. "The Development of Political Stability within the United Auto Workers Union." Ph.D. dissertation, University of Wisconsin, 1957.

Smith, Constance. "A Five-Year Study from 1941 to 1945, of Children with Behavior Problems who were Brought to the Juvenile Court for the First Time." Master's thesis, University of Michigan, 1948.

Straub, Eleanor. "Government Policy toward Civilian Women during World War II." Ph.D. dissertation, Emory University, 1973.

Thomas, Richard H. "From Peasant to Proletarian: The Formation and Organization of the Black Industrial Working Class in Detroit, 1915–1945." Ph.D. dissertation, University of Michigan, 1976.

Van de Water, Peter E. "'Peacemaker:' President Alexander G. Ruthven of Michigan and His Relationship to His Faculty, Students, and Regents." Ph.D. dissertation, University of Michigan, 1970.

Wilburn, James Richard. "Social and Economic Aspects of the Aircraft Industry in Metropolitan Los Angeles during World War II." Ph.D. dissertation, University of California, Los Angeles, 1971.

Wolff, Thomas D. "Safeguarding the Arsenal of Democracy: A History of the Detroit Office of Civilian Defense in World War II." Master's thesis, Wayne University, 1952.

Yenney, Freda Seifert. "Areas of Tension in the John R. Fisher Homes as Revealed by One Hundred Wives Living on the Project." Master's thesis, Wayne University, 1944.

BOOKS AND ARTICLES

Adler, Selig. *The Isolationist Impulse: Its Twentieth-Century Reaction.* New York: Collier-Macmillan, The Free Press, 1957.

"Adventures of Henry and Joe in Autoland." *Fortune,* vol. 33, March, 1946, p. 96.

Akers, E. R., and Fox, Vernon. "Detroit Rioters and Looters Committed to Prison: Summary of Prison Data on Their Background." *Journal of Criminal Law and Criminology*, vol. 35 (1944): 105–10.

Amidon, Beulah. "Battle of Detroit." *Survey Graphic*, vol. 31, April 1942, 198.

Andriola, Joseph. "Mental Health Problems in a War Production Area." *Mental Hygiene*, 26 (1942): 560–70.

"Anniversary of Hate." *Newsweek*, vol. 23, June 26, 1944, pp. 49–50.

"Of Arms and Automobiles." *Fortune*, vol. 22, December, 1940, p. 56.

Arnow, Harriet. *The Dollmaker*. New York: Macmillan, 1954.

Automobile Manufacturers Association. *Freedom's Arsenal: The Story of the Automotive Council for War Production*. Detroit: The Association, 1950.

Baber, Ray E. "Marriage and the Family after the War." *Annals of the American Academy of Political and Social Science*, 229 (1943): 164–75.

Bald, F. Clever. *Michigan in Four Centuries*. New York: Harper Brothers, 1954.

Banner, Warren N. *Observations on Conditions among Negroes in the Fields of Education, Recreation, and Employment in Selected Areas of Detroit, Michigan*. Washington, D.C.: National Urban League, 1941.

Baskin, Alex. "The Ford Hunger March-1932." *Labor History*, 13 (1972): 331–60.

"Battle of Detroit." *Time*, vol. 39, March 23, 1942, pp. 10–14.

Beatty, Jerome. "A City Gets a New Job." *American Magazine*, vol. 134, July, 1942, pp. 44–45.

Benedek, Therese. *Insight and Personality Adjustment: A Study of the Psychological Effects of War*. New York: Ronald Press, 1946.

Benedict, Murray. *Farm Policies of the United States, 1790–1950*. New York: Columbia University Press, 1953.

Bernstein, Barton J. "The Automobile Industry and the Coming of the Second World War." *Southwestern Social Science Quarterly*, 48 (1966): 20–32.

———. "The Debate on Industrial Reconversion: The Protection of Oligopoly and Military Control of the Economy." *American Journal of Economics and Sociology*, 16 (1967): 159–72.

———. "The Removal of War Production Controls on Business, 1944–1946." *Business History Review*, 39 (1965): 243–60.

———. "Walter Reuther and the General Motors Strike of 1945–46." *Michigan History*, 49 (1965): 260–77.

———, ed. *Towards a New Past: Dissenting Essays in American History*. New York: Random House, 1968.

Bernstein, Irving. *Turbulent Years: A History of the American Worker, 1933–1941*. Boston: Houghton Mifflin, 1970.

Beynon, Erdmann D. "The Southern White Laborer Migrates to Michigan." *American Sociological Review*, 3 (1938): 338–48.

Blum, Albert A. *Drafted or Deferred? Practices Past and Present*. Ann Arbor: Bureau of Industrial Relations, University of Michigan, 1967.

Blum, John Morton. *V Was for Victory: Politics and American Culture during World War II*. New York: Harcourt Brace Jovanovich, 1976.

Bober, Joseph F., and Glasser, Cary. "Work and Wage Experience of Willow Run Workers." *Monthly Labor Review*, 61 (1945): 1074–90.

Boykin, Ulysses W. *A Handbook on the Detroit Negro*. Detroit: Minority Study Associates, 1943.

Brean, H. "Prophet Jones in Church and at Home." *Life*, vol. 17, November 27, 1944, pp. 57–63.

Bremner, Robert H., ed. *Children and Youth in America: A Documentary History*. 3 vols. Cambridge, Mass.: Harvard University Press, 1970–74.

Brennan, B.C. "Fighting Ships from Bay City." *Inland Seas*, I (1945): 21–25.

Brody, Clark L. *In the Service of the Farmer: My Life in the Michigan Farm Bureau*. East Lansing: Michigan State University Press, 1959.

Brody, David. "The Emergence of Mass Production Unionism." In John Braeman, Robert H. Bremner, and David Brody, eds. *Change and Continuity in Twentieth-Century America*. Columbus: Ohio State University Press, 1964, pp. 242–62.

———. "The New Deal in World War II." In John Braeman, Robert H. Bremner, and David Brody, eds. *The New Deal*. vol. 1. *The National Level*. Columbus: Ohio State University Press, 1975, pp. 267–305.

Bromberg, Walter. "The Effects of the War on Crime." *American Sociological Review*, 8 (1943): 685–91.

Brown, Earl. "Detroit's Armed Camps." *Harper's*, vol. 191, July, 1945, pp. 1–9.

———. "The Truth about the Detroit Riot." *Harper's*, vol. 187, November, 1943, pp. 488–98.

Bruner, Jerome S. *Mandate from the People*. New York: Duell, Sloan, & Pearce, 1944.

Buchanan, Russell. *The United States in World War II*. New York: Harper & Row, 1964.

Burns, James MacGregor. *Roosevelt: The Soldier of Freedom*. New York: Harcourt Brace Jovanovich, 1970.

Calder, Angus. *The People's War: Britain, 1939–1945*. New York: Random House, Pantheon Books, 1969.

Campbell, Brewster, and Pooler, James. "Hallelujah in Boomtown." *Collier's*, vol. 113, April 1, 1944, p. 18.

Cantril, Hadley, ed. *Public Opinion, 1935–1946*. Princeton: Princeton University Press, 1951.

Capeci, Dominic J., Jr. *The Harlem Riot of 1943*. Philadelphia: Temple University Press, 1977.

Carr, Lowell J., and Stermer, James E. *Willow Run: A Study of Industrialization and Cultural Inadequacy*. New York: Harper & Brothers, 1952.

Catton, Bruce. *The War Lords of Washington*. New York: Harcourt, Brace, & Co., 1948.

Cavnes, Max Parvin. *The Hoosier Community at War*. Bloomington, Ind.: Indiana University Press, 1961.

Chafe, William Henry. *The American Woman: Her Changing Social, Economic, and Political Roles, 1920–1970*. New York: Oxford University Press, 1972.

Chinoy, Eli. *Automobile Workers and the American Dream*. Garden City, N.Y.: Doubleday & Co., 1955.

Cliŋansmith, Michael S. "The Black Legion: Hooded Americanism in Michigan." *Michigan History*, 55 (1971): 243–62.

Clinard, Marshall B. *The Black Market: A Study of White Collar Crime*. New York: Rinehart & Co., 1952.

Cole, Wayne S. *America First: The Battle Against Intervention, 1940–1941*. Madison: University of Wisconsin Press, 1953.

Coles, Robert. *Migrants, Sharecroppers, Mountaineers. Children of Crisis*, vol. 1. Boston: Little Brown, 1967.

———. *The South Goes North. Children of Crisis*, vol. 3. Boston: Atlantic, Little Brown, 1972.

Connolly, Vera. "Job for a Lady." *Collier's*, vol. 113, June 10, 1944, p. 18.

Conot, Robert. *American Odyssey*. New York: William Morrow, 1974.

Cormier, Frank, and Eaton, William J. *Reuther*. Englewood Cliffs, N.J.: Prentice-Hall, 1970.

Craig, Richard B. *The Bracero Program: Interest Groups and Foreign Policy*. Austin: University of Texas Press, 1971.

Cuff, Robert A. *The War Industries Board: Business-Government Relations during World War I*. Baltimore: Johns Hopkins University Press, 1973.

Dalfiume, Richard M. *Desegregation of the United States Armed Forces: Fighting on Two Fronts, 1939–1953*. Columbia: University of Missouri Press, 1969.

———. "The Forgotten Years of the Negro Revolution." *Journal of American History*, 55 (1968): 90–106.

Dancy, John C. *Sand Against the Wind: The Memoires of John C. Dancy*. Detroit: Wayne State University Press, 1966.

Davenport, Walter. "Detroit Strains at the Federal Leash." *Collier's*, vol. 110, October 31, 1942, p. 15.

———. "War Rides the Assembly Lines." *Collier's*, vol. 110, July 11, 1942, p. 13.

Davies, Richard O. *Housing Reform during the Truman Administration*. Columbia: University of Missouri Press, 1966.

Deford, Frank. *There She Is: The Life and Times of Miss America*. New York: Viking Press, 1971.

Denisoff, R. Serge. *Great Day Coming: Folk Music and the American Left*. Urbana: University of Illinois Press, 1971.

Derber, Milton. *The American Idea of Industrial Democracy, 1865–1965*. Urbana: University of Illinois Press, 1970.

Despert, Louise. *The Emotionally Disturbed Child, Then and Now*. New York: R. Brunner, 1965.

"Detroit Has a Race Riot." *Life*, vol. 12, March 16, 1942, pp. 40–41.

"Detroit is Dynamite." *Life*, vol. 13, August 17, 1942, pp. 15–22.

"Detroit: New Era Beings." *Time*, vol. 39, February 9, 1942, p. 18.

"Detroit Reconverts Slowly." *The Labor Market*, August, 1945, pp. 26–27.

"Detroit: Six Months After." *Life*, vol. 14, March 1, 1943, pp. 28–29.

Diamond, Sander A. *The Nazi Movement in the United States, 1924–1941*. Ithaca, N.Y.: Cornell University Press, 1974.

Disbrow, Donald. *Schools for an Urban Society.* Lansing: Michigan Historical Commission, 1969.

Divine, Robert A. *Roosevelt and World War II*. Baltimore: Johns Hopkins University Press, 1969.

Dos Passos, John. *State of the Nation*. Boston: Houghton Mifflin, 1944.

Dratch, Howard. "The Politics of Child Care during the 1940s." *Science and Society*, 38 (1974): 167–204.

Dunbar, Willis F. *Michigan: A History of the Wolverine State*. Grand Rapids: William Eerdmans, 1970.

Eldridge, Hope T. "Problems and Methods of Estimating Post Censal Population." *Social Forces*, 24 (1945): 41–46.

Fairchild, Byron, and Grossman, Jonathan. *The Army and Industrial Manpower.* Washington, D.C.: U.S. Government Printing Office, 1959.

Fine, Sidney. *The Automobile under the Blue Eagle: Labor, Management and the Automobile Manufacturing Code*. Ann Arbor: University of Michigan Press, 1963.

———. *Frank Murphy: The Detroit Years.* Ann Arbor: University of Michigan Press, 1975.

———. *Sit-down: The General Motors Strike of 1936–1937*. Ann Arbor: University of Michigan Press, 1969.

Finkle, Lee. "The Conservative Aims of Militant Rhetoric: Black Protest during World War II." *Journal of American History*, 60 (1973): 692–713.

———. *Forum for Protest: The Black Press during World War II*. Rutherford, N.J.: Fairleigh Dickinson University Press, 1975.

Fletcher, Ralph Carr. "Runaway Youth to Detroit during the War." *Social Service Review*, 22 (1948): 349–54.

Foner, Phillip. *Organized Labor and the Black Worker, 1619–1973*. New York: Praeger Books, 1974.

Foster, James Caldwell. *The Union Politic: The CIO Political Action Committee*. Columbia: University of Missouri Press, 1975.

Galenson, Walter. *The CIO Challenge to the AFL: A History of the American Labor Movement, 1935–1941*. Cambridge, Mass.: Harvard University Press, 1960.

Garfinkel, Herbert. *When Negroes March: The March on Washington Movement in the Organizational Politics for FEPC*. New York: Atheneum, 1966.

Gates, William B. *Michigan Copper and Boston Dollars: An Economic History of the Michigan Copper Mining Industry, 1845–1949*. Cambridge, Mass.: Harvard University Press, 1951.

Gelfand, Mark I. *A Nation of Cities: The Federal Government and Urban America,*

1933–1965. New York: Oxford University Press, 1975.

Goldman, Eric F. *Rendezvous with Destiny: A History of American Reform*. New York: Random House, Vintage Books, 1959.

Goodman, Jack, ed. *While You were Gone: A Report on Wartime Life in the United States*. New York: Simon & Schuster, 1946.

Grayson, Harry. *A Region in Upheaval*. Detroit: Detroit Edison Co., 1941.

Green, James. "Fighting on Two Fronts: Working-Class Militancy in the 1940s." *Radical America*, 9 (1975): 7–47.

Gregory, Chester W. *Women in Defense Work during World War II: An Analysis of the Labor Problem and Women's Rights*. Jericho, N.Y.: Exposition Press, 1974.

Gruenberg, Sidone M., ed. *The Family in a World at War*. New York: Harper & Brothers, 1942.

Hachey, Thomas E. "The Wages of War: A British Commentary on Life in Detroit in July, 1943." *Michigan History*, 59 (1975): 227–38.

Hamby, Alonzo L. *Beyond the New Deal: Harry S. Truman and American Liberalism*. New York: Columbia University Press, 1973.

———. "Sixty Million Jobs and the People's Revolution: The Liberals, the People, and World War II." *Historian*, 30 (1968): 578–98.

Hanawalt, Leslie L. *A Place of Light: The History of Wayne State University*. Detroit: Wayne State University Press, 1968.

Harris, Seymour E. *Inflation and the American Economy*. New York: McGraw-Hill, 1945.

Havens, Thomas R.H. "Women and War in Japan, 1937–45." *American Historical Review*, 80 (1975): 913–34.

Havighurst, Robert J., and Morgan, H. Gerthon. *The Social History of a War-Boom Community*. New York: Longman's Green, 1951.

Hawley, Amos H. *Intrastate Migration in Michigan, 1935–1940. Michigan Governmental Studies No. 25*. Ann Arbor: University of Michigan Press, 1953.

———. *The Population of Michigan, 1840 to 1960: An Analysis of Growth, Distribution, and Composition. Michigan Governmental Studies No. 19*. Ann Arbor: University of Michigan Press, 1949.

Heath, Jim F. "Domestic America during World War II: Research Opportunities for Historians." *Journal of American History*, 63 (1971): 384–414.

Hill, Reuben. *Families under Stress: Adjustment to the Crises of War Separation and Reunion*. New York: Harper & Brothers, 1949.

"Hitler or the U.S.?" *Time*, vol. 40, August 24, 1942, p. 17.

Holli, Melvin C. "The Impact of Automobile Manufacturing Upon Detroit." *Detroit in Perspective*, 2 (1976): 176–81.

Howe, Irving, and Widick, B.J. *The UAW and Walter Reuther*. New York: Random House, 1949.

Jackson, Kenneth T. *The Ku Klux Klan in the City, 1915–1930*. New York: Oxford University Press, 1967.

Janeway, Eliot. *The Struggle for Survival: A Chronicle of Economic Mobilization during World War II*. New Haven: Yale University Press, 1951.

Jennings, Ed. "Wildcat! The Wartime Strike Wave in Auto." *Radical America*, 9 (1975): 77–105.

Jones, Robert C. *Mexican War Workers in the United States: The Mexico-United States Manpower Recruiting Program and its Operation*. Washington, D.C.: Pan American Union, 1945.

Kandel, I. L. *The Impact of the War upon American Education*. Chapel Hill: University of North Carolina Press, 1948.

Katz, Alfred H. "Counseling Outpost for War Workers." *Family*, 26 (1945): p. 43.

Katzman, David M. *Before the Ghetto: Black Detroit in the Nineteenth Century*. Urbana; University of Illinois Press, 1973.

Kennedy, Susan E. *The Banking Crisis of 1933*. Lexington: University Press of Kentucky, 1973.

Kesselman, Louis C. *The Social Politics of FEPC: A Study in Reform Movements*. Chapel Hill: University of North Carolina Press, 1948.

Killingsworth, Charles. *State Labor Mediation Acts*. Chicago: University of Chicago Press, 1948.

Kirkendall, Richard S. *The United States, 1929–1945: Years of Crisis and Change*. New York: McGraw-Hill, 1974.

Klemmer, Harvey. "Michigan Fights." *National Geographic*, 86 (1944): 677–715.

Koistinen, Paul A.C. "Mobilizing the World War II Economy: Labor and the Industrial-Military Alliance." *Pacific Historical Review*, 42 (1972): 443–78.

Kuhn, Madison. *Michigan State: The First Hundred Years, 1855–1955*. East Lansing: Michigan State University Press, 1955.

Lee, Alfred McClung, and Humphrey, Norman D. *Race Riot*. New York: Dryden Press, 1943.

Leuchtenburg, William E. *Franklin D. Roosevelt and the New Deal, 1932–1940*. New York: Harper & Row, 1963.

Lever, Harry, and Young, Joseph. *Wartime Racketeers*. New York: G.P. Putnam's Sons, 1945.

Lindbergh, Charles A. *The Wartime Journals of Charles A. Lindbergh*. New York: Harcourt Brace Jovanovich, 1970.

Lingeman, Richard R. *Don't You Know There's A War On? The American Home Front, 1941–1945*. New York: G.P. Putnam's Sons, 1970.

Litchfield, Edward H. "Case Study of Negro Political Behavior in Detroit." *Public Opinion Quarterly*, 5 (1941): 267–74.

Lowell, Jon. "The Paducah Express." *Newsweek*, vol. 85, January 20, 1975, p. 20.

Marcus, Sheldon. *Father Coughlin: The Tumultuous Life of the Priest of the Little Flower*. Boston: Little Brown, 1973.

Markowitz, Norman D. *The Rise and Fall of the People's Century: Henry A. Wallace and American Liberalism, 1941–1948*. New York: The Free Press, 1973.

Martin, John Bartlow. *Call It North Country: The Story of Upper Michigan*. New York: Alfred A. Knopf, 1944.

Martin, Louis E. "Detroit—Still Dynamite." *Crisis*, 51 (1944).

Marwick, Arthur. *Britain in the Century of Total War: War, Peace, and Social Change, 1900–1967*. Boston: Little Brown, 1968.

Maternal Health League of Michigan. *A Study of Detroit's Defense Area*. Detroit, 1941.

Matthews, Elmora M. *Neighbor and Kin: Life in a Tennessee Ridge Community*. Nashville: Vanderbilt University Press, 1965.

May, George S. *'A Most Unique Machine': The Michigan Origins of the American Automobile Industry*. Grand Rapids: William B. Eerdmans, 1975.

McKelvey, Thelma. *Women in War Production*. New York: Oxford University Press, 1942.

McWilliams, Cary. *Ill Fares the Land: Migrants and Migratory Labor in the United States*. Boston: Little Brown, 1942.

Meier, August, and Rudwyck, Elliott. *CORE: A Study in the Civil Rights Movement, 1942–1968*. New York: Oxford University Press, 1973.

Menefee, Seldon. *Assignment: U.S.A.* New York: Reynal & Hitchcock, 1943.

Mennel, Robert M. *Thorns and Thistles: Juvenile Delinquents in the United States, 1825–1940*. Hanover, N.H.: University Press of New England, 1973.

Merrill, Frances E. *Social Problems on the Home Front: A Study of Wartime Influences*. New York: Harper & Brothers, 1948.

Meyer, Agnes E. *Journey Through Chaos*. New York: Harcourt, Brace, & Co., 1944.

Michigan Bell Telephone Company. "A New Index of Business Activity in Michigan." *Michigan Business Review*, 5 (1953): 24–29.

Mowrer, Ernest R. "War and Family Solidarity and Stability." *Annals of the American Academy of Political and Social Science*, 229 (1943): 100–106.

Murphy, Irene E. "Detroit's Experience with the Wartime Care of Children." In National Conference of Social Work. *Proceedings of the National Conference of Social Work: Selected Papers*. Edited by Cordelia Trimble. New York: Columbia University Press, 1943, pp. 133–39.

Murphy, T.E. "Orphans of Willow Run." *Saturday Evening Post*, vol. 218, August 4, 1945, p. 20.

Murray, Florence, comp. and ed. *The Negro Handbook, 1944: A Manual of Current Facts and General Information Concerning Negroes in the United States*. New York: Current Reference Publications, 1944.

National Manpower Council. *Womanpower: A Statement by the National Manpower Council with Chapters by the Council Staff*. New York: Columbia University Press, 1957.

Nelson, Donald M. *Arsenal of Democracy: The Story of American War Production*. New York: Harcourt, Brace & Co., 1946.

Nevins, Allan, and Hill, Frank Ernest. *Ford: Decline and Rebirth, 1933–1962*. New York: Charles Scribner's Sons, 1962.

————. *Ford: Expansion and Challenge, 1915–1933.* New York: Charles Scribner's Sons, 1957.

————. *Ford: The Times, the Man, the Company.* New York: Charles Scribner's Sons, 1954.

Northrup, Herbert. *Organized Labor and the Negro.* New York: Harper & Brothers, 1944.

———— et al. *Negro Employment in Basic Industry.* 6 vols. Philadelphia: University of Pennsylvania Press, 1970.

Novik, David; Anshen, Melvin; and Truppner, W.C. *Wartime Production Controls.* New York: Columbia University Press, 1949.

Ogburn, William F., ed. *American Society in Wartime.* Chicago: University of Chicago Press, 1943.

O'Neill, James, and Krauskopf, Robert. *World War II: An Account of Its Documents.* Washington, D.C.: Howard University Press, 1976.

Oppenheimer, Valerie. *The Female Labor Force in the United States: Demographic and Economic Factors Governing its Growth and Changing Composition. Population Monographs Series No. 5.* Berkeley: University of California Institute of International Studies, 1970.

Ortquist, Richard T. "Unemployment and Relief: Michigan's Response to the Depression during the Hoover Years." *Michigan History,* 57 (1973): 209–36.

Osborn, Hazel. "Problems in Teen-Age Hangouts; Observations in Some Detroit YWCA Centers." In National Conference of Social Work, *Proceedings of the National Conference of Social Work: Selected Papers.* Edited by Cordelia Trimble. New York: Columbia University Press, 1944, pp. 148–59.

Ottley, Roi, *'New World A-Coming': Inside Black America.* Boston: Houghton Mifflin, 1943.

Peckham, Howard H. *The Making of the University of Michigan, 1817–1967.* Ann Arbor: University of Michigan Press, 1967.

"Peace Arrives at Gar Wood." *Fortune,* vol. 32, October, 1945, p. 152.

Perrett, Geoffrey. *Days of Sadness, Years of Triumph: The American People, 1939–1945.* New York: Coward, McCann & Geohegan Inc., 1973.

Polenberg, Richard. *War and Society: The United States, 1941–1945.* Philadelphia: J. B. Lippincott, 1972.

Pollock, James K., and Eldersveld, Samuel J. *Michigan Politics in Transition: An Areal Study of Voting Trends in the Last Decade. Michigan Governmental Studies No. 10.* Ann Arbor: University of Michigan Press, 1942.

Pringle, Henry F. "Not Enough Doctors." *Ladies' Home Journal,* vol. 60, September, 1943, p. 22.

Quick, Paddy. "Rosie the Riveter: Myths and Realities." *Radical America,* 9 (1975): 115–21.

Rae, John B. *The American Automobile: A Brief History.* Chicago: University of Chicago Press, 1965.

Redl, Fritz, and Wineman, David. *Children Who Hate: The Disorganization and*

Breakdown of Behavior Controls. Glencoe, Ill.: The Free Press, 1951.

Reuther, Victor G. *The Brothers Reuther and the Story of the UAW: A Memoir.* Boston: Houghton Mifflin, 1976.

Richter, Irving. "Detroit Plans for Chaos." *Nation,* vol. 160, June 30, 1945, pp. 719–21.

Rogers, Malcolm B. "For War Workers' Children." *Michigan Education Journal,* 21 (1944): 444–48.

Rose, Joseph R. *American Wartime Transportation.* New York: Thomas Y. Crowell. 1953.

Rose, Marc A. "Detroit: Million Man Arsenal." *Forbes,* vol. 49, April 15, 1942, p. 15.

Ross, Davis R. B. *Preparing for Ulysses: Politics and Veterans during World War II.* New York: Columbia University Press, 1969.

Ruchames, Louis. *Race, Jobs, and Politics: The Story of FEPC.* New York: Columbia University Press, 1953.

Rupp, Leila J. *Mobilizing Women for War: German and American Propaganda, 1939–1945.* Princeton: Princeton University Press, 1978.

Sarasohn, Stephen B., and Smith, Carl O. "Hate Propaganda in Detroit in the 1945 Election." *Public Opinion Quarterly,* 10 (1946): 24–52.

Schlabach, Theron F. *Edwin E. Witte: Cautious Reformer.* Madison: State Historical Society of Wisconsin, 1969.

Schlebecker, John T. *Whereby We Thrive: A History of American Farming, 1607–1972.* Ames, Iowa: Iowa State University Press, 1975.

Schramm, Leroy H. "Union Rivalry in Detroit in World War II." *Michigan History,* 54 (1970): 201–15.

Schwantes, Carlos A. "'We've Got 'Em on the Run, Brothers!': The 1937 Non-Automotive Sit Down Strikes in Detroit." *Michigan History,* 56 (1972): 179–99.

Scott, Mel. *American City Planning since 1890.* Berkeley and Los Angeles: University of California Press, 1969.

Seidman, Joel. *American Labor from Defense to Reconversion.* Chicago: University of Chicago Press, 1953.

Shogan, Robert, and Craig, Tom. *The Detroit Race Riot: A Study in Violence.* Philadelphia: J. B. Lippincott, 1964.

Shryock, Henry S., Jr. "Internal Migration and the War." *Journal of the American Statistical Association,* vol. 38 (1943): 16–30.

———. *Population Mobility in the United States.* Chicago: Community and Family Studies Center, University of Chicago, 1964.

———, and Eldridge, Hope T. "Internal Migration in Peace and War." *American Sociological Review,* 12 (1947): 27–39.

Sissman, L. E. "'Into the Air, Junior Birdman!'" *Atlantic,* vol. 236, November, 1975, pp. 26–27.

———. "Missing the Forties." *Atlantic,* vol. 232, October, 1973, p. 35.

Sitcoff, Harvard. "The Detroit Race Riot of 1943." *Michigan History,* 53 (1969): 183–206.

———. "Racial Militancy and Interracial Violence in the Second World War." *Journal of American History*, 58 (1971): 661–81.

Sloan, Alfred P., Jr. *My Years with General Motors.* New York: Doubleday, 1964.

Sobel, Robert. *The Age of Giant Corporations: A Microeconomic History of American Business, 1914–1970.* Westport, Conn: Greenwood Press, 1972.

Speer, Albert. *Inside the Third Reich: Memoirs.* New York: Avon Books, 1970.

Stadtfeld, Curtis K. *From the Land and Back.* New York: Charles Scribner's Sons, 1972.

Stone, I. F. *Business as Usual: The First Year of Defense.* New York: Modern Age Books, 1941.

Straub, Eleanor. "United States Government Policy towards Civilian Women during World War II." *Prologue*, 5 (1973): 240–54.

Stromberg, Roland N. "American Business and the Approach of War, 1935–1941." *Journal of Economic History*, 13 (1953): 58–78.

Sward, Keith T. *The Legend of Henry Ford.* New York: Rinehart, 1948.

Swarthout, Glendon F. *Willow Run, A Novel.* New York: Thomas Y. Crowell, 1943.

Tobias, Sheila, and Anderson, Lisa. "Whatever Happened to Rosie the Riveter?" *Ms.*, vol. 1, June, 1973, pp. 92–97.

United Automobile Workers (CIO). *Proceedings of the Ninth Annual Convention, September 11–17, 1944.* Detroit: UAW, 1945.

"U.S. Radio at War." *Time*, vol. 38, December 15, 1941, p. 48.

Van Wagoner, Murray D. "Operating the Toolshop of America." *Vital Speeches*, 8 (1942): 660–64.

Veenstra, Theodore A. "Defense Housing Policies and Progress." *Monthly Labor Review*, 52 (1941): 1061–64.

Walton, Francis. *Miracle of World War II: The Story of American War Production.* New York: Macmillan, 1956.

"War Worker Migration Shifts Population." *The Labor Market*, June, 1944, p. 15.

Watters, Mary E., ed. *Illinois in the Second World War.* 2 vols. Springfield: Illinois State Historical Society, 1951–52.

Weaver, Robert C. *Negro Labor, A National Problem.* New York: Harcourt, Brace & Co., 1946.

Werth, Alexander. *Russia at War: 1941–1945.* London: Barrie & Rockliff, 1964.

Whitehead, Don. *The Dow Story: The History of the Dow Chemical Company.* New York: McGraw-Hill, 1968.

Wiers, Paul. *Economic Factors in Michigan Delinquency.* Edited by William Fuson. New York: Columbia University Press, 1944.

———. "Wartime Increases in Michigan Delinquency." *American Sociological Review*, 10 (1944), 515–23.

Wilcox, Walter W. *The Farmer in the Second World War.* Ames, Iowa: Iowa State College Press, 1947.

Wilson, Edmund. *The American Earthquake: A Documentary of the Twenties and*

Thirties. Garden City, N.Y.: Doubleday, 1958.

Wilson, Marion. *The Story of Willow Run.* Ann Arbor: University of Michigan Press, 1956.

Wolf, Anna. *Our Children Face War.* Boston: Houghton Mifflin, 1942.

Woodford, Frank B., and Woodford, Arthur M. *All Our Yesterdays: A Brief History of Detroit.* Detroit: Wayne State University Press, 1969.

Woodward, C. Vann, ed. *The Comparative Approach to American History.* New York: Basic Books, 1968.

Work Projects Administration, Federal Writers' Program in the State of Michigan. *Michigan, A Guide to the Wolverine State.* New York: Oxford University Press, 1941.

Wright, Gordon. *The Ordeal of Total War, 1939–1945.* New York: Harper & Row, 1968.

Wynn, Neil A. *The Afro-American in the Second World War.* New York: Holmes & Meier, 1976.

———. "Black Attitudes toward Participation in the American War Effort, 1941–1945." *Afro-American Studies,* 3 (1972): 13–19.

———. "The Impact of the Second World War on the American Negro." *Journal of Contemporary History,* 6 (1971): 42–53.

Young, Clarence H., and Quinn, William A. *Foundation for Living: The Story of Charles Stewart Mott and Flint.* New York: McGraw-Hill, 1963.

Index

Addes, George, 27, 73, 82, 83, 167
Agriculture, 42–50. *See also* Rural areas
Allie, Betty, 199
Almanac Singers, 60
America First Committee, 15, 16
American Farm Bureau Federation, 49
American Federation of Labor, 12, 13, 14, 56, 57, 63, 71, 78, 143
American Protective Association, 10
Anderson, John, 77
Ann Arbor, 108, 109, 205, 206, 217
Army, 21, 29, 31, 48, 60, 67, 96, 116, 119, 155, 205
Association of Catholic Trade Unionists, 73
Automobile industry: community role of, 97–98; conversion of, 25–29; during defense period, 18–25; during depression, 10, 12–14; impact of war on, 1, 35, 236–37; profits of, during war, 33; reconversion, 221–25, 227–28; rise of, 6–7; war production of, 16, 29–31
Automobile Manufacturers Association, 16

Automotive Council for War Production, 16

Ballinger, John, 164, 166
Battle Creek, 31, 96, 116, 119, 145, 155, 217
Bay City, 31, 75
Bennett, Harry, 13, 56, 57, 69, 110
Benton Harbor, 48
Biddle, Francis, 140, 162
Black Cabinet, 147
Black Legion, 11
Black market, 93
Blackney, Joseph, 84
Blacks, 10, 207; and Detroit city election, 1943, 162–64; and Detroit city election, 1945, 166–67, 168; and labor, 141, 142–44; attitude toward war, 130–32; Detroit riot, 1943, 156–62, 166, 180, 207; during depression, 10–11; employment, 8–9, 133–38, 167–68; federal policy toward, 132–33, 134–35; hate strikes, 141–42, 143, 157; health, 115; housing, 132, 144–54, 169; impact of war on, 130, 168–69, 240–41; in armed forces, 131,

291

Blacks (*continued*)
    154–55; in early twentieth-
    century Michigan, 8, 10;
    interracial committees, 156, 161,
    164–66, 168; migrant attitudes
    toward, 162, 180; migration, 8,
    133, 162; press, 131–32, 135;
    reaction to, of whites, 130, 132,
    138–39, 155–56, 162; Sojourner
    Truth riot, 148–49, 151;
    unemployment, 10, 136; women,
    137
Blandford, John H., Jr., 109, 110,
    111, 149
Bomber City, 109–10, 153
Bomber Local 50, 69, 73, 80, 121
Briggs Corporation, 20, 69, 186,
    188, 226
Briggs Local 212, 59, 69, 88–89
Brown, Prentiss M., 83
Buchanan, 155
Buffa, Joseph, 146, 147
Bulware, Lemuel, 222
Bureau of Labor Statistics, 62
Byrnes, James, 223

Cadillac Motors Division, 222
Calhoun County, 96
California, 1, 82, 181
Campbell, Harvey, 18
Carter, Robert, 80
Centerline, 24
Charlotte, 120
Chevrolet Gear and Axle Divison,
    139
Children. *See* Youth
Christopher, George, 66
Chrysler Corporation, 10, 13, 20,
    27, 29, 30, 58, 86, 215, 216, 231
Chrysler tank arsenal, 21, 24, 97,
    101, 137
Civilian defense, 91–92, 98, 128
Colman, William, 154–55
Committee for Industrial
    Organization, 13

Committee for Congested
    Production Areas. *See* President's
    Committee for Congested
    Production Areas
Commodity shortages, 118–19
Communists, 22, 59, 72–73, 81, 85
Communities: federal involvement
    in, 97, 98–103, 126–29, 239;
    impact of war on, 90, 96, 125–29,
    239. *See also under names of
    individual communities*
Congress, 16, 32, 78, 79, 82, 99,
    100, 112, 125, 128, 135, 145, 190,
    196, 220, 225
Congress of Industrial
    Organizations, 13, 14, 63, 71, 74,
    78, 140, 161, 163, 165, 238
Connally, Tom, 78
Continental Motors, 20, 67
Controlled Materials Plan, 30, 32
Conversion. *See* Automobile
    industry
Cost of living. *See* Workers
Cost-plus contracts, 32–33
Coughlin, Charles E., 11, 16, 139–
    40
Crime, 93, 156
Cross and the Flag, The, 140
Currier Lumber Company, 58
Cushman, Edward, 167

Davis, William H., 60
Day care, 193–98
Dearborn, 7, 12, 14, 56, 151–54,
    209, 240
Dearborn Independent, 10
Defoe, J. W., shipyards, 31
Democratic Party, 11, 82, 83
Depression: automobile industry
    during, 10, 12–14; Michigan
    during, 10; politics during, 11
De Soto Local 227, 61
Detroit, 6, 7, 8, 9, 10, 11, 12, 15, 21,
    26, 27, 40, 62, 75, 80, 83, 99, 101,
    131, 134, 173, 195, 219, 226, 233,

239; city election, 1943, 162–64; city election, 1945, 166–67, 168; cost of living in, 65, 232; fascist activities in, 139–41; food shortages in, 118; growth of, 7–8; health in, 116; housing, 103–8, 125, 128, 145–51, 152–53; migrants in, 9, 94; population, 7, 94; problems of, 88, 97–98, 126; relations with federal government, 101, 102, 123–25; riot, 1943, 156–62, 166, 180, 207; Sojourner Truth riot, 148–49, 151; symbol of victory, 2, 16, 28; transportation, 112–14; war production in, 34; wartime life, 95
Detroit Board of Education, 198, 206
Detroit Common Council, 145, 146, 147, 150, 151, 153, 161, 163, 165, 167, 169, 198
Detroit Council of Churches, 180·
Detroit Federation of Labor, 72
Detroit Free Press, 16, 98
Detroit Housing Commission, 103, 104, 106, 108, 125, 180; racial policy, 144, 145, 146, 147, 150, 151, 153, 169
Detroit Interracial Committee, 165, 167
Detroit Lions, 52
Detroit News, 16, 55, 162, 183, 191, 192, 199, 226
Detroit Street Railway Company, 112, 113, 114
Detroit Tigers, 37, 227
Detroit Tribune, 131, 148
Detroit Urban League, 135–36, 167, 180
Detroit Victory Council, 97, 114
Dewey, Thomas E., 83
Dickinson, Luren, 98
Divorce. *See* Marriage and Divorce
Dodge plants, 137, 138

Doll, Tracy, 166, 167, 168
Dollmaker, The, 177–78, 180
Dondero, George, 84
Double V campaign, 131, 240
Dow Chemical Corporation, 31
Dowling, William, 157, 161
Dybwad, Gunnar, 196

East Lansing, 206
Ecorse, 59
Ecorse Township, 153, 154
Edgecomb, Charles, 181
Education, 36, 117–18, 205–6, 216–17
Edwards, George, 166, 167, 168
Elections: congressional, 1942, 83, 140; Detroit city, 1943, 162–64; Detroit city, 1945, 166–67, 168; presidential, 1944, 81–84, 220. *See also* Politics
Elliott, Eugene, 205, 206
Emergency Farm Labor Program, 43
Emergency Maternal and Infant Care Program, 116
Employment. *See* Manpower
Employment Act of 1946, 225
Equal Rights Amendment, 190

Fair Employment Practice Committee. *See* President's Committee on Fair Employment Practice
Family, impact of war on, 212–13, 241–42. *See also* Marriage and Divorce
Farming. *See* Agriculture
Fascist activities, 139–41
Federal government. *See* United States government
Federal Housing Administration, 107, 236
Federal Public Housing Authority, 105, 109, 110, 111, 121, 150, 151, 152, 153, 154

Federal Works Agency, 99, 100, 101, 116, 117, 118, 123, 124, 145, 146, 194, 198
Ferguson, Homer, 33, 140, 153, 218
Ferndale, 47
Ferrazza, Jess, 69, 85
Fisher Homes, John R., 105–6, 172, 175, 177, 180, 183
Fitzgerald, Frank, 163, 164, 168
Flint, 7, 9, 13, 21, 27, 72, 80, 173, 215, 219, 226
Flint Local 599, 80, 191–92
Ford, Edsel, 57
Ford, Henry, 7, 8, 10, 12, 13–14, 19, 21, 24, 56, 57, 58, 102, 108, 110, 224
Ford, Henry, II, 224
Ford Local 600, 56, 80, 85
Ford Motor Company, 10, 30, 36, 56, 70, 133, 136, 146, 147, 153, 173, 216, 228, 229, 231; strike at, in 1941, 57. *See also* River Rouge plant
Fort Brady, 119, 154
Fort Custer, 48, 96, 119, 131
Fowlerville, 46
Frankensteen, Richard, 73, 82, 83, 166–67, 168
Frazer, Joseph, 224
Fry, Edward, 84

Ganley, Nat, 81
Garrison, Ben, 80, 81
Gar Wood Industries, 227
General Motors Corporation, 10, 13, 18, 19, 25, 29, 58, 70, 86, 189, 191, 200, 216, 221, 271 n.20; strike at, in 1945–46, 229–32
Genesee County, 34
Germany, 16, 34
GI Bill of Rights. *See* Servicemen's Readjustment Act
Grand Haven, 32
"Grand Ole Op'ry," 176, 264 n.12

Grand Rapids, 21, 52–53, 81
Gratiot Township, 94
Great Depression. *See* Depression
Green, William, 86
Greenberg, Hank, 227
Guthner, John, 159, 161

Harden, Walter, 142
Hastie, William, 147
Hastings, 214
Hatcher, Raymond, 180
Hawes, Baldwin, 60
Health, 101, 115–16; venereal disease, 96, 116, 208. *See also* Sanitation
Henderson, Leon, 23, 25–26, 113
Highland Park, 7
Hill, Charles, 146, 149, 166, 167, 168
Hillman, Sidney, 13, 20, 26, 66, 82
Hoffa, James, 143–44
Hoffman, Clare, 84
Home front, mobilization of, 90–93
Housing, 103–12, 125, 128; black, 9, 132, 144–54, 169; federal program, 99, 105–6; migrant, 105–6, 174–75; opposition to federal program, 107–10, 112; rent control, 104–5; Willow Run, 108–11, 125, 150, 151, 217
Hubbard, Orville, 152
Hudson Motors Corporation, 24, 139, 196, 224
Hudson naval arsenal, 24, 101, 141
Hummel, Russell, 124
Hutchinson, B. E., 86

Immigration, 8
Income, personal, 50–51
Industry. *See* Automobile Industry; War production
Industrial Manpower. *See* Manpower
Ingham County, 34
Inkster, 94, 157

International Brotherhood of Teamsters. *See* Teamsters Union

Ionia, 32

Jackson, 32
Japan, 16, 225, 242
Jeffrey, Mildred, 190
Jeffries, Edward J., Jr., 15, 79, 91, 99, 101, 107, 146, 147, 148, 149, 151, 156, 159, 161, 163–64, 165, 166–67, 168
Jenkins, Bill, 80, 85
Johnson, Charles, 169
Johnston, Eric, 86
Juvenile delinquency, 207–12, 242

Kaiser, Henry, 224
Kaiser-Frazer Corporation, 224, 271 n.20
Kalamazoo, 21
Kanzler, Ernest, 26, 27
Kellogg Company, 31
Kelly, Harry, 84, 159, 210, 211, 219
Kelsey-Hayes Wheel Corporation, 137, 228, 229
Kentucky, 9, 173, 177, 179, 181, 183
Knudsen, William S., 19–20, 23, 24, 25, 26, 28
Krech, August, 159
Krug, Julius, 223, 224, 225
Ku Klux Klan, 10, 11, 139, 142

Labor: and Army, 60, 67; and blacks, 141, 142–44; and federal wage policy, 63–64; and manpower policy, 40–41, 66; and politics, 81–84, 88, 163, 166, 168; cooperation with business, 67–68; during defense period, 55–60; during depression, 12–14; during reconversion, 228–32; federal representation of, 65–66; impact of war on, 73, 75, 86–89, 237–38;

interunion rivalry, 56, 58–59, 71–72, 87; intraunion rivalry, 72–73; national service legislation, 79. *See also* Labor relations; No-strike pledge; Strikes; *and under names of individual unions and locals*
Labor-management committees, 3, 69–70
Labor relations: and Smith-Connally Act, 78; wartime, 67–71, 86–87. *See also* Regional War Labor Board, Michigan
La Guardia, Fiorello H., 91
Lanham Act, 99–100, 194, 195, 196, 198, 239
Lanham, Fritz, 99, 100
Lansing, 27, 61, 120, 210, 214, 219
Larned, Abner E., 217
Lewis, John L., 13, 56, 60, 64, 78
Lindbergh, Charles, 30
Little Steel formula, 64, 74, 75, 82, 228
Livingston County, 46
Louis, Joe, 11
Louisville Courier-Journal, 183
Ludington, 31
Lyons, Charles "Little Willy," 157, 158, 164

McClendon, James, 134, 161
McGill, John, 80
McLaury, Frank M., 124
McNutt, Paul V., 40
Macomb County, 24, 94, 96–97, 101, 124, 133, 157, 159
McRae, William, 154–55
Maintenance of membership policy. *See* War Labor Board
Manpower: agricultural, 44–49; industrial, 36–42, 133, 232
March on Washington Committee, 134
Marriage and Divorce, 187, 201–2
Martin, George, 209

Martin, Homer, 14, 238
Marysville, 31
Maternal Health League of
    Michigan, 175
Maverick, Maury, 107
Mazey, Emil, 89
Mead, James, 154
Meader, George, 109
Mechanics Educational Society of
    America, 72
Mecosta County, 50
Merrill-Palmer School, 193, 194
Metropolitan Detroit Fair
    Employment Practice Committee,
    136, 138
Mexico, 46
Michener, Earl, 99
Michigan, impact of war on, 234–43
Michigan Bell, 92, 118
Michigan Commonwealth
    Federation, 82, 84
Michigan Chronicle, 131, 157, 167
Michigan Council of Defense, 47,
    66, 98, 194, 219
Michigan Department of Labor and
    Industry, 206
Michigan Department of Public
    Instruction, 117
Michigan Department of Social
    Welfare, 193–94, 196
Michigan National Defense
    Council, 98
Michigan Regional War Labor
    Board. *See* Regional War Labor
    Board, Michigan
Michigan State CIO Council, 79
Michigan State Police, 67
Michigan State Troops, 149, 159
Michigan Unemployment
    Compensation Commission, 184,
    199, 226, 227
Michigan War Council, 98
Michigan Youth Guidance
    Commission, 211, 212

Midland, 31
Migrants: adaptation problems of,
    170, 174–78; agricultural, 45–46;
    assistance to, 180–81; at Willow
    Run, 170, 173–74, 180, 181–82;
    attitude toward blacks, 11, 162;
    conflict with natives, 9, 121, 170,
    179–83, 241; demographic data
    on, 171–72; departure of, 183–
    84, 226–27; housing, 105–6, 174–
    75; religion, 138–39, 178–79; role
    in 1943 riot, 180; southern, 9,
    171, 173, 174–84; travels of, 173;
    wages, 175; youth, 176–77
Migration: black, 133, 162; during
    depression, 10, 171–72; intrastate,
    7, 94, 170; motivation for, 172–73
    predepression, 7, 9; wartime, 93–
    95, 108, 170–72, 226–27, 238–39
Mining industry, 10, 53
Miriani, Louis C., 71
Miss America, 202
Monroe, 32, 173
Mooney, Edward Cardinal, 140
Morse, Wayne, 230
Murphy, Frank, 13
Murphy, Irene, 194, 197, 198
Murray Corporation, 20, 137
Murray, Philip, 56, 81, 86, 231
Muskegon, 21, 37, 40, 62, 125, 174
Muskegon County, 94

Nash Motors, 224
National Association for the
    Advancement of Colored People,
    131, 136, 150, 152, 157, 162, 164,
    166
National Defense Advisory
    Commission, 19
National Defense Mediation Board,
    58, 59–60
National Housing Agency, 100, 102,
    105, 106, 111, 129, 149, 152, 153
National Industrial Recovery Act, 12

National Labor Relations Board, 13
National Resources Planning
  Board, 128
National Workers League, 139
National Youth Administration, 36
Navy, 141, 205
Neighborhood War Clubs, 91
Nelson, Donald, 26, 69, 110, 221,
  222, 223
New Deal, 3, 4, 11, 19, 82, 99, 196,
  235, 236
New York, 1, 34, 82, 83
Nisei internees, 46
Norris, J. Frank, 139, 140, 178
No-strike pledge, 60, 74, 82, 86,
  228; referendum, 81, 85–86

Oakland County, 94, 101, 124, 133,
  159
Oceana County, 46, 47
Office of Civilian Defense, 91, 100
Office of Community War Services,
  100, 116
Office of Defense Transportation,
  100, 113
Office of Emergency Management,
  100
Office of Government Reports, 27
Office of Price Administration, 26,
  33, 52, 100, 225, 231, 232;
  gasoline rationing program, 113–
  14; price control program, 92–93;
  rent control program, 104–5
Office of Price Administration and
  Civilian Supply, 23
Office of Production Management,
  19, 26, 32, 38, 66, 135
Office of Scientific Research and
  Development, 206
Office of Veterans' Affairs, 217
Office of War Information, 102,
  132, 179
Office of War Mobilization, 223
Olds, Ransom E., 7

Organized labor. *See* Labor
Oscoda, 154

Packard Motors Corporation, 18,
  20, 29, 66, 69, 137, 138, 139,
  141–42, 188, 218, 224
Packard Local 190, 142
Paradise Valley, 9, 11, 12, 145, 159,
  160, 166
Paterson, Robert, 24
Pearl Harbor, 1, 15, 16, 22, 25, 28,
  53, 123, 139
Petoskey, 31
Pittsburgh Courier, 131
Political Action Committee, 82–84,
  166, 168, 238
Politics: during depression, 11. *See
  also* Elections; Labor
Pontiac, 29, 71
Pratt and Whitney, 30, 56
President's Committee: for
  Congested Production Areas,
  124–25, 128; on Fair Employment
  Practice, 135, 136, 138, 143–44,
  165
Prisoners of war, 48
Production. *See* War production
Propaganda, 90–91, 188
Prosperity, return of, 50–53, 234–
  25
Public housing. *See* Housing
Public Works Administration, 101

Race riots. *See* Riots
Railway Express Agency, strike at,
  59
Randolph, A. Philip, 134, 135, 164
Rank and File caucus, 80–81, 82, 85
Rationing, 92–93, 112; of gasoline,
  113–14
Reconstruction Finance
  Corporation, 224
Reconversion: economic revival
  during, 232–33; fears of postwar

Reconversion (*continued*)
  depression, 217–18; national
  controversy on, 222; national
  legislation on, 220; of automobile
  industry, 221–25, 227–28; state
  policy on, 219–20
Recreation, 118
Red Cross, 91, 123, 131, 201
Redl, Fritz, 212
Regional War Labor Board,
  Michigan, 70–71, 72, 75
Religion. *See* Migrants
Republican Party, 11, 82, 84, 140
Reuther, Victor, 74, 232
Reuther, Walter, 22, 66, 73, 83, 85,
  86, 229, 230, 231, 232, 237
Reuther Plan, 3, 22–23
Richards, William, 27
Rickenbacker, Eddie, 39
Ringwald, John, 69
Riots: Detroit, 1943, 156–62, 166,
  180, 207; Sojourner Truth, 148–
  49, 151
River Rouge plant, 7, 9, 12, 14, 20,
  56, 57, 67, 80, 105, 108, 133, 141,
  152, 224
Rolls-Royce, 19, 20
Roosevelt, Dorothy Kemp, 192
Roosevelt, Eleanor, 133, 161, 165,
  230
Roosevelt, Franklin D., 1, 2, 3, 4, 11,
  14, 18, 19, 26, 33, 140, 214, 223,
  240; and automobile industry, 20,
  24; and blacks, 132, 134, 155,
  160, 162; and community
  problems, 99–100, 124, 127; and
  Economic Bill of Rights, 220; and
  labor, 56, 58, 59, 64–65, 78, 81;
  presidential election, 1944, 81–
  84, 220
Ross, Malcolm, 143
Royal Oak, 11, 140
Royal Oak Township, 151
Rural areas, 117–18. *See also*
  Agriculture; Upper Peninsula

Saginaw, 21, 58, 98, 195
St. John, 122
St. Joseph County, 45
Sanilac County, 45
Sanitation, 101–2. *See also* Health
Sault Ste. Marie, 16, 119, 154; lock
  canal, 53, 119
Second World War. *See* World War
  II
Selective Service Act, 44, 215
Selective Service System, 37, 44–45,
  115, 216
Selfridge Field, 154
Servicemen's Readjustment Act, 216
Seven Mile-Fenelon Neighborhood
  Improvement Association, 145,
  146
Sewers. *See* Sanitation
Shulman, Harry, 191
Sloan, Alfred P., Jr., 221, 232
Small business, 32
Smaller War Plants Corporation, 32
Smith, Gerald L. K., 140, 141
Smith, Howard, 78
Smith, Matthew, 72
Smith-Connally Act, 78, 82
Snyder, Baird, 147
Social Justice, 16, 139, 140
Sojourner Truth Homes, 145–50,
  156, 164
Sojourner Truth riot, 148–49, 151
Sorenson, Charles, 21
Southern migrants. *See* Migrants
Soviet Union, 15, 34, 59
Springer, Harvey, 141, 178
Stalin, Joseph, 33
State Day Care Committee, 194,
  196, 198
State government, war effort of, 98
Steel Workers Organizing
  Committee, 59
Stimson, Henry, 33
Strikes: defense period, 58–60;
  during reconversion, 228; Ford
  Motor Company, 1941, 57;

General Motors, 1945–46, 229–32; public attitude toward, 77–78, 230; racial, 141–42, 143, 157; soldier attitude toward, 79; wartime, 55, 70, 75–78, 86, 271 n.29
Suburbs, 94, 96–97
Superior Township, 109
Supply, Priorities and Allocation Board, 26
Supreme Court, 12, 13, 56, 216

Taxes, 33, 51, 97
Taylor, Fay, 69
Teamsters Local 299, 143–44
Teamsters Union, 58–59, 74
Tenerowicz, Rudolf, 145, 146, 147, 150
Tennessee, 9, 173, 179, 181
Thomas, R. J., 14, 73, 74, 80, 81, 83, 86, 142, 143, 161, 190, 218, 221, 228, 229, 230, 232, 237, 238
Tipton, Leo, 158, 164
Tourist industry, 52
Transportation, 112–15
Traverse City, 48
Trotskyites, 73
Truman Committee, 110
Truman, Harry S, 214, 220, 228, 229, 230, 231

"UAW-CIO," 60–61
Unemployment: black, 136; during conversion, 28; during defense period, 23, 24–25; during reconversion, 226, 227, 228, 232; statistics of, 11, 50
Unionism. *See* Labor
United Automobile Workers (AFL), 14, 56, 58, 71
United Automobile Workers (CIO), 27, 38, 56, 59, 65, 71, 186, 237, 238; and blacks, 57, 141, 142–43, 152, 160; and premium pay issue, 63–64; and veterans, 215–16; and

women workers, 189, 190, 191, 197, 200, 268 n.37; Communists in, 59, 72–73, 81, 85; community role, 87–88, 109; convention, 1942, 64, 81, 190; convention, 1943, 143; convention, 1944, 79–81; convention, 1946, 232; decline of militants in, 88–89; factionalism in, 14, 72–73, 86; Ford organization drive, 56–58; General Motors strike, 1945–46, 229–32; no-strike pledge debate, 79–81; no-strike pledge referendum, 81, 85–86; origins of, 13–14; political role of, 84, 88; reconversion program, 221; recreation program, 118. *See also under names of locals*
United Automobile Workers International Executive Board, 80, 86, 200, 216, 228
United Automobile Workers War Policy Division, 143, 190
United Construction Workers Organizing Committee, 58–59
United Electrical Workers, 189, 231
United Mine Workers, 60
United Mine Workers District 50, 71
United Rubber Workers, 71
United Service Organization, 118, 154
United States Children's Bureau, 194, 203
United States Conciliation Service, 57
United States Department of Agriculture, 42, 44, 47
United States Employment Service, 36, 40, 47, 95, 143, 167, 183, 187, 216, 220, 226, 228
United States government: and blacks, 132–33, 134–35; and community problems, 97, 98–103, 121, 123–29, 239; and women

United States government
    (*continued*)
    workers, 187; and youth, 204–5;
    education program, 117; health
    program, 115–16; housing
    program, 99, 105–6; impact of
    war on, 235–36; manpower
    policy, 40–42
United States Housing Authority,
    145, 146
United States Public Health Service,
    115, 121
University of Michigan, 30, 217
Upgrading, 136–37
Upper Peninsula, 10, 53, 119

Van Wagoner, Murray D., 16, 23,
    53, 57, 58, 83, 91, 219
Veterans, 125, 215–17, 233
Victory Farm Volunteers, 47
Victory Gardens, 118
V-J Day, 214–15

Wages, 61–65, 175, 189–90
Wagner Act, 12, 56, 58
Wallace, Henry, 83, 243
War Food Administration, 43
War Industries Board, 19
War Labor Board, 38, 60, 70, 87,
    228; maintenance of membership
    policy, 74–75; regional boards,
    70–71, 72, 75; wage policy, 64–
    65, 76, 79, 189
War Manpower Commission, 40, 41,
    66, 114, 135, 187, 193, 222
War Manpower Commission,
    Minority Group Service, 135
War production, 29–36; and
    manpower, 36–42; and small
    business, 32; catalyst for change,
    242–43; cutbacks in, 218, 225;
    stimulus of prosperity, 53
War Production Board, 26, 30, 34,
    41, 52, 102, 107, 110, 114, 118,

119, 123, 190, 192; reconversion
    policy, 221–24, 225
Warren Township, 21, 118, 175
War Workers. *See* Workers
Washtenaw County, 21, 24, 94, 102,
    108, 109, 121, 123, 124, 125, 133
Wayne County, 24, 83, 94, 108, 123,
    124, 133, 159, 194, 195
Wayne County CIO Council, 88,
    163
Wayne University, 194
Weaver, Robert, 142, 147
White, Dr. Edna Noble, 194
White, Walter, 161
Widman, Michael F., Jr., 56
Willitts, Ethel, 178
Willkie, Wendell, 11, 56, 243
Willow Lodge, 111, 121, 122, 123,
    173, 174
Willow Run, 31
Willow Run, 126, 127, 170, 182;
    conditions at, 108, 120–23, 212–
    13, 239; housing, 108–11, 125,
    150, 151, 217; transportation
    problems, 112
Willow Run Community Council,
    123
Willow Run plant: construction of,
    21, 24; cutbacks at, 219;
    described, 30–31; labor force at,
    36, 102–3, 137, 186; labor
    relations at, 68, 69; labor union
    at, 73–74; postwar disposition of,
    224, 271 n.20; problems at, 31
Willow Village, 111, 121, 151
Wilson, Charles E. (president of
    General Electric), 222, 223
Wilson, Charles E. (president of
    General Motors), 25, 70, 86
Wineman, David, 212
Wishart, James, 65
Witherspoon, John, 161, 164
Witte, Edwin E., 70, 71, 77
Wolcott, Jesse, 84

Women: attitudes toward war, 202; Emergency Maternal and Infant Care Program, 116; impact of war on, 185, 200–203, 241–42; in 1943 Detroit riot, 160; marriage and divorce, 187, 201–2; migrant, 177–78; problems of war wives, 188, 201. *See also* Women workers

Women workers, 63, 114; and day care, 193–98; and unions, 189, 190, 191–92, 197, 200, 268 n.37; black, 137; discharge of, 200; employment of, 185–89, 200; federal policy toward, 187; motivation of, 188; out-of-plant problems, 192–93; postwar plans, 199–200; public attitude toward, 190–92; wages of, 189–90

Women's Army Auxiliary Corps, 201

Women's Bureau, 199

Women's Land Army, 47

Work Projects Administration, 193, 194

Workers: attitude toward blacks, 138; attitude toward strikes, 76–77, 78, 85; attitude toward unions, 73–74, 75, 85; attitude toward war, 27, 60–61; cost of living, 65, 232; criticism of, 218; employment conditions of, 66–67; praise for, 65; spending habits of, 51–52; wages of, 61–65, 175, 189–90. *See also* Women workers

World War I, 19, 42

World War II: attitude toward, 15; historiography of, 2–6; impact of, summarized, 234–44

Yost, Larry, 80, 85

Youth: and day care, 193–98; education of, 117–18, 205–6; Emergency Maternal and Infant Care program, 116; employment of, 206–7; federal policy toward, 204–5; female, 205, 207, 208; impact of war on, 203; in agriculture, 47; juvenile delinquency, 207–12, 242; migrant, 176–77; volunteer war activities of, 205

Ypsilanti, 21, 108, 109, 115, 121, 122, 173, 195

Ypsilanti Township, 120

Zupan, John, 80